Africa Bible Commentary Series

General Editors

Old Testament
Dr Nupanga Weanzana

New Testament
Dr Samuel Ngewa

Advisors

Tokunboh Adeyemo, Solomon Andria, Issiaka Coulibaly,
Tewoldemedhin Habtu, Samuel Ngewa, Yusufu Turaki

DEDICATION

To the Africa Inland Mission and Africa Inland Church, and their partner missions and church organizations

Their guarding of the truth of the gospel has produced many in Africa who believe and teach the truths found in the book of Galatians – justification by faith alone, sanctification as the fruit of the Spirit, and a striving for holiness without claiming perfection.

Africa Bible Commentary Series

GALATIANS

Samuel Ngewa

© 2010 Samuel Ngewa

Published 2010 by HippoBooks, an imprint of ACTS and Langham Publishing.

Africa Christian Textbooks (ACTS), TCNN, PMB 2020, Bukuru 930008, Plateau State, Nigeria. **www.actsnigeria.org**

Langham Publishing, PO Box 296, Carlisle, Cumbria, CA3 9WZ, UK
www.langhampublishing.org

ISBNs:
978-1-78368-828-9 Print
978-1-78368-666-7 ePub
978-1-78368-667-4 Mobi
978-1-78368-668-1 PDF

Samuel Ngewa has asserted his right under the Copyright, Designs and Patents Act, 1988 to be identified as the Author of this work.

All rights reserved. No part of this publication may be reproduced, stored in a retrieval system or transmitted, in any form or by any means, electronic, mechanical, photocopying, recording or otherwise, without the prior written permission of the publisher or the Copyright Licensing Agency.

All Scripture quotations, unless otherwise indicated, are taken from the Holy Bible: Today's New International Version™. TNIV®. Copyright © 2001, 2005 by International Bible Society®. All rights reserved worldwide.

British Library Cataloguing-in-Publication Data
A catalogue record for this book is available from the British Library

ISBN: 978-1-78368-828-9

Cover Design: projectluz.com

Cover Design: To a Tee Ltd, www.2at.com

The publishers of this book actively support theological dialogue and an author's right to publish but do not necessarily endorse the views and opinions set forth here or in works referenced within this publication, nor guarantee technical and grammatical correctness. The publishers do not accept any responsibility or liability to persons or property as a consequence of the reading, use or interpretation of its published content.

CONTENTS

Introduction to the Africa Bible Commentary Series . . ix
Acknowledgements xi
Abbreviations xii

Introduction to Galatians 1
    Recipients 2
    Author and Date 3
    Structure 3

Unit 1   Galatians 1:1–5

A Message from a Leader 5
    Paul the Apostle 6
    Paul's Team 8
    Paul's Prayer 9
    Paul's Gospel 10

Unit 2   Galatians 1:6–10

The Galatians and Their Teachers 13
    The Galatians 13
    The False Teachers 15
    The Gospel 18
    The Issue of Approval 23

Unit 3   Galatians 1:11–24

The Source of Paul's Gospel 27
    Received by Revelation 27
    Not Based on Human Wisdom 37

| Unit 4 | Galatians 2:1–5 |

A Visit to Jerusalem 45
Paul and Jerusalem 46
Paul's Companions 47
The Reason for the Visit 48
The Nature of the Visit 50
Problems during the Visit 51
Response to the Problems 53

| Unit 5 | Galatians 2:2, 6–10 |

Unity of Purpose 55
Paul's Action 56
Paul's Purpose 56
The Outcome 57

CASE STUDY – Rivalry Instead of Team Spirit 67

| Unit 6 | Galatians 2:11–14 |

Clash of Two Great Men 69
Background 69
Peter's Role 70
Paul's Assessment 72
Paul's Action 74

| Unit 7 | Galatians 2:15–21 |

Justification by Faith 77
Areas of Agreement 78
Evidence of Agreement 82
Answering an Objection 83
The Real Violation of the Law 83
The Real Meaning of Justification by Faith 85
The Implications of Justification by Works 88
Summary 89

Contents vii

Introduction to Galatians 3 and 4..................... 91
 CASE STUDY – Father–Child Relationships.................... 93

Unit 8 Galatians 3:1–5

Arguments Based on the Galatians' Experience 95
 Their Understanding of Jesus Christ 95
 Their Reception of the Holy Spirit....................... 96
 Their Starting Point in Their Spiritual Journey 97
 Their Suffering in the Past............................... 98
 The Miracles They Have Seen 99

Unit 9 Galatians 3:6–14

Arguments Based on Scripture...................... 101
 The Case of Abraham 102
 Our Relationship to Abraham 103
 The Testimony of Scripture............................. 105
 Faith and Blessing.................................... 106
 The Only Alternative.................................. 107
 Our Redemption..................................... 108
 The Choice 109

Unit 10 Galatians 3:15–4:11

Arguments Based on Everyday Life.................. 111
 Promise and Law..................................... 112
 Son and Slave 117

 CASE STUDY – What Matters Most?....................... 123

Unit 11 Galatians 4:12–31

Arguments from Relationships...................... 125
 The Galatians' Relationship to Paul....................... 126
 The Relationship of Hagar and Sarah...................... 128

Unit 12 — Galatians 5:1–15

Three Choices 133
- Choice of Status: Slave or Free 134
- Choice of Leader: Consistent or Confusing? 137
- Choice of Lifestyle: Indulging or Serving 141

Unit 13 — Galatians 5:15–26

Three Ways of life 143
- Life under the Law 144
- Life Led by the Sinful Nature 144
- Life Led by the Spirit 148
- The Tension and the Cure 154
- **CASE STUDY** – Balancing the Burden and the Load 156

Unit 14 — Galatians 6:1–10

Three Key Relationships 157
- Relationship with Others 157
- Relationship with Self 163
- Relationship with God 165

Unit 15 — Galatians 6:11–18

The Essence of Christianity 167
- The Gospel 168
- The Preacher 170
- Concluding Prayer 173

Notes 175
Bibliography 195

INTRODUCTION TO THE AFRICA BIBLE COMMENTARY SERIES

The church of Christ in Africa rejoiced at the launch of the *Africa Bible Commentary (ABC)* in 2006. This one-volume commentary was unique in being a product of African soil. Seventy African scholars representing many countries and denominations contributed commentaries on each of the sixty-six books of the Bible as well as articles on various themes of relevance to the African context.

But even as the *ABC* was being released, the ABC Board was looking ahead. A one-volume commentary does not provide enough space to deal with many important issues. Thus was born the Africa Bible Commentary Series.

This series provides more depth of study, width of explanation, and variety of application than was possible in the *ABC*. The contributors are Anglophone or Francophone African scholars, all of whom adhere to the statement of faith of the Association of Evangelicals in Africa.

Besides the African authorship, there are a number of other features that make this commentary series distinctive. First, each commentary is divided into preaching units to help pastors develop a series of sermons on that particular book of the Bible. The main text deals with issues that could come up in such a series, while more complex academic issues relating to the original languages and academic controversies are discussed in the comprehensive endnotes. Each unit ends with questions that can be used to stimulate discussion of the themes in that unit. Each book in the series also contains a number of case studies and brief articles expanding on the practical application of points mentioned in the text.

It is hoped that this combination of features will make these books valuable to pastors, students, and small group Bible study leaders, as well as to ordinary Christians who are interested in getting a fuller understanding of God's Word.

The Africa Bible Commentary Series will be published under the HippoBooks imprint, named in honour of the great African theologian Augustine of Hippo. This imprint is owned by a consortium of African publishers from across the continent (currently WordAlive in Kenya, ACTS in Nigeria and Step in Ghana). The aim is to ensure that the series will be widely available in Africa. In the West, the books will be distributed by Zondervan.

The general editor for the New Testament series is Dr. Samuel Ngewa of the Nairobi Evangelical Graduate School of Theology (NEGST), Kenya, while the editor for the Old Testament series is Dr. Nupanga Weanzana of Bangui Evangelical School of Theology (BEST), in Bangui, Central African Republic.

The Africa Bible Commentary Series is based on Today's New English Version (TNIV). Its main goal is to relate the best biblical scholarship to the African context. This is no easy task. May the Lord bless the work of our hands and use it to strengthen his church in Africa. May our words also bring insight and encouragement to our fellow-believers around the world.

Samuel Ngewa
Easter 2009

ACKNOWLEDGEMENTS

As with my earlier commentary on Timothy and Titus, so also with this commentary on Galatians. The encouragement of Pieter Kwant and the thorough copy-editing of Isobel Stevenson and Debbie Head have been a treasured part of the process of producing this book.

The support of my wife Elizabeth and our beloved daughters and son have also kept me going till the work was completed. Elizabeth allowed me to spend long evenings in the office, and my children were constantly asking how the writing was going. Their support made the work much easier.

My parents, James and Tabitha Mutyandia, and my Sunday school teachers taught me the way of salvation in my tender years. Their teachings and nurture have made my acceptance of the truths expressed in the book of Galatians easy and joyous. These truths have many times caused me to burst into praise even in the privacy of my study.

My students, colleagues and teachers in seminary have helped me to reflect on Scripture and make this commentary far more than merely a paraphrase. I have been constantly challenged to ask myself, How does this relate to me? How does it relate to the church? How does it relate to the nations?

The gracious and justifying God presented in Paul's letter to the Galatians is the same God who has planned my life – giving me my parents, my teachers, my wife and children and the colleagues who have come alongside to help me produce this book. To him be praise, glory and honour.

ABBREVIATIONS

Books of the Bible

Old Testament (OT)
Gen, Exod, Lev, Num, Deut, Josh, Judg, Ruth, 1–2 Sam, 1–2 Kgs, 1–2 Chr, Ezra, Neh, Est, Job, Ps/Pss, Prov, Eccl, Song, Isa, Jer, Lam, Ezek, Dan, Hos, Joel, Amos, Obad, Jonah, Mic, Nah, Hab, Zeph, Hag, Zech, Mal

New Testament (NT)
Matt, Mark, Luke, John, Acts, Rom, 1–2 Cor, Gal, Eph, Phil, Col, 1–2 Thess, 1–2 Tim, Titus, Phlm, Heb, Jas, 1–2 Pet, 1–2–3 John, Jude, Rev

Translations of the Bible

Abbreviation	Translation
ESV	English Standard Version
HCSB	Holman Christian Standard Bible
KJV	King James Version
Message	The Message
NASB	New American Standard Bible
NEB	New English Bible
NIV	New International Version
NKJV	New King James Version
NRSV	New Revised Standard Version
Philips	J.B Philips The New Testament in Modern English
RSV	Revised Standard Version
TNIV	Today's New International Version

INTRODUCTION TO GALATIANS

In our heart of hearts, most of us long for our parents' blessing and try to do things that will bring it. If this is the case with our human parents, how much more is it true of our relationship with God who gives us life. But what do we have to do to earn his approval? This is the great question that Paul addresses in his letter to the Christians in Galatia.

Some Jewish believers in Galatia seem to have been teaching that Christians could gain God's approval by obeying the law that God had given to his chosen people, the Jews. In particular, they insisted that all male believers should be circumcised. Paul recognized that this type of teaching had very serious implications. So he wrote to remind the believers about the great truths of justification by faith and freedom in Christ.

Today we are not told that we have to obey the Old Testament law to win God's approval, but "the law" has been replaced by other things that we have to do to be saved. Many Africans are convinced that they are saved by being baptized and given an English name. Some preachers suggest that we can earn God's love and blessing by donating money to their church. Others demand that we follow regulations prescribed by the leader or founder of a particular group.

Do these actions really earn us God's approval? Paul reminds the Galatians, and us, that it is faith that makes us acceptable to God, not faith plus works. Justification brings freedom, not bondage, and so there is no rule that we have to do certain things in order to be saved. However, it is also true that while we no longer need the law to force us to do what God wants, those who love God will want to do what he wants.

Paul had taught these truths to the Galatians, but, as often happens today, some of the believers had forgotten what they had been taught and were being led astray by wrong teaching. So Paul sends them this short but powerful letter, urging them to remain true to the gospel.

In its concern for the believers' doctrine and lives, this letter is a model for pastoral practice. Paul presents his teaching with a clarity that is matched only in his letter to the Romans, but also with deep love and concern for the Galatian believers. Nearly all who read this letter carefully are blessed by it.[1] It reminds us that any attempt to earn God's love undermines the truth that God loves us freely. We can be refreshed and encouraged, rather than weighed down with obligations, when we reflect on what God needs from us in order to open his hands and give us a warm welcome.

Recipients

The letter is addressed *"to the churches in Galatia"* (1:2). Galatia was originally the name of a district in north-central Asia Minor from which the Romans recruited many mercenaries. When the Romans established a Roman province in Asia Minor, they applied the name Galatia to the entire area bordered by the Black Sea and the Mediterranean Sea (a region that is now part of Turkey). In Paul's day, "Galatia" could thus be either the specific area of Asia Minor that had initially been called Galatia or the larger province. This causes problems when we try to decide who exactly Paul was writing to. Was this letter addressed to the churches in the northern area that was originally called Galatia, or was he writing to the churches in the whole province of Galatia?

Some commentators think that it was written to the northern Galatians because the people in that area had a reputation for being fickle (probably because of their willingness to serve as mercenaries for whoever paid them, rather than being loyal to one particular cause or to particular principles).[2] This would fit with Paul's accusation that the believers there are ready to change their allegiance from the gospel he preached to an alternative gospel. Those who support this position also argue that in Acts 16:6 and 18:23, Phrygia and Galatia are referred to as different places, although both were parts of the larger province known as Galatia. However, we have no record of Paul ever ministering in the northern district known as Galatia, and the words in Acts can also be translated as "Phrygia that is in Galatia", meaning that it is difficult to base an argument on this verse.

By contrast, Acts 13 and 14 show that Paul served extensively in the southern region of the province known as Galatia. I would thus argue that Paul addresses this letter to the churches in the south.[3] He regarded the believers there as his spiritual children because he had personally founded the churches in Antioch, Iconium, Lystra and Derbe, and probably elsewhere. When they abandoned his teaching, he felt like a father whose children had abandoned his instruction. Certain that what he had taught them was the truth, Paul writes to lovingly rebuke them.

Author and Date

New Testament scholars are almost unanimous that this letter was written by Paul, as is claimed in 1:1.[4] This question of when he wrote it is directly tied to the question of who it was addressed to. If it was addressed to the churches in the southern part of the province of Galatia, it could have been written as early as AD 49, following Paul's visits to Antioch, Iconium, Lystra and Derbe in AD 46–47 during his first missionary journey (Acts 13–14). However, if it was addressed to the churches in the northern region that had originally been known as Galatia, it would probably not have been written until after his second missionary journey around AD 51–52.

I support the earlier date, in part because it makes it easier to explain the activity of the false teachers in Galatia. The type of teaching they seem to have been propagating was addressed by the Jerusalem Council in AD 50. Paul would have been able to refer to the decision of that council if the letter had been written after that date.

Structure

This letter is divided into three sections of two chapters each. In chapters 1 and 2, Paul defends his right to preach the gospel – a right that exists independently of the apostles with whom Jesus walked the streets of Palestine and of their acceptance of his right to preach. Paul has to write very personally and autobiographically here because his authority is under attack.

In chapters 3 and 4, Paul defends his teaching that we are justified by faith in Christ alone, without any need to do anything else to earn salvation. He shows that his teaching is rooted in the Old Testament and in the Galatians' own experience when they believed in Christ, and that it is the only feasible way of being acceptable to God.

In chapters 5 and 6, Paul exhorts the Galatians not to exchange the freedom that is theirs in Christ for bondage to a set of laws that they cannot possibly keep. He reminds them that their freedom is not a licence to sin. They are to live lives worthy of those called to be Christ's followers.

UNIT 1
GALATIANS 1:1–5

A MESSAGE FROM A LEADER

In every culture or setting, someone is seen as being in charge. In most African societies, a father is in charge of a family and an elder is in charge of a community. The elders have chiefs over them, and the chiefs in turn report to a district officer, who reports to a provincial commissioner, and so on all the way up to a president or prime minister. People may take turns being the one in charge, but no two people ever equally share one position of authority. (True, in some families authority is shared by the mother and father, but trouble sets in unless both agree on some delegation of authority.)

The person in authority may be appointed by God (as when he appoints the husband to lead the family), by a human authority (as when provincial commissioners appoint chiefs), by voters (as when they elect a president), or by circumstances (when the founder of an organization continues to run it). Once someone is given authority, anyone else who tries to operate at the same level of authority in the same organization at the same time causes confusion. When this happens, the original leader has to decide whether to give in and resign or to assert his or her authority. The choice may be determined by the importance of the issues at stake. Some things may be too important to allow for any compromise.

Paul views his authority in relation to the churches of Galatia as something that cannot be compromised. He does not feel this way because he wants personal gain but because of his concern for the welfare of the Galatians. With the Lord's help, he has led the Galatians into a safe place. Those agitating to replace him are luring the Galatians to jump off a cliff! So Paul treats the matter with the seriousness it deserves and asserts his authority.

Paul the Apostle

The first step in asserting his authority is to remind the readers of the letter of who he is. When we write letters today, we do this by using our full names and titles (for example, I would sign a friendly letter as "Sam", but a formal one as "Prof. Samuel M. Ngewa, Ph.D). Paul signals that this is an important letter by signing it with his name and title. He is *Paul, an apostle* (1:1).

He does not start all his letters in this way. He begins 1 Corinthians and his letters to the Thessalonians with just "Paul", and his letters to the Romans, Philippians and Titus with "Paul, a servant". Thus his decision to use his official title here suggests that all is not well in Galatia.[5]

In the course of the letter it becomes clear that some Galatians are questioning both Paul's authority and the accuracy of his message (see, for example, 1:7; 3:1–5; 4:12–20). So Paul feels it necessary to remind them that he is an "apostle", a title that in Greek means "one who is sent".[6] But he is no ordinary messenger. He is like the Hebrew *shaliach*, a messenger who spoke and acted with the authority of the one who sent him.[7]

We are still familiar with this situation today. We know that someone sent to speak to us by a school principal does not have the same power as someone sent to us by the president of our country. So who was it who sent Paul? By whose authority does he speak?

Not sent by other people

Paul's opponents seem to have been saying that he received his message from human sources – either the apostles who had been with Jesus when he walked the streets of Palestine for three years or the church in Antioch, which commissioned him (Acts 13:1–3). They were saying that he represented a human group.

Paul insisted otherwise. He had not come *with a human commission*, or, more literally, his authority was "not from men" (1:1a).[8]

Paul's opponents may have responded that, even if he had not been commissioned by some group, he had still received his authority through the agency of a human being. So Paul explicitly rejects this possibility too, saying that he did not receive it *by human authority*.[9] It is possible that the person who was suspected of commissioning him was someone like Ananias (Acts 9:15–18) or Barnabas (Acts 9:27, 12:25), for these men had encouraged Paul early in his ministry. Alternatively, his opponents may have been thinking of some individual speaking on behalf of a group like the original apostles or the church at Antioch. Paul is adamant that no such person was involved in his call to be an apostle.

To understand why Paul stresses this point, think of a time when you went to hear a prominent speaker. Maybe it was a bishop, a president, or a famous preacher. You waited and waited for the speaker to arrive, and then someone else stepped onto the stage. He announced that the speaker could not come, and he was to deputize for him. How did you feel? Were you disappointed? Did what was said feel less important because the important person was not there? Did some people leave without waiting to hear what the substitute had to say? Even if the meeting continued and achieved its general purpose, your level of satisfaction was probably far lower than it would have been if the leader you wanted to hear had been present. Paul is aware of this psychological reaction, and that is one reason why he stresses that no one sent a representative to bestow on him the authority he exercises.

After dismissing the human possibilities, Paul uses a strong *but* to introduce the contrast:[10] his authority was given to him *by Jesus Christ* himself.

Sent by God

But it was not just Jesus who commissioned Paul. Rather, his apostleship comes from *Jesus Christ and God the Father, who raised him from the dead* (1:1b). Jesus Christ met Saul (also known as Paul[11]) on the road to Damascus and then commissioned him to preach to the Gentiles, as Paul recounts when he stands before King Agrippa (Acts 15:9–17).[12] God the Father sent Jesus into the world (John 3:16, 17:3; Acts 3:20; Rom 8:3) and "raised him from the dead". If God had not performed this miracle, Paul would not have had a gospel to preach or any apostolic authority to exercise (1 Cor 15:17).

While Paul can speak of Jesus Christ and God the Father as separate beings, he does not consider them separate agents.[13] In the mystery of the Trinity, they share one will and purpose (John 6:44; 17:4; see also Matt 28:19; 2 Cor 13:14). They only differ in terms of function. The Son submits to the Father (John 17:2) and carries out the Father's plan of redemption. Thus Jesus Christ and God the Father are both the source and the agents of Paul's apostleship. They work together in perfect harmony.

Paul's Team

Jesus and God the Father are the joint source of Paul's apostolic authority (1:1) and of blessings for believers (1:3), and they are joint agents of our redemption (1:4). They work together, not in isolation. In the same way, Paul does not see himself as acting in isolation but as part of a team, and so he sends this letter to the Galatians from himself and *all the brothers and sisters with me* (1:2). These may have been members of the church he was with at the time of writing, or fellow-missionaries who were travelling with him.[14]

Not only is a leader without followers not a leader, but neither is a leader without associate leaders. Teamwork is needed if any of us are to achieve our goals. Senior pastors should not be so focused on their seniority that they do not recognize the contribution of those who work with them. If they do not acknowledge this, they may shine for a few days but will eventually fail. The same principle applies in other situations, including our homes. A husband who misunderstands Paul's statement about the husband being the head of the household (Eph 5:23; 1 Cor 11:3) and ignores his wife's ideas and involvement in family affairs is running a race he will eventually lose.

When we lead, we must encourage each member of our group to share the same motivation and to work hard to achieve our common goal. Every player must regard the victory as their own. We see this illustrated every time we watch a soccer match, but we often forget to apply it in our own lives. Remember, a player who plays alone may put on a short-lived show but will rarely score! It is the team that coordinates its efforts and treats every player as important that performs well.

Paul's Prayer

In Paul's day, Jewish people typically greeted one another with *shalom*, which means "peace" (Ezra 4:17; 5:7), while Greeks used *charein*, which means "greetings" (Acts 15:23; 23:26; Jas 1:1). But Paul modifies this greeting, changing *charein* to *charis*, to imbue what would normally be a mere greeting with theological significance. He prays that the Galatians may receive *grace and peace* (1:3a).[15]

We all need grace. We need it to speak words that build others up. I have heard people say, "In my culture we speak the truth", and then express the truth in words that totally alienate their listeners because they speak without grace.

We also need grace to listen to strong words that are spoken for our good. The Galatians will need God's grace not to react defensively when Paul calls them foolish (3:1). It is very easy to take criticism personally. A gracious spirit will enable us to listen, carefully evaluate what is said, and take action as prompted by the Holy Spirit.

Grace will prevent criticism from disturbing our peace and leading to enmity. That is also why Paul prays for peace for the Galatians. He does not want his words to destroy their inner peace or the harmony between him and them.

Given our fallen natures, it is difficult for us to consistently accept and offer constructive criticism. Doing this requires the grace and peace that comes *from God our Father and the Lord Jesus Christ* (1:3b). God is the giver of the grace that can receive any criticism and communicate any truth in a manner that builds the listener up. He is the giver of the peace that can withstand any word, deed or circumstance.

Africa has seen many bad leaders. And we have often criticized them from the pulpit and in newspapers, and also while riding in buses and taxis and so on. But have we given this criticism in a gracious way that will correct and mould these people? It is all very well to say that bad leaders will not accept criticism graciously, but that does not relieve us of our responsibility to offer it graciously. This is true in the church as well. I know of a pastor who says he was fired because he "criticized immorality", but there is clear indication that he did not do so using words that were gracious as well as honest.

May the Lord help us to reach the point where we can speak words of grace even to those who hate us most. May he also help us as listeners to reach that point where even the strongest words to or about us do not take away our peace – peace within ourselves and peace towards those who criticize us.

Paul's Gospel

Paul cannot end his greeting without summarizing the core of his message, namely what Christ did when he *gave himself* (1:4). This giving was costly, for he had to leave heaven, suffer the hardships of earthly life and endure the cross.[16] Paul briefly spells out why this gift was needed, Christ's purpose in offering it, and the motives of the giver.

The need

The need that led Christ to give himself was *our sins* (1:4a).[17] He came in response to our sins and died as our representative, even our substitute (see 3:13).[18]

Sin was also the reason why Paul needed to preach the gospel, and why we still need to preach it. Like him, we must begin by acknowledging that sin exists and that it must be dealt with. It festers within us, for we do not always love others the way we should. And it is all around us. At times, it manifests itself in terrible ways such as attacks on someone's character or in murder and rape. Christ died to deal with all sin, and has made available all that is needed to change the worst of characters into the best of characters.

The purpose

The purpose of Christ's coming was *to rescue us* (1:4b). We deserved God's judgment because of our sins, but through his death, Jesus rescued us from judgment and put us into a right standing with the holy God.[19]

Paul describes what we are rescued from as *the present evil age*. Jewish teachers at the time spoke of two ages: the present age (in which we await the Messiah) and the age to come (after the Messiah has come).[20] Christian teachers like Paul announce that the Messiah, Christ Jesus, has already come, but that we still live in an evil age in which the devil keeps us from living as we should. Yet Christ is already at work in our lives, rescuing us from this evil age and preparing us for the new age in which he will rule in perfect purity and happiness (see Mark 10:30; Luke 18:30).

In African traditional beliefs, any calamity signalled that a sin had been committed or a taboo violated. The response was to urgently seek for some remedy to rescue people from the consequences of their actions. Surely we should be equally urgent in seeking to rescue men and women from sin, which kills?[21] If believers saw life from this perspective, we would see more urgency and involvement in proclaiming the good news of salvation in Christ.

The motive

Christ gave himself *according to the will of our God and Father* (1:4c). He did not seek to benefit himself but voluntarily conformed to the will of the one who is both the great and majestic God and also the loving and kind Father.[22] It is to this great and loving God that Paul attributes glory in 1:5.

As human leaders, we should model ourselves on these divine leaders. Christ did not seek to enrich himself or to cling to power, but sought only to do what his Father wanted. At the same time, the Father is not so caught up in his great power that he ignores those who serve him. When human leaders focus on power and ignore the needs of those they lead, they are falling far short of the example that God has set. Many African political leaders have failed in this matter and have become dictators, so determined to maintain power that they eliminate any threat to their power, even if they have to commit murder to do so. The danger of clinging to power is also present in the church, where power struggles are sadly not unknown.

The type of leader of whom God approves is one who follows in his footsteps, and comes alongside his people. In the Old Testament, God is referred to as both *Elohim* (the Almighty) and *Yahweh* (the Covenant God). He is both transcendent and immanent; on the throne and on the streets with his people. This became literally true with the coming of Jesus, who is "Immanuel, which means, 'God with us'" (Matt 1:23). The true leader, the true pastor, the true bishop must be both "up there" and "down here", simultaneously, a person of power and also a person of the people. It is a requirement without which one cannot pass the test of leadership in God's examination.

God exercises his power as a loving father who seeks to rescue his children from the danger into which they have fallen. This is where God's heart is, and where Paul's heart was. Paul's mission should now be our mission. Working with this perspective will keep us from being easily discouraged by our circumstances. When we are working to fulfil the mission of God, we can be assured of the Lord's presence.

Thank God for those churches in Africa that have missionary boards and send missionaries to unreached areas. They are carrying out the same rescue mission that led Christ from heaven to earth. At times, the task may demand that we leave a comfortable place to work in a difficult situation, but any rescue involves risks – many men and women have lost their lives while rescuing those they love.

Whether in a foreign or familiar setting, rescuing lives is what we are doing as believers on this earth. Many are still lost in sin and are heading towards eternal death. We should not spare any effort as we seek to rescue them.

Questions for Discussion

1. As team leaders or team members, we may be tempted to try to outshine others or to gain personal recognition. How would being a team player who submits to God's authority change our attitude? What impact would this have on our church staff, our families or our colleagues?
2. Think about how you receive and communicate criticism. Share an example from your experience in which those involved did or did not use grace. How did graciousness, or the lack of it, affect the results?
3. How would you carry out an urgent rescue mission? How does this compare with how you have participated in the rescue mission of the gospel? Have you supported the work as best you can? Share how you could improve your participation.

UNIT 2
GALATIANS 1:6–10

THE GALATIANS AND THEIR TEACHERS

On May 10, 2004, a headline in the *East African Standard* read, "Illegally Imported Fake Drugs Flood Kenya". Traders were smuggling in suitcases full of counterfeit pills, which they sold at a much lower price than the legal drugs. Those who sold the legal drugs lost much of their business, and the buyers were not helped by taking pills that contained only chalk dust. There was an urgent need to warn the public to beware of cheap pills.

This portion of Galatians could equally well be entitled, "Illegally Imported Fake Gospel Floods Galatia." Paul writes to warn the Galatians that a fake gospel will not save them. Only the true one will do that. He is no longer defending his apostleship as he did in 1:1–5, but is defending the gospel he preached. This gospel is under attack, and some of the Galatians are beginning to swallow what the attackers are saying about the gospel and about Paul.

Paul responds by showing the Galatians what they are doing, describing the activities and motives of the false teachers, and setting out the true nature of the gospel.

The Galatians

Paul paints a clear picture of the spiritual state of the members of the church in Galatia.

Recipients of the true gospel

The Galatians have heard the correct gospel. It was preached to them by Paul and his associates in the course of his first missionary journey (Acts 13:13–14:20).[23] Thus the "we" in *we preached* (1:8) probably includes Barnabas, who was with Paul at that time. The tense of the verb allows for the possibility that this message was presented not just in one sermon but throughout the entire ministry of Paul and his team.[24]

Not only had the Galatians heard the gospel, they had also *accepted* it (1:9) and made it their own.[25] But now the situation is changing.

Easily influenced by another gospel

The Galatians are behaving like children who have inherited some family treasure and are now listening to someone who is encouraging them to exchange it for something that looks like the original but is actually a fake. Paul is amazed that they are falling for this trick.[26] Why would they want to exchange real treasure for counterfeit treasure? Would someone who has dollars, shillings, pounds or nairas be willing to exchange that money for new, uncrumpled notes without asking why the person offering the new notes wants to make the exchange and without carefully examining the new notes to see that they are genuine? But this is what the Galatians are doing as they exchange the true gospel for a fake one.

Paul is also astonished that the Galatians have made this exchange *so quickly* (1:6a). How quickly? It is likely that it has happened in less than two years![27] That was all the time that had elapsed between Paul's first missionary journey and the date of this letter. If he is referring to the time since the false teaching started in Galatia, it is even less than two years. The false teachers were moving in fast. Paul needed to respond urgently, and that is why he speaks so bluntly. Believers with only two years in the faith have very shallow roots, and their growth can easily be stunted by error.

It is not that people should never change their thinking after coming to faith. Rather, it is important that we examine all new ideas very carefully before changing our minds about something. We should heed the Apostle John's words: "Do not believe every spirit, but test the spirits to see whether they are from God" (1 John 4:1). We must be open to learn, but we must examine and test what is taught.

Students who come to a Bible school or seminary will inevitably be challenged with new ideas and may have to modify some parts of what they believe. But students should always be like the Bereans, who both "received the message with great eagerness and examined the Scriptures every day to see if what Paul had said was true" (Acts 17:11). The Galatians needed to test what the new teachers were telling them against the gospel Paul preached. We, too, must examine what we hear very carefully, comparing it to the Scriptures. Certain fundamentals of the faith must remain constant even as we learn new ideas. These fundamentals include who Jesus is (God incarnate), how he saves (by faith) and his promise of coming again (physically).

Turning away

The Galatians' behaviour is equivalent to *deserting the one who called you by the grace of Christ* (1:6b).[28] "Deserting" carries the idea of defecting or changing allegiance. God had graciously extended salvation to the Galatians, but they are now abandoning him and increasingly giving their allegiance to false teachers.[29] In human terms, the Galatians are acting like people who were happy to receive kindness and help at a time when they needed it, but then turn their backs on the one who gave the help. Those who witness such behaviour will be right to condemn it. The Galatians have begun to turn away from a gracious God, and Paul writes to arrest that motion.

The False Teachers

After challenging the Galatians about what they are doing, Paul goes on to outline the type of behaviour being engaged in by the false teachers who are corrupting the church.

Their activity

The false teachers are preaching another gospel. Paul uses the word for preaching three times in 1:8–9: *If we or an angel from heaven should preach a gospel other than the one we preached to you ... If anybody is preaching to you a gospel other than what you accepted.* Clearly, someone in Galatia is preaching a message contrary to what Paul preached. The "if" at the start of 1:8 does not disprove this: It is the type of conditional statement that assumes that what is being talked about is a fact.[30] Someone is preaching another gospel.

Think of a time when you had a really bad headache. Advertisers will try to sell you dozens of different headache tablets, each better than the next. You will be encouraged to ignore the medication that your doctor prescribes and take whatever brand the salesman can sell you. The false teachers in Galatia were acting like these salesmen. They were telling the Galatians that Paul had presented a gospel, but not the best gospel. Theirs is much better and will offer a faster cure for their spiritual problems than the one Paul preached.

In our day, too, false teachers urge us to try a gospel, any gospel. They say that any of them will resolve our problems and lead to God. "Don't think that you have to choose one religion over another," they say, "all religions lead to God. Just choose whichever religion gives comfort to your soul." But what they are offering is a fake gospel. The fake drugs smuggled into Kenya could not cure headaches or other diseases; neither can the fake gospel cure sin.

Paul's view is different. If God has prescribed a certain medicine to cure what is wrong with us, that is the medicine we must take. All other medicines will offer only symptomatic relief and will not treat the underlying disease. For Paul, the prescription is Christ alone.

The false teachers' preaching was troubling the Galatians, or *throwing you into confusion* (1:7b).[31] The same verb is used to describe Herod's response to the news that a new king had been born (Matt 2:3). He felt so threatened that he ordered the killing of all baby boys two years old and under (Matt 2:16). It is also used of Jesus as he agonized in the garden of Gethsemane (John 12:27) and of the confusion to which the Jerusalem Council was a response (Acts 15:24).

These examples illustrate the type of agitation and restlessness that the false preachers were stirring up. It began with planting doubts in people's mind about their allegiance, which caused confusion and made them vulnerable to attack.

This type of approach is very common in politics. Politicians put a lot of effort into showing how poorly their opponent is performing. If he or she is already in office, doubts are planted as to whether he or she has actually achieved anything positive. Each politician offers their own promises about what they will do differently, and more successfully. The voting public can easily become confused in the welter of claims and counter-claims.

In Christian circles, the same approach is used by those who want to destroy what the Christian faith has always stood for, such as the uniqueness of Jesus Christ. Those who want to challenge this begin by planting doubts in the mind of their hearers about whether and how he can be God. Once the mind has been confused by being presented with a problem it cannot solve (for there is a divine mystery here), the challenger presents a solution that denies the deity of Christ – making him no more than an exceptional man.

Believers have to be alert to the first steps in this strategy. Paul is very aware of it, and he sets out to warn the Galatians before they become prey to the false teachers.

Their motives

The motive of the false teachers is spelled out in 1:7c: it is *to pervert the gospel of Christ*.

The false teachers were strategists. Their first step was to cause mental disturbance or confusion. Their second step was to persuade the Galatian Christians to desert the one who called them, and the third was to establish them in a different gospel, that is, a perverted gospel.

It seems that their message was that faith in Jesus Christ is only part of what is needed for salvation. In addition to exercising faith in him, Gentiles have to observe the Jewish law. In other words, in order to belong to the household of faith, a Gentile must become a Jew. These people did not deny the gospel, but they complicated it with additions.

This mistake is still made today by people who do not feel satisfied that faith in Christ is sufficient for salvation. They want to do this, that or the other in order to make themselves fully accepted by God. Paul would label that as perversion. Faith in Christ alone is the basis for our full acceptance by God. What we do follows from that relationship, but it is not the basis for establishing it.

The Gospel

The TNIV is right to translate Paul's words in 1:7c as saying that these teachers were *trying to pervert the gospel*.[32] They could never realize their goal because the content of the gospel is set and will never change. Paul makes this clear as he lists five features that characterize the true gospel.

Unique

The true gospel is distinct from all others in its focus on Christ, in the calling of believers by God the Father, and in the fact that it is based in grace.

The focus on Christ is clear from Paul's stress that it is *the gospel of Christ* (1:7). This can mean two things. On the one hand, it is the gospel Christ proclaimed.[33] He is its source. He is the one who described himself as the Shepherd who lays down his life to save his sheep (John 10:11, 14–15) and as the gateway to salvation (10:9). These truths are central to the gospel and need to be passed on without any distortion if we claim to owe our allegiance to Christ.

On the other hand, Christ is also the content of the gospel.[34] The gospel is about Christ. He is the one it proclaims as risen from the dead and giving himself for our sins (1:1, 4). This second interpretation of the words "of Christ" best fits the context of this letter. The gospel Paul preached and that the Galatians were deserting concerns the one who died for them and rose again, a sign of victory over death. Without Jesus, there is no gospel.

When we listen to sermons, the question we must ask ourselves is, "Am I learning more about Christ, or only more about some man or woman of God?" If from Sunday to Sunday all I hear about is the miracles and wonderful deeds that the preacher has done, then I am wasting my time. My focus is not being drawn to the one who matters most – my Saviour who died for me and is the Lord of my life.

The true gospel is also distinct from all others in that believers are *called* into faith by God the Father (1:6). Given that the importance of any position is related to the importance of the one who has placed us there, we have good grounds to be proud of our calling! We could not hope for a better position. But the Galatians were abandoning this position in a move that amounted to moving away from God. Those perverting the gospel were telling them that they would be in a better position and show more zeal for God if they defected from the gospel preached by Paul and adopted a "Christ plus works" type of gospel. But they would actually be departing from God rather than drawing nearer to him.

Finally, the gospel is distinct because it comes by grace. Paul tells the Galatians that God the Father called them *by the grace of Christ* (1:6c).[35] This phrase could mean that the gracious work of Christ is the means by which God saves, or that they were saved solely by grace and not by works, or that although they did not deserve salvation, God in his mercy stretched out his hand and called them out of their helpless situation. All three of these ideas overlap, but the last one seems the most important in the context. Paul describes the Galatians as people who have quickly forgotten the unmerited kindness God has shown in welcoming them as his children. Instead of rejoicing in his grace, they are seeking to supplement this grace with works.

In summary, therefore, the Father calls, Christ gives us grace, and we respond in faith, becoming members of the community of believers. John teaches the same thing when he says that the Father draws us (John 6:44), Jesus satisfies us (John 6:35) and our part is to believe (John 6:40). In 1 John 1:3, John describes this beautiful fellowship believers enjoy as being "with us" (the apostles and other believers) and "with the Father and with his Son, Jesus Christ". The Father and the Son not only make salvation possible but also welcome us into their family.

Let me give an illustration of what this means. Over the years, several of the students I have trained have undertaken further study and taken up posts in theological institutions. Some of them are now full professors. When we talk, we recognize that I was once their teacher, and that we are now also co-teachers or co-professors. Yet most of them still address me as their teacher because of our past relationship.

The relationship between teacher and student is analogous to that between the Creator and the people he has created. We are helpless and ignorant, yet he saves us and draws us into the fellowship he has established. Within that fellowship, we are co-workers with God to bring salvation to others, who will in turn become part of that fellowship. We are, therefore, not just in the mission of God but also missionaries with God. This is quite a privilege!

Another example would involve adult children who work alongside their parents. A child can never be the same age as his or her biological father, yet the two of them can work together in a business, a law firm, a school or a church. The father has nurtured and educated the child to be able to carry out the same functions as he does, yet without erasing the distinction between father and child. In the same way, God develops us to be like him in those attributes that we can share, and to work alongside him even as we remain his creation.[36]

Irreplaceable

There are two Greek words that can be translated as "different", and Paul uses both of them when talking to the Galatians. The ESV translation brings this out well: *I am astonished that you are ... turning to a different gospel – not that there is another one* (1:6–7a ESV). The word translated "different" means something of a completely different kind, while the word translated "another" means "another example of the same kind".[37] In 1:6 Paul denies that there is any other kind of gospel, and in 1:7 he denies that there is any similar gospel – which is why the TNIV describes any attempt to formulate such a gospel as *really no gospel at all* (1:7a). It is as if you were talking about an orange and someone illustrated your talk with a picture of a lemon. Yes, both are fruits, but they are not interchangeable. Paul has set an orange before the Galatians and now others are asking them to exchange the orange for a lemon, while pretending that it is just a different type of orange.

The particular form of the perversion of the gospel in Galatia was adding law (especially circumcision) as a basis for acceptance before God. Instead of accepting that Christ's work was all that was needed for salvation, they were saying that the salvation required both Christ's death and obedience to the law of Moses. They were presenting completely different grounds for people's acceptance by God.

Paul insists that this is a different gospel. It is not even another gospel of the same kind as the true one. It is a fake. There is only one true, effective gospel. It centres on Christ alone as the basis for salvation. It is the same everywhere and for all – for rich and poor, master and slave, men and women, the president and the ordinary citizen, the oppressor and the oppressed, the wise and the foolish, the educated and the uneducated, the Gentile and the Jew, the Galatian and the African. No alternative gospel is effective in offering salvation.

Recognition that the content of the gospel is Christ and that the gospel applies to all means that no preacher should ever feel a need to modify a sermon just because the president or a leading politician or a celebrity is present. We preach Christ, and all need Christ.

Immovable

So convinced is Paul of the truth of the gospel he preached to the Galatians that he boldly states that they should reject any alternative, even if it comes from what might seem to be an impeccable source like Paul and his team (*we*) or like *an angel from heaven* (1:8).[38]

Angels have fallen before (Jude 6) and they can fall again and bring a message contrary to the true gospel. Paul and his companions (see 1:2) might also fall away from the truth and advocate a perverted gospel. Should that happen, the Galatians are not to listen to them. Even Paul should be ignored if he comes to them a second time and says that he was wrong in what he preached before. The issue is sealed and cannot be modified.

Paul's words reveal the depth of his conviction and commitment. He had no further investigation to do. He had analyzed every aspect of the matter from every perspective and is utterly convinced of the truth of his position. Not even the wisest person on earth can shake his conviction.

We need to seek to be as convinced as Paul was of the truth of what we proclaim. Those of us who study theology will need to wrestle with questions about whether the Bible is the word of God in the sense of coming "from God" or merely being "about God". We will also have to wrestle with the views of those who distinguish between the Christ we believe in (the Christ of faith) and the Jesus who walked on the streets of Palestine (the Jesus of history). We should pray that we will emerge from these debates with the same depth of conviction that Paul had regarding the truth of the gospel. For Paul, the message he preached was the unchangeable truth from God (2 Tim 3:16) and the Christ he preached was the God who came from heaven to save humanity (Phil 2:6–11).

Paul broadens the scope of his prohibition, saying that the Galatians are to reject *anybody ... preaching to you a gospel other than what you accepted* (1:9). No one is excluded, regardless of who they are. Paul may have had someone specific in mind when he wrote this, but it is more likely that he is speaking in general terms.[39] However, it is also true that this is already happening in Galatia.[40] Someone is teaching a different gospel there.

This pattern has been common throughout history. As soon as the truth is presented, some form of distortion or denial follows. God instructed Adam and Eve on how they ought to live (Gen 2:16–17) and Satan brought in a lie, destroying their lives (Gen 3:4–5). Paul taught the truth in Galatia and the false teachers set out to distort it. John taught the truth in Ephesus, but false prophets undermined it (1 John 4:1–3). Satan is still working to destroy the faith of our youth, the leaders of tomorrow. We must be alert for the danger posed by those who do his work and must refuse to listen to them.

Dangerous to Distort

Whether it is Paul, his team members, an angel, or anyone else who attempts to distort the gospel, that person is *under God's curse* (1:8). The Greek word translated "curse" is *anathema*. This is the Greek translation of the word used in the Old Testament with reference to setting something or someone apart for God, usually by destruction (Lev 27:28–29; Deut 7:26; Josh 6:17–18, 7:1). This is also how Paul is using the word here,[41] which is why the NIV translates what he says as "let him be eternally condemned."

Paul does not utter such dire words because he hates people who distort the gospel but because of the seriousness with which he takes the gospel. Perverting it is a major crime in the divine judicial system.

Paul's words do not entitle us to go about cursing people (or inviting God to curse them), but they do challenge us in terms of how we respond when we hear perversions of the gospel. How do we respond when cartoonists or comedians make jokes about the Bible or the gospel? Do we strongly condemn such behaviour?

Given that the mission of the gospel and of those who preach it is a rescue mission, someone who distorts it to make Christ appear less than a Saviour is like someone cutting a rope that has been let down by rescuers to pull someone out of danger. Such behaviour is tantamount to murder, because it prevents the person from being rescued. That is why Paul sees such behaviour as deserving a curse.

Paul's pronouncement of a curse on anyone who perverts the gospel is not a new thing. He introduces the curse in 1:9 with the words, *As we have already said*. Though we do not know when Paul said this, the fact that he has done so indicates that his words are not motivated by resentment of Judaizers in Galatia as individuals. No, his attitude to them is a matter of principle. They were doing something against which Paul had already pronounced a curse.

There is a helpful lesson here. Actions based on principles established earlier avoid any appearance of being personal vendettas. Our action has nothing to do with whether we like or dislike the person, but on whether what was done was right or wrong.

The Issue of Approval

Paul finishes this section by asking an important question: *Am I now trying to win human approval, or God's approval?* (1:10a). The word translated "win approval" can be interpreted as relaxing requirements so as to induce people into friendship.[42] This is what some teachers do when they lower standards and give high grades in order to curry favour with their students. Paul is not attempting anything of this kind.

Nor is he like other teachers who deliberately add requirements to the curriculum to make it difficult for students to move on to higher levels of education. Paul would see the Judaizers as doing something like this when they add observance of the law (and especially circumcision) to the set standard.

The Judaizers might accuse Paul of lowering the standard by leaving out observance of the law so as to please people. But Paul insists that he is working to a set standard (salvation by faith in Christ) and consequently pleasing God, who has set the standard. His motive "now" as he writes this letter is simply to guard the purity of the gospel.[43]

Paul asks a second question, which is a variant of the first part of his first questions: *Am I trying to please people?* (1:10b). If he were interested in general approval, he would be less concerned about truth than about being popular. His motive would be selfish. But Paul dismisses any such motive: *If I were still trying to please people, I would not be a servant of Christ* (1:10c).⁴⁴ He is not interested in pleasing people. Nor is he interested in satisfying his own desires at the expense of God's truth. All that he is interested in is the gospel that God approves. That gospel was preached to the Galatians by Paul and others with him. He preached it to them then and he defends it now because it is what pleases God.

Paul's point is one that we, too, should adopt: we should be guided by principles based on truth, not by what will please people. If we judge that something is right, we must stand by it even if that means that we are in the minority. If we judge that something is wrong, we must oppose it, even if the majority accept it. Whenever there is a choice between pleasing God and keeping our popularity with others, we must always choose pleasing God.

This is not easy. It can be costly. Those who stand against corruption may find themselves socially isolated and may even lose their jobs. But there is a great reward from God, either in the present or in the future.

God in his wisdom made the chameleon and gave it the ability to change its colour to conform to its environment for protection. But when I watch one and reflect on people I know, I am often drawn to pray, "Lord, help me not to be like the chameleon." A chameleon has no colour of its own and those who are like it at the moral level have no principles of their own. They move with every wind that comes their way. They are driven by popularity, not truth. Paul knew what was true and he stuck to it no matter the odds. May the Lord help us to do likewise!

Questions for Discussion

1. Which of the following are important when judging whether the gospel being preached is genuine?
    a) It gives prominence to Jesus.
    b) The pastor is eloquent and full of charisma.
    c) It teaches that Jesus is God, took human nature, and died for us.
    d) It teaches that we must give tithes to the church if we want to be blessed by God.

2. Have you ever found yourself in a situation where you had to choose between pleasing a person and pleasing God? What did you do and what were the results?
3. What are some matters of belief or practice on which we should never compromise?

UNIT 3
GALATIANS 1:11–24

THE SOURCE OF PAUL'S GOSPEL

In Africa, curses are not taken lightly. My grandfather, on his deathbed, thought it necessary to forbid any of his descendants ever pronouncing a curse on any of their children. He was determined to try to prevent the damage a curse causes to the one who pronounces it and to the one on whom it is pronounced.

Paul, however, has just pronounced a curse on anyone who dares distort the gospel that he preached to the Galatians. This is a very serious matter. What can possibly make him feel so convinced of the truth of his own position?

The answer is related to the source from which he obtained *the gospel I preached* (1:11).[45] These words could be translated literally as "the gospel, the one I preached". The emphasis contrasts the gospel Paul preaches and defends with any other gospel the Galatians are hearing or may hear in the future. His gospel, whose central message is "Jesus Christ is the Son of God; Jesus Christ is the risen Lord"[46] and whose chief characteristic is that it is "law-free",[47] did not come to him by ordinary channels.

Received by Revelation

Paul's gospel is not something he scraped together on his own or learnt from other people. It was something he received *by revelation from Jesus Christ* or, as the ESV puts it, "through a revelation of Jesus Christ" (1:12b). The difference between these two translations reflects two possible interpretations of these words: a) Jesus revealed the gospel to Paul, or b) Jesus was the content of the gospel that was revealed to Paul by God the Father (see 1:16).[48] Both interpretations are grammatically and theologically plausible, but the former seems more likely in this context, where Paul is refuting his opponents' claim that he obtained his gospel from a human being.

If Christ revealed the gospel to Paul, what are we to make of 1:15–16, where he says that God the Father was involved in this revelation? It seems likely that what Paul is saying is that the Father revealed Jesus to him, and Jesus in turn revealed the gospel to him. This double divine intervention makes Paul who he is as a person (one changed by Jesus who was revealed to him by the Father) and as a preacher (one with a gospel revealed to him by Jesus Christ). He has this special privilege because of the special mission the Lord had for him.

Most of us who teach about Christ have had our eyes opened by the Father to see who Christ is (John 6:44), but we have had someone else instruct us about Christ, whether directly as we read the Scripture or indirectly as Scripture is interpreted to us. These people are the instruments God uses to train us.

But God is also still able to miraculously bless certain individuals who have never attended school with a divine ability to read and interpret the Scriptures when he has a special mission for them, just as he had a special mission for Paul. The difference with Paul's situation is that Paul was taught directly by Jesus, while today the Lord passes on his instruction through Paul's writings and the other Scriptures.

This distinction is important because it means that although we can understand Scripture and teach from it, we cannot add to it. Beware of those who claim that their teaching has the same authority as the Bible because God tells us that adding to it is a distortion of the gospel (Deut 4:1, 2; Matt 5:17–19).

Paul's Testimony

Paul gives more information about the divine source of his gospel by giving his testimony and describing what he was like before his conversion, how he came to be converted, and what he was like after his conversion.

Paul before conversion

Before his conversion Paul was immersed *in Judaism* (1:13).[49] It governed his thinking, actions, and attitudes. He reminds the Galatians of this fact (which they already knew – *you have heard*, 1:13a[50]) to show that he was a very unlikely candidate for change. In fact, he was more into Judaism than the Judaizers who are now troubling the Galatians.

Paul was as deeply into Judaism as a witchdoctor is into African traditional religion.[51] His conversion would be as startling to those who knew him as it would be for us to see the best known witchdoctor in our village sitting in the front row at church. We would all be asking "what happened?" and thinking that his presence must be the result of some miracle that only the living God could perform.

Paul's life before his conversion was characterized by three things: hatred of the church of God, a promising career in Judaism, and zeal.

Paul's hatred of the church is demonstrated by the intensity with which he *persecuted the church of God* (1:13b). He constantly devoted all his energy to seeing that those who belonged to Jesus suffered (Acts 8:1, 3; 9:1–2, 21; 22:4, 19; 26:10, 11).[52] He describes those he persecuted as "the church of God", that is, the church that belongs to God, as do all who believe in Jesus as the Messiah.[53] Of course, Paul did not know that the church belonged to God at the time when he was persecuting it. He was acting in ignorance (1 Tim 1:13b).

By persecuting the church, Paul *tried to destroy it* (1:13c).[54] He put all his determination, energy and zeal into this project, but he could not succeed – not because he lacked the will to do so but because of who owns the church. Not even Satan is able to destroy something that is owned by God himself (Matt 16:18). This reminds us of the witchdoctor again. It is common knowledge that witchdoctors are among the worst enemies of a village church. They speak evil of it and seek to undermine it by claiming that even the Christians come to them for healing or other services. But no matter what they do or say, they cannot destroy the church. The church belongs to God, and the one in us as believers is greater than the one in the world (1 John 4:4). The church's mission is to continuously and bravely proclaim the word of God, even when opposed by the powers of evil. The same God who drew Paul to salvation is able to save even the most stubborn enemies of the church. We thank God for those he has saved and the witness they have been to the church of Christ.

Paul's zeal and commitment to Judaism were noted by others, so that he can safely say, *I was advancing in Judaism beyond many of my own age among my people* (1:14).[55] He was his teachers' top student. He was highly intelligent and demonstrated a "dedication to excellence and to the most careful exposition of and living in accordance with the law".[56] The classmates he compares himself to could be his fellow Pharisees or, more likely, "other Jews of Paul's age generally, without any attempt to rank his progress among the Pharisees specifically".[57] If there had been a vote, he would have been judged the student most likely to succeed.

Most people who abruptly change course do so because they have tried something and failed. But when someone who is enjoying great success suddenly turns away to pursue something else, it is a clear signal that he or she has found something of greater value. Paul abandoned the field in which he was successful because he had met a master for whom it was worth leaving all behind.

At one time, there was a perception in Africa that people entered the ministry because they were unqualified for other professions like law, medicine and architecture. Increasingly, however, I am meeting people who have left successful professional careers in order to enter the ministry or who are undertaking additional theological study to enrich their professional service. We need men and women serving God in every field, but those whom the Lord has called into full-time ministry from successful legal, medical and business practices have been used tremendously to reach those of their own background.

Paul was a rising star in his field, but he submitted to the Lord's call to serve the Gentiles. May we be as willing to hear the Lord's call.

The TNIV describes Paul as *extremely zealous*. But this is an interpretation of the Greek. What Paul actually says is that he was "a zealot". This has led to much discussion of whether he was using this word to refer specifically to the political group known as Zealots, who were so zealous for the Mosaic law that they did not shrink from using violence in its defence.[58] Was Paul a member of this party, or was he merely using their name generically, to indicate that he was zealous about his faith?

Most commentators take the term in the general sense. Paul would have seen himself as belonging to the same company as Simeon and

Levi, who zealously avenged the defilement of their sister Dinah (Gen 34); as Phinehas, whose zeal for the law led him to take strong action when an Israelite man married a Midianite woman (Num 25); as Joshua who led the Israelites into the Promised Land and upheld God's decrees (Josh 7);[59] as Elijah as he challenged the four hundred and fifty prophets of Baal on Mount Carmel (1 Kgs 18:19–46); and as Mattathias, an elder who led a rebellion against Antiochus IV and his forces in the second century BC because he could not stand the humiliation of the Jewish people and the defilement of their place of worship.[60]

The word translated "zealot" is itself neutral. It may become bad or good depending on what it leads to.[61] For example, the acts of Phinehas, Joshua, Elijah, and Mattathias may be seen as acceptable expressions of zeal, while the actions of Levi and Simeon may be judged unacceptable. But it cannot be denied that all these acts sprang from zeal. Paul would have seen himself as like these men in his determination to preserve "Israel's purity and distinctiveness".[62] He thought that what he was doing was good and acceptable. Now, however, he knows it was against God. He has received fuller revelation and can better judge the acts prompted by his zeal.

When we judge extremely zealous groups harshly, it might do no harm to reflect that they put most of us to shame in that we seem to be zealous for nothing at all. It is a good quality to be so consumed by something that we spare no effort in achieving our goal. True, zeal for the wrong thing is dangerous, but if we are under God's control, our zeal will focus on right things. When it comes to studying as students, evangelising as evangelists, dispensing justice as judges, instructing as teachers, or anything that we do, zeal is the key to moving ahead. It plays an important role in attaining success in any task. A pastor who has zeal for the ministry and makes wise decisions in exercising that zeal will always succeed. Zeal in pastoral work shows itself in well-prepared sermons and in visiting the sick and bereaved, without neglecting other responsibilities.

Paul was zealous for *the traditions of my fathers* (1:14c), that is, the many traditions recorded in the Mishnah, the ancient interpretation of the Jewish law.[63] Unfortunately for Paul, his zeal for these ancestral traditions was actually a zeal directed against Jesus and God the Father.

To sum up, Paul was not a beginner in Judaism but an advanced scholar, and he was not on the periphery of Judaism but was fully and zealously involved. His dedication to the cause showed itself in the way he devoted his energy to destroying the church. For him to be changed into someone who advocates a path of salvation that is not dependent on keeping the Jewish law must be the result of some superhuman power. He would not have listened to any human being advancing this argument. The only one who could have convinced him to change was God himself.

Paul's testimony is a warning that it is possible for zeal to be misguided. In Paul's case, this was understandable because he had only the Old Testament to guide him, and had not yet received the full revelation of the will of God in the form of the Old and New Testaments. We, however, have fuller revelation. So before we spend our energy on anything, we must first search the Scriptures to make sure that what we are planning to do will be approved by God. Many movements and associations will ask us to join them in their work. But before we consent to do so, we must ask ourselves: How does this relate to God's will? When it promotes God's will, we should be as zealous as we can possibly be.

I am always impressed by believers who seek their pastor's counsel when an organization they are involved with seems to be moving into something morally dubious. Their action shows that they want to live in accordance with the will of God. And what do we know about God's will? The first thing we know is the general principle laid down in Micah 6:8: we are to "act justly and to love mercy and to walk humbly with your God." This should be our beginning point, even before we seek counsel from a pastor or some other advisor.

- Justice means treating others the way I would want to be treated. That was not the way Paul treated the church. Nor is it the way we sometime treat others, particularly when we give in to greed.
- Kindness means that when I am in the right and the other person is in the wrong, I still treat that person with consideration. I do not persecute them. Nor do I demand that other person puts things right overnight. While such a demand may be within my "rights", it is not kind.

- Humility must make us present all that we do to God, acknowledging that we are not perfect and may fail.

Paul's testimony is included in Scripture so that we can learn from his example. As we read about his zeal, we should examine our own level of zeal and its focus. Paul regrets that his zeal was directed against God. May the Lord help us to have zeal, and may that zeal be used to promote the kingdom of God!

Paul's conversion

Paul describes what happened to bring about the change from what he was to what he now is. He stresses that his conversion did not involve any action on his part. Rather, it was all the result of God's activity, beginning before his birth when God set him apart (1:15a).[64] Paul uses the same phrase in Romans 1:1, where he describes himself as having been set apart for the gospel of God". The literal meaning of the Greek verb is "determined beforehand".[65] If we take this literal meaning, Paul is saying that God decided in the past what Paul would be, and that is what he now is as he writes this letter.

This setting apart by God began when Paul was still in his mother's womb. This same idea is expressed several times in the Old Testament. Samson told Delilah that he was set apart to God "from my mother's womb" (Judg 16:17). Isaiah spoke to Israel on behalf of the God "who made you, who formed you in the womb" (Isa 44:2). In one of the Servant passages, Isaiah says, "Before I was born the Lord called me" (Isa 49:1). Paul may or may not have had one of these passages in mind as he wrote, but what is clear is that he sees God's call as dating from before he was born: "God destined him from his birth to his vocation, no matter how wayward and unlikely had been the career of his youth".[66] The fact that this "setting apart" took place before Paul could think for himself is further evidence that his gospel is not of his own making.[67]

The aspect of being set apart is one of the mysteries of our lives. Many times we assume that our own training has brought us to our present position. But the truth is that our training is merely the means the Lord used to bring us to the ministry he set us apart for. It is also important to note that leaders who work themselves into positions by manipulating other people or rigging elections through misrepresenting votes and ruthlessly eliminating rivals cannot claim to have been set apart for their ministry by the Lord. The place the Lord has for us comes as we follow the path of righteousness and is confirmed by an inner peace and conviction that the Lord has brought us there. This truth applies to the political leader and the church leader. Until Paul became an apostle to the Gentiles, he was on his own. Now that he is an apostle, he gives God credit for setting him apart for this position. What about you? Has God set you apart for what you are involved in, or are you on your own?

In addition to God's setting Paul apart for ministry, Paul says that he *called me by his grace* (1:15b). The setting apart took place before Paul had reached the years of discretion, but the "calling" took place on the road to Damascus. As discussed when dealing with 1:1 and 1:12, this call involved both Jesus and God the Father. Here, however, Paul focuses on God the Father's action. This calling included the meeting with Jesus on the road to Damascus (Acts 9:1–9) and all God's providential working out of the details associated with this, such as the assignment of Ananias to help Paul (Acts 9:10–19). In all these things, God was at work to make Paul who he had been designated to be.

Paul was called by God's grace, or literally, "through his grace".[68] Paul has already mentioned God's grace in 1:6, where he spoke of the manner in which the Galatians were called into God's family. Here the focus is on the manner in which Paul was called into the same family. But whereas in 1:6 he spoke of the grace of Christ, here in 1:15 he speaks of the grace of God the Father. As said when discussing 1:1, the activity of the Father is also the activity of the Son. What is important in both cases is that the initiative lies with God. He is the one who calls Paul into salvation and simultaneously into service. So Paul can confidently claim that he does not owe his commission to any human being.

Just as Paul needed the Galatians to take note that he was a person in whom God was at work behind the scenes, so also in our day the world needs to be assured that we are not operating on our own. People are watching to see whether God is at work before they will believe what we say and join the faith. A preacher who performs miracles on Sunday but offers bribes on Monday has no credibility. Nor does a church member who sings praises on Sunday but cheats his or her employer on Monday. Our claim that God is with us must be backed up by every aspect of our lives (including our response to public criticism).

Paul's commissioning

Paul's setting apart and calling were followed by God's revelation of his Son in Paul and God's commission to Paul.[69] Here, too, the initiative is all from God's side. Paul speaks of this in 1:15–16, saying *When God ... was pleased to reveal his Son in me*. The most likely occasion for this revelation was his encounter with Jesus on the road to Damascus.[70]

Paul's conversion and post-conversion experiences both took place on the same occasion. But the sequence is important. Before his conversion, Paul opposed Jesus; once his eyes have been opened, he received this revelation. It is, of course, possible that while Paul received the essence of the revelation here, its meaning gradually became clearer over time. But we are not told anything about this.

Paul describes his revelation in an intriguing way when he says that God revealed "his Son in me".[71] What does this mean? Some interpreters take it as indicating that Paul received an internal, subjective revelation of Jesus that changed the way he thought about Jesus.[72] Others see it as meaning that God has used Paul to reveal Christ to others, so that the "in me" might be better translated "through me".[73] To my mind, the subjective interpretation fits the context better. Paul is speaking about how he received the gospel, not about how he proclaimed it.[74] The revelation referred to here is one of the things God did to transform the old Paul into a new Paul. This new Paul was not merely someone who had been converted; he was someone whose life goal had been transformed. Instead of seeking to persecute Christ's followers, he would now seek to nurture them.

What was it that was revealed to Paul? To be sure, it was "his Son", but does this mean that God revealed Jesus himself to Paul, or was Jesus the topic of the revelation, so that Paul learned more about Jesus?[75] Obviously, these two positions overlap to some extent, so that it is possible to say that the content of this revelation is "Jesus Christ himself and the gospel he entrusted to Paul".[76] But the view that Jesus himself is the content of the revelation must take precedence. Paul's greatest need was not to know facts about Jesus, for he knew some of these already, but to know that Jesus was actually the Messiah, God's Son. The encounter with Jesus was what changed Paul from a zealous Jew into a believer.

The question we have just asked about Paul is also relevant in our day. What is it that transforms us – the person of Christ or what we know about Christ? For the answer, we can reflect on the fact that it is possible to obtain a doctoral degree in theology without having any personal knowledge of Jesus. When we do know him, he changes our character by transforming our heart, and the information we learn about him changes our minds. For successful Christian ministry, it is more important to know Christ than to know a lot about him.

There is an unfortunate saying that theological seminaries are like cemeteries, because those who go there bury their excitement about knowing Christ as they delve into theoretical theology. Sadly, this is sometimes true, especially at those seminaries that question the uniqueness of Christ. Head knowledge, without reflection that feeds the heart, kills. This is a danger we must avoid in all our theological institutions in Africa. What we teach about Christ must always rest on a growing walk with him.

This principle also applies as regards believers in general. On Sundays, they want more than just to hear about Christ; they want to see him. A place of worship where Christ and his love are not visible might just as well be used as a supermarket. Paul's inward experience of Christ became the basis for his ministry. So it should be for us all.

The purpose for which God revealed his Son to Paul was *so that I might preach him among the Gentiles* (1:16b). Did Paul fully understand what that meant at the time of the assignment? Possibly not, but he must have been given the essence of this commission during his encounter on the Damascus road. It is safe to say that "this commission was an integral part of the disclosure given to Paul by the risen Christ both on the road to Damascus and later in Paul's temple vision in Jerusalem (Acts 9:15; 22:17–21)".[77] However, the fuller implications of this commission probably came to him gradually. Longenecker says, "Paul's own letters suggest that his understanding of Christ developed throughout his life as a Christian, and the Acts of the Apostles indicates that there were stages in his comprehension of what a mission to Gentiles involved".[78]

Up to this stage in his description of what God has done for him, Paul has been using past tenses ("God set me apart ... called me ... was pleased") but now he suddenly changes to a present tense in the verb translated "I might preach".[79] The tense indicates that this is what Paul is doing and will continue to do. And what he is to do is "preach", or literally "announce good news" about "him", that is, the Son whom the Father revealed to him. The good news in this context is identified as "him". The new Paul gives his time and energy to no other message but the good news which centres on the redeeming work of Christ.

The people to whom Paul was to preach were "the Gentiles" (or literally, "the nations").[80] The general concept among the Jews of the time was that the Messiah was for the Jews and those others who went through the requirements set by the Jews for initiation into Judaism. It was a very limited group. Paul's mission opens this club to everyone! It was not that he was never to preach to Jews. We know that he longed to see them converted too (Rom 9:3). His strategy during his missionary journeys was always to begin his ministry in the synagogues (Acts 13:5, 24; 14:1; 17:2, 10; 18:4, 19; 19:8). He knew that converted Jews would have a good understanding of the Old Testament and would help to provide a strong basis on which to build the church. Clearly, he did not form a new club for Gentiles only, but rather opened the old club to include both Jews and Gentiles with the only ticket for membership being faith in Jesus Christ as the means of acceptance before God.

Summary

Paul has been giving his personal testimony to remind the Galatians that he is what he is because of God's ordination (setting apart), calling, revelation and commissioning. It was through the revelation that he received his assignment to preach to the Gentiles. His testimony makes it abundantly clear that his position as an apostle and the gospel he preaches derive directly from the Father and the Son (Jesus Christ), and not from a human source.

Not Based on Human Wisdom

Paul underlines the point he is making about the source of his gospel by stressing that it *is not of human origin* (1:11). No earthly authority imparted it to him and it was not the product of his own reasoning. It is not "a philosophical system, or a religious faith created by some religious genius."[81] This is what sets the Christian gospel apart from all other religions. It does not start with a human being who discovers some special things about God and passes them on to others; it starts with God revealing himself to us.

Neither inspired nor taught by a human being

To underscore his point in 1:11, Paul repeats it in 1:12, beginning with an emphatic "I": *I did not receive it from any human source.* No human being had any role in giving him the gospel message.[82]

Some may suggest that Paul is contradicting himself here, for in 1 Corinthians 15:3 he says that "what I received I passed on to you", with what he received defined as "that Christ died for our sins according to the Scriptures". But the one from whom he received this teaching could well have been the Lord himself, just as it is in 1 Corinthians 11:23, where Paul says: "I received from the Lord what I also passed on to you."

Paul adds to his denial of a human source by saying *nor was I taught it* (1:12b). In the education system of Paul's day, great importance was attached to being able to say that "Rabbi X says this, but Rabbi Y says that". But Paul has no human instructor to cite. He was not taught his gospel by one of the twelve apostles or by anyone else. He got it directly from the Lord, just as he got his apostleship from the Lord (1:1).

We sometimes hear someone read a speech as a representative of some higher authority. For example, on important occasions in Kenya, provincial commissioners sometimes read the president's speech to people gathering in the provinces. On such occasions, the one doing the reading has no authority to modify what is said, for it is not his or her speech. We also hear presidents and prime ministers deliver speeches that were written for them by professional speech writers. The only input from the president is likely to have been the modification of a few words and confirmation of a few facts. The president may even learn some technical details from the speech written for him! Paul denies that he is in this kind of relationship with any human being. He is not passing on a message given to him by someone else, or filling in an outline provided to him by another human being. The gospel he preaches comes directly from the Lord.

Note that Paul is not saying that it is wrong to learn from others. He is simply giving his testimony about how the Lord prepared him to preach. He nowhere suggests that his experience sets a precedent for others. He himself became the teacher and mentor of others like Timothy, Titus and the Galatians, and instructed them to teach others.

Most of us learn from others but we should not be envious when someone, for the Lord's own reasons, is taught by the Lord himself. Nor should we dismiss Paul's testimony as untrue simply because we ourselves learn from other human beings. We should be content with how God wants to work in our lives and should glorify him in whatever we do.

More of Paul's testimony

After receiving his revelation, Paul did not *consult any human being* (1:16), or more literally, he did not consult "flesh and blood".[83] In other words, he did not immediately seek out "someone who was recognised as a qualified interpreter about the significance of some sign – a dream or omen, or portent" in order to get "a skilled or authoritative interpretation".[84] Paul had no need to do this because he had received both the message and its interpretation in one package from the Lord himself. To be sure, Ananias and the believers in Damascus who are mentioned in Acts 9:10–22 helped the newly converted Paul, but he did not consult them about the content of the gospel he was to preach. Nor did he go to Jerusalem to consult those who were already apostles before him (1:17).

Instead, immediately after his conversion and commissioning, *Paul went into Arabia*. Some time later, he *returned to Damascus* (1:17–18). A full three years elapsed before he went to Jerusalem (1:18a). Paul is giving these details to show the Galatians that he was engaged in preaching the gospel long before he met any of the twelve apostles. Thus he could not have received his gospel from them.

Paul adds that *I was personally unknown to the churches of Judea that are in Christ* (1:22).[85] If he had gone to Judea, the region where Jerusalem was located, large numbers of believers would have wanted to meet the new Paul, who was no longer their persecutor. They knew about his conversion and were glorifying God because of him (1:23–24). The fact that they did not know him is further proof that he did not interact with the twelve apostles based in Jerusalem.

Paul goes on to give details of how he spent the first fourteen years after his conversion (2:1). His aim is to prove that his visits to Jerusalem were so brief and infrequent that they would not have allowed enough time for him to have been taught what he should preach by the apostles. His comings and goings can be summarized like this:

- Conversion and brief stay in Damascus (Acts 9:19–25)
- Journey to Arabia (1:17b)
- Return to Damascus (1:17c)
- First post-conversion visit to Jerusalem (three years after conversion (1:18)
- Journey to Syria and Cilicia (1:21)
- Second post-conversion visit to Jerusalem (2:1).

Paul's stay in Arabia

Paul's statement that *after three years I went up to Jerusalem* (1:18) means that in those three years he must have fitted in a brief stay in Damascus (Acts 9:19b), the stay in Arabia (Gal 1:17b) and a second stay in Damascus before going to Jerusalem (1:17c). (Unless, as some argue, the "three years" were the time he spent in Damascus on his return to that city and do not include his time in Arabia.)

It is impossible to say how long he spent in Arabia. It may have been only a few weeks or it may have been many months. Complicating the issue is the Jewish way of reckoning time, with part of a year being treated as a year (the same principle applied to any segment of time – part of a day counted as a full day, part of a month as a full month, and so on). Thus the three years was not necessarily equivalent to thirty-six months. The time could even have been as short as fourteen months, if it included just the end of one year and the start of another.

The only guideline we have for judging how long he spent in Damascus is the statement in Acts 9:19 that he spent "several days" there immediately after his conversion, and the statement in 9:23 that he spent "many days" in Damascus, presumably during his second stay there. This does not help us much, but the fact that the author uses "days" suggests that these visits did not run to many months.

Paul does not give us a detailed itinerary because all he wants to do is prove that he stayed away from Jerusalem in the years immediately after his conversion and commissioning. Yet he was already proclaiming the gospel – so much so that his preaching aroused the opposition of the Jews in Damascus before he even set foot in Jerusalem after his conversion (Acts 9:23–25).

There is disagreement about what region Paul called "Arabia". Was it the Sinai peninsula, the place where the law was given to Moses and where Elijah meditated?[86] Or was it the Nabatean kingdom, extending from the Red Sea to the River Euphrates, with Petra in the south and Bosra in the north as the main cultural centres.[87] Those who argue for the Sinai peninsula point out that Damascus was part of Nabatea, and so it would be odd for Paul to say that he left Arabia and returned to Damascus (1:17). (Of course, given that boundaries are flexible, it is possible that by the time Paul wrote Galatians, Damascus was no longer part of the Nabatean kingdom and that Paul's words reflect the situation at the time of writing.)[88]

There is also disagreement about what Paul did in Arabia. Some commentators think that this was his first (undocumented) missionary journey, and that he was preaching there. He had been sent to the Gentiles, and there were plenty of them in Nabatea, some in the cities and some living as nomads.[89] Others, in fact the majority of scholars, argue that Paul used his time in Arabia to think. His life and belief system had been turned upside down, and he needed time to reflect on the change and "to seek through meditation a fuller understanding of the meaning of his call".[90] In support of this position they argue that Arabia was a desert area and thus sparsely populated, so Paul must have gone there to avoid people and thus by implication to consult God.[91]

Either position is possible. Paul does not tell us, and thus we cannot know.

The first visit to Jerusalem

It was only three years after his conversion that Paul returned to Jerusalem as a believer (Acts 9:26–30).[92] He had been preaching the gospel he received from the Lord before this date, but now he thought it was time *to get acquainted with Cephas* (1:18a).[93] Cephas, which means "rock", was the name that Jesus gave Peter in John 1:42.

The translation "get acquainted" suggests that the primary reason for the visit was to establish a personal relationship between Paul and "the leader of the original apostles, who was also at this time the unchallenged leader of the Jerusalem church."[94] The purpose was not to learn from Peter. As one commentator puts it, "Paul did not go to consult Cephas, or get any information essential to the validity of his office and work, but to visit him as a noted apostle – one whom it would be gratifying to know through private and confidential intercourse".[95]

While much of the talk between the two apostles must have centred on Jesus and their mission, this does not mean that Paul was being tutored by Peter. However, the meeting may have given Paul more information about the background of the Jesus movement, supplementary information about Jesus, and access to ways of expressing the gospel that were already being formulated by Peter and others.[96] But it was more a meeting of minds than a teacher–learner relationship. Paul and Peter shared as equals and each learned more about the other's mission and vision.

This type of interaction is important for people who are in the same mission. Co-operation is the goal, even when our areas of concentration differ. Thus in the institution in which I teach, there is a tradition that each year each academic department gives a one-hour presentation to the entire student body gathered in the chapel. One thing that comes across in these presentations is the interdependence of biblical studies, theological studies, translation studies, mission studies, pastoral studies, and historical studies. No matter the area of concentration, our calling is one: to build the kingdom of God.

What a contrast with a situation I observed recently, where one congregation was building their house of worship not more than three hundred feet from another congregation. Both were each using amplifiers to broadcast their services to the neighbourhood. Sadly, the main message they were communicating was one of competition, not co-operation. Paul and Peter consulted each other so that their ministry would be unified despite the fact that Peter focused on reaching Jews and Paul on reaching Gentiles.

This particular visit to Jerusalem lasted a mere fifteen days (1:18b). The contrast between "fifteen days" and the "three years" preceding the visit impresses on the reader how short this visit was. There is no way that two weeks would have been long enough for Peter to teach Paul everything he needed to preach.

Paul does not want to leave out anyone whom he met on this visit, and so when he specifies that *I saw none of the other apostles,* he hastily adds *only James, the Lord's brother* (1:19).⁹⁷ James was a leader in the church, whom the Galatians would know and whom Paul will mention later in this letter (2:9, 12). It is interesting that Paul classes James among the apostles, as the more literal NASB translation shows: "I did not see any other of the apostles except James, the Lord's brother". Here the word "apostle" is being used in the non-technical sense in which it simply means "one who is sent". In this sense it is used of several people in the New Testament (Rom 16:7; 2 Cor 8:23; Phil 2:25). This usage should not be confused with the technical title of apostle applied to the Twelve and Paul who got their teaching directly from Jesus himself. There is thus nothing wrong with contemporary preachers calling themselves "apostles", provided they do not claim to speak with the same authority as Peter, Paul, John, and others who learned from Jesus directly.

James was not an apostle in the technical sense, and so was not Paul's instructor. Nor were any of the Twelve, for Paul did not meet any of them except Peter – and he met Peter as a colleague. A brief account of this visit is given in Acts 9:26–30.

Paul spends so much time on the source of his gospel because the Judaizers were planting doubts in the minds of the Galatian believers. They were insinuating that Paul had been taught the gospel by the Twelve and had now departed from it to teach his own ideas, with which the others would not agree. So Paul stresses that his message was given to him directly by the Lord.

This matter is of such importance that Paul not only argues it but also swears to the truth of what he says: *I assure you before God that what I am writing you is no lie* (1:20).⁹⁸ Oaths like this were commonly used in Roman law courts to testify to the truthfulness of what was being said.⁹⁹ Paul utters similar assurances in Romans 9:1, 2 Corinthians 11:31 and 1 Timothy 2:7. However, this is the only time that he includes the phrase "before God", which intensifies the power of the oath. Given the seriousness of the matter and the fickleness of the Galatians, they need the strongest possible assurance.¹⁰⁰

Some people would argue that Paul is acting contrary to Christ's instructions against uttering oaths: "Do not swear – not by heaven or by earth or by anything else." (Matt 5:34–37; see also Jas 5:12). But this prohibition is against using oaths to deceive or because we cannot be trusted to tell the truth. This is not the case with Paul. He is trustworthy, but the Galatians are suspicious. He will do whatever it takes to convince them of the truth of his words. Their continuance in salvation depends on it.

Journey to Syria and Cilicia

After leaving Jerusalem, Paul travelled to the Roman region known as *Syria and Cilicia* (1:21).[101] He was hundreds of miles away from the mother church in Jerusalem and the apostles there, but closer to the region where he had grown up, for his home town, Tarsus, was located in Cilicia. That was where he was sent to escape death threats (Acts 9:30). That was where Barnabas found him and invited him to come to Antioch (Acts 11:25–26), the town where the label "Christian" was first applied to the followers of Christ (Acts 11:26). Antioch became the missionary base for Paul and Barnabas (Acts 13:1–3).

Paul mentions his time in this region to remind the Galatians that he stayed away from Jerusalem, but it is worth pausing to reflect that his time there was a necessary preparation for a life full of spiritual energy and ministerial experience. It is a reminder to us that God brings experiences into our lives for a good reason. Paul's rejection in Jerusalem (Acts 9:29) led him to his home town for leave and from there to Antioch, his missionary base. God is a wonderful moulder of both our lives and our ministries.

Questions for Discussion

1. What other faiths are you familiar with besides Christianity? What similarities and differences do they have with Christianity? Would Paul accept the equation of Christianity with any other religion? Why or why not?
2. Has your authority ever been undermined? How did you go about defending it, and how does your approach differ from or match the way in which Paul goes about defending his authority in this section of Galatians?
3. Have you ever been so concerned about someone needing to know the truth that you went to extremes to try to convince them of the truth? What was the issue and what were the results? What is Paul's concern here?

UNIT 4
GALATIANS 2:1–5

A VISIT TO JERUSALEM

In Africa important negotiations are traditionally done before witnesses who are related to one of the negotiating parties. Few negotiations are taken more seriously than those relating to a marriage.

Some years ago, I was a member of a group accompanying a friend to the negotiations with the family of the girl his son wanted to marry. The journey to their home was long and difficult, and several times our cars got stuck in mud. Then one of the cars broke down. This was disastrous, for the girl's father had specified the exact time he wanted us to arrive because some of the witnesses with him had to travel later that same day. We prayed that the girl's family would not decide that habitual lateness was a trait of the boy's family and refuse to negotiate a marriage.

Our fears were well-founded. When we got there two hours later than scheduled, we found the gate locked. We were no longer welcome. We persisted in knocking until eventually someone came out of the house with the message: "The rest of you can stay outside, but one of you can come in and explain why you are late." My friend looked to me for support, and I quickly slipped in beside him. The gatekeeper was a bit surprised but did not use force to keep me out.

We introduced ourselves to the girl's parents, described the difficulties of the journey, and reminded them that they should not be too hasty to judge because we were dealing with the future of two people we loved. Our words melted their hearts, and the gate was opened to admit everyone in our party. The negotiations began.

We soon found out that those most determined to oppose the negotiations were not the girl's parents but some of their neighbours.

The negotiations were going to be difficult. However, the Lord used three things to turn the situations around.

The first was my friend's answer to the traditional question, "Can you tell us why you have made this visit?" (Everyone knows the reason, but this question marks the start of the actual negotiations.) My friend answered with such humour that everyone had to laugh. The mood lightened – this could be a happy occasion after all.

Next, my friend introduced all of those who had come with him. When he mentioned my name, someone asked whether I was the pastor who had preached at his church several times. I said that I was, and he responded enthusiastically. The atmosphere warmed still more.

Finally, African hospitality took over. We shared food, and a cow was slaughtered for an all-night celebration. By the next morning, the negotiations were not only complete but everyone was very full and happy.

This incident illustrates the importance of knowing the purpose for a visit and choosing the right companions, as well as the effect of the disposition of those visited. This holds true whether the purpose of our visit is to establish relationships, achieve reconciliation, raise funds, or anything else. So when Paul tells us about his visit to Jerusalem, he describes its purpose, his companions, the complications and the solution.

Paul and Jerusalem

In the letter so far, Paul has been stressing that he did not get his gospel from the apostles and the leaders in Jerusalem but got it directly from the Lord. However, he does not want anyone to think that he is hostile to the other leaders, so he explains that they support each other's work. In evidence he mentions the events associated with the visit he made to Jerusalem *fourteen years* after his conversion (2:1).[102]

In the years between these two visits, Paul preached the gospel in Syria and Cilicia (1:21).

Paul's Companions

Paul's main companions on this visit to Jerusalem were Barnabas, a Jew, and Titus, a Gentile (2:1b). *Barnabas* was a Levite from Cyprus who became a Christian in Jerusalem (Acts 4:36–37). The references to him in Acts make it clear that he was a key figure in helping bridge the gap between the mission to the Jews and the mission to the Gentiles (Acts 9:27; 11:22; 13:1–14:28; 15:2–4, 12, 36–41).[103] *Titus* is not mentioned in Acts. We are, however, told that he was not Jewish but an uncircumcised Greek (2:3), who had probably been converted by Paul (Titus 1:4). He became an important associate of Paul (2 Cor 2:12–13; 7:5–16; 8:6–24; 9:35; 12:18; Titus 1:5).

Paul seems to have been the one in charge, the one who chose his companions.[104] But why would he include Titus, whose presence would certainly arouse controversy among the Jewish Christians in Jerusalem? Paul does not tell us his reason, but scholars have suggested several possibilities:

- He wanted to test whether the Jewish Christians in Jerusalem and their leaders would accept a Gentile in his team.
- He wanted to demonstrate the peaceful co-existence of the circumcised and the uncircumcised in Christ.
- He wanted to demonstrate that he was "all things to all men" – a Gentile as he related to Titus and a Jew as he related to Barnabas.

All of these would be acceptable strategies for Paul, and for us if we are engaged in a ministry which some people oppose. We should provide practical examples of what our ministry accomplishes and should carefully observe how others respond to our ideas or practices. Paul's message was that both Jews and Gentiles belong together, and his team demonstrated that.

When we proclaim that we are all one in Christ, no matter what our colour, race or tribe, do our ministry teams match our words? Do we include people from every group? Are ministries staffed mainly by missionaries and non-Africans? Do our teams include people from various language groups? And if we are all one in Christ and have all received spiritual gifts, why are many churches dominated by men? If we are not showing our own acceptance of diversity, we are not "walking the talk". In saying this, I am not arguing that we should appoint people to positions regardless of their qualifications, but I am saying that we should check that we actually demonstrate the oneness of Christ that we proclaim.

Paul specifically mentions Titus when writing to the Galatians because he wishes to make the point that the fact that Titus was not circumcised did not result in his being rejected or lead to any conflict between Paul and the key leaders in Jerusalem. Paul explicitly states that *not even Titus, who was with me, was compelled to be circumcised, even though he was a Greek* (2:3).

There is some debate about whether Paul is saying that Titus chose to remain uncircumcised or whether he voluntarily submitted to circumcision.[105] In the context of this letter, it seems likely that Titus was not circumcised during or after the visit, and that the leadership in Jerusalem did not make an issue of it. However, regardless of whether he was or was not circumcised, the principle remains clear: circumcision is not essential for salvation. There is no objection to Gentiles choosing to be circumcised, but they should not be forced to do so.

There is a very important principle at play here. Whenever the Christian faith is planted in a new area, there is always something equivalent to circumcision, that is, some practice that is insisted on which keeps people from grasping the core of the gospel, which is faith in Christ. For example, Christians who smoke are sometimes treated as unbelievers. While smoking may be a bad habit (and a sign of failure to care for the body the Lord has given to us – 1 Cor 6:19), it is wrong to link smoking and salvation. The same applies to how much clothing believers wear in cultures where the people traditionally wear little. Our salvation is not dependent on how much of our body is exposed.

The Reason for the Visit

Paul says that he went to Jerusalem *in response to a revelation* (2:2). What does he mean? Who received this revelation and how was it received? Paul does not tell us, but that has not prevented scholars from discussing it. Some think that Paul is referring to the revelation to Agabus that famine was coming (Acts 11:28).[106] However, given the emphasis Paul lays on his dependence on the Lord alone for both his apostleship and his message, it seems likely that he has some more direct revelation in mind.[107] He was certainly familiar with various modes of revelation, for example, prophecy (1 Cor 14:6, 26, 30), visions or dreams (Acts 16:9–10; 18:9–10; 23:11; 27:23–24), and God-given conviction (Phil 3:15; Acts 16:6–7; 20:22).

We are living in days when many preachers claim to have become prophets because God has revealed this, that or the other to them. Some of the revelations have to do with other people's lives. When evaluating such revelations, believers must consider the following points:

- Revelation will not contradict Scripture. If it does, it must immediately be dismissed.
- God does not reveal his will only to preachers. If a preacher gets a revelation concerning you, the best response is to ask the preacher to pray that God will affirm it through a revelation to you also. There are wolves among the shepherds, and believers should be careful not to be deceived.
- Any prophet who claims to have a revelation about you must be someone whose known walk with God makes it likely that God would use them in this special way.
- We should walk so closely with God that he can speak to us directly and not need to relay his messages through someone else.

Much of God's will for our lives has already been revealed in Scripture. The areas in which we tend to look for or receive revelations concern issues like whom we should marry (for the single) or when to begin a family (for the married). Our aim should always be to live in the Lord's will. When we do this, he is with us as we walk the journey of life, no matter how difficult the path.

Paul has no doubt that his visit to Jerusalem was in the Lord's will. He did not go there because he had been summoned by the leaders or because of any human urging. He went there following divine guidance.[108]

Paul makes this statement in defence of his own authority but it is worthy applying to life in general. There is nothing as good as being certain one is doing the Lord's will. People may urge us to do various things and tell us their opinions, but at the end of the day, our path must be guided by a good sense of what God's will is. When the church approaches someone about a particular assignment and the person says that he or she does not sense the Lord leading that way, the church must back off and pray that the Lord will lead them in the right direction. For example, when the mission board of a local church wants to send a missionary to a particular field and the missionary does not hear the Lord's voice directing him or her there, the transfer should not be forced. When the right time comes, the revelation will come.

The Nature of the Visit

Before looking at the details of what was accomplished during this visit, it is worth trying to work out whom Paul met. The translation in the TNIV makes it appear that he met only with the leaders: *meeting privately with those esteemed as leaders, I set before them* (2:2a).[109] But the original Greek text is ambivalent. The NKJV gives a more literal translation: "I … communicated to them … but privately to those who were of reputation …". The "them" in 2:2a could refer to the whole Jerusalem Christian community, and not just the leaders.[110] If so, Paul met with the larger group before meeting with the leaders (literally, "those reputed to be important").[111] The total picture may be something like this:

1. Paul and his team met with the Jerusalem church in something like a general church meeting.
2. During this meeting, it became apparent that a smaller group, equivalent to a church board, needed to meet in private to talk to Paul about his ministry.
3. The smaller group of church leaders gathered under the leadership of James, Cephas (Peter) and John (2:9), who functioned like the executive committee of a council or board in our day.
4. The demands of the false believers were rejected, and James, Cephas and John gave Paul and his team their hand of fellowship, endorsing his ministry.

Problems during the Visit

Not everything went smoothly during the visit. Some troublemakers attended the meetings to promote the cause of those demanding that all male believers be circumcised.

Paul refers to these troublemakers as *false believers* (2:4), but provides no further clues to their identity. Nor does he say whether this problem first arose in Jerusalem or in Antioch, or whether it was before, during or after his visit to Jerusalem. Once again, commentators have had to attempt to reconstruct events. The more common view is the one I have outlined above, namely that this problem arose during his second visit to Jerusalem (the next most popular view is that they arose in Antioch).

Assuming that the first view is correct, three key parties were involved: 1) Paul, Barnabas and any others who agreed with their position on circumcision; 2) the false believers causing the problem; and 3) the leaders with whom Paul and Barnabas were meeting. In this unit we will concentrate on what we know about the false believers.

The first thing we know is that they were insisting that circumcision was a requirement for salvation, and that accordingly Paul's Greek companion, Titus, must be circumcised. This is clear from 2:3–4, and Paul's words that *this matter* (that is, Titus' circumcision) came up because of the presence of *some false believers*.[112]

The second thing we know is that these people had set out to spy on the freedom Paul and his companions had in Christ (2:4b). They were like spies or traitors, worming their way into an organization or an army camp in order to learn enough about it to be able to destroy it.[113] It is not clear whether what they had *infiltrated* was the church in general, the church in Antioch, or the consultation in Jerusalem.

If the correct answer is the church in general, then some people had joined the church and attached themselves to Paul's mission to the Gentiles for sinister motives. This could have happened either in Antioch, where Paul had been working, or in Jerusalem.[114] However, the simplest interpretation of this passage is that false believers sneaked into a meeting between Paul and Barnabas and representatives of the Jerusalem church.[115] They pretended to be genuinely concerned about maintaining unity in the church's outreach, but in fact they wanted to push the point that Gentiles must be circumcised in obedience to the law. So they insisted that Titus must be circumcised. His lack of circumcision had not been an issue before they arrived.

This type of situation still happens today. When we are serving on some committee, it is very important to be alert to the contribution of every committee member. I have known church councils where some members would sleep through long meetings and have to be woken up to vote! That is dangerous. We need to be listening to determine whether a speaker is genuine in what he says. Otherwise, speakers with ulterior motives may hijack a committee. Nor is it enough just to instruct people to stay awake. We may also need to schedule meetings in such a way that they do not become exhausting for the participants. Elders who tire fast should even consider resigning to allow younger members to assume office. The same holds true for our theological institutions. We must take care when appointing faculty that no one slips in whose motive is to destroy. (In saying this, I am not saying that we should not be open to new ideas; but there are certain fundamentals on which we should not compromise.)

Jesus told his disciples to "watch and pray" (Matt 26:41), for it is when we sleep that the devil sneaks in. We must constantly be alert to any deviations from the truth that the devil may cleverly attempt to introduce.

The infiltrators immediate target may have been Titus and his lack of circumcision, but Paul sees their goal in broader terms: they had come *to spy on the freedom we have in Christ Jesus* (2:4c). The verb translated as "spy" is used of watching something with an evil intent (2 Kgs 10:3; 1 Chr 19:3).[116] These men were spying on Paul's freedom in order to be able to take it away. The result would be that they would *make us slaves*, or as the NASB put it, "bring us into bondage" (2:4c).

The freedom that Paul refers to here is not freedom in general but freedom from the need to obey the law of Moses in order to be accepted by God. True freedom comes by way of Christ and is enjoyed in Christ.[117] He took care of all the demands of justice and obeyed the law perfectly on our behalf.

Response to the Problems

Paul and his associates had no hesitation about how to respond to this attack on them: *We did not give in to them for a moment* (2:5a).[118] They were not prepared to consider forcing Titus to be circumcised. Why were they so adamant on this point? The answer was that they recognized that this was a situation where *the truth of the gospel* (2:5b) was at stake.[119] If Paul, Barnabas and the others who were with him had given in to this demand, they would have endorsed the false principle that justification is by way of works.

Paul tells the Galatians about this incident and the response to it because they are in the similar situation. Their freedom in Christ is being threatened by the Judaizers, and they too must stand firm and resist all attempts to bring them back into bondage. The same principles apply regardless of the context.

Paul's stress that *we* did this so that the truth of the gospel *might remain with you* (2:5b) brings out the importance of doing what is right for the sake of future generations. Leaders who never give a thought to how their decisions will affect what happens in the future should not be in office. Yet there are many such leaders. They pursue short-term goals and show no concern for long-term consequences. We see this in the financial sphere, where reckless borrowing brings disaster on individuals and nations. We see it in the environmental sphere, where degradation of the environment today will result in hunger and disease in the future. Sadly, we even see it in the church when church leaders fail to think beyond the immediate problem. We need leaders who are concerned about today's needs but who also think about the needs of tomorrow.

Is Paul being inconsistent here? He had Timothy circumcised (Acts 16:3), so why not do the same with Titus in order to avoid causing unnecessary offence? But Timothy's circumstances were very different. His mother was Jewish, whereas both Titus' parents were Gentiles. Also, Timothy was circumcised because Paul was going to be preaching in Jewish synagogues, and some Jews would have objected to Timothy's presence there. So the decision to have him circumcised was based on the needs of Paul's evangelistic ministry. However, in the case of Titus, these believers were insisting that circumcision was necessary for salvation. This Paul refused to accept.

Paul's willingness to seem inconsistent is highly relevant to the way we make decisions. Some leaders assume that once a precedent has been set, we must never deviate from it. But it is wrong to assume that we must always make the same decision. Every situation is different, and different facts have to be taken into account. While precedents can provide useful guidelines, they should not dictate our actions, which should be based on careful analysis of what is best for the new situation. The precedent set by Timothy's circumcision does not apply in Titus' case because a higher principle is at stake.

Questions for Discussion

1. Has anyone ever demanded that you do something that you knew was wrong? For example, have you been told to pay a bribe in order to get a job, change the numbers in an account in order to illegally divert money, or lie to protect someone who has done wrong? How did you respond? What qualities does it require to stand firmly for what is right, especially in Africa today?
2. How inclusive is your circle of friends or your ministry team? Did you select them for secondary reasons (they have similar likes and dislikes and you have known them for a long time), or even for the wrong reasons (they come from the same people group or clan and are easy to manipulate)? Or did you choose them for good reasons, because their gifts complement yours, or to demonstrate oneness in the body of Christ, or because they can make a real contribution to building the kingdom of God? How do you evaluate the church or institution you belong to in this regard? How can areas of strength be strengthened still more and areas of weakness corrected?
3. What current issues are attacking our unity in the church? Are these attacks equivalent to what the false believers tried to do in sowing discord between Peter's and Paul's teams to stop them cooperating? As you mention each issue, evaluate whether it is something on which you need to take a stand or whether it is an issue on which church members should accommodate each other. Explain your thinking.

UNIT 5
GALATIANS 2:2, 6–10

UNITY OF PURPOSE

On 27 June 2009 a large group of Kenyans gathered in the town of Nakuru in the Rift Valley. They were there to meet with the former president of Kenya, Daniel Toroitich arap Moi. The theme of the meeting was reconciliation.

Eighteen months before this meeting, Kenya had been convulsed with violence. There had been no clear winner in the national election in December 2007, and the electoral process had been hijacked by the premature announcement that Mwai Kibaki had won. Supporters of Raila Odinga rioted, and two months of violence followed. Many lost their lives. Those who supported one of the candidates tortured and killed those they suspected of supporting the other. Those who had been attacked launched revenge attacks. Kenya was tearing itself apart. Thank God, Kofi Annan, the retired general secretary of the United Nations, was able to restore some degree of peace.

Those attending the meeting in June 2009 were gathered to declare that the people of the Rift Valley were determined to live together in peace and never repeat what had happened. We pray that they will keep their word, and that the rest of the population of Kenya will uphold the peace.

In all such situations, the key issue is how people handle differences of opinion. When people react emotionally, they strike out at others and before we know it innocent people are being murdered. Kenya is not the only place where this has happened. We saw it in Nigeria in the late 1960s and in Rwanda in the early 1990s. Those who respond emotionally end up hating, and sometimes harming, those with whom they differ. It would be far better to deal with the issues before they give birth to misunderstandings, and these misunderstandings lead to hatred or war.

The early church was also in a situation that could easily have led to serious in-fighting between Jews and Gentiles. But the leaders of the two parties used their God-given wisdom to reach mutual understanding before these differences produced chaos in the church. Paul, the apostle to the Gentiles, and Peter, whose mission was to the Jews, agreed to support each other in the tasks God had assigned them. They set an example not only to the church but also to politicians. We should not only study how they did it but should seek to apply their principles to every sphere of our lives.

Paul's Action

At his meetings in Jerusalem, Paul reported on *the gospel that I preach among the Gentiles* (2:2b). In doing this, he was not acting like a subordinate reporting to his supervisors. The Greek verb translated *set before them* is the same one used when Porcius Festus "discussed Paul's case" with King Agrippa (Acts 25:14).[120] Paul speaks as an equal of the Jerusalem apostles. He is simply comparing notes with them to make sure that they are all on the same page.

His use of the present tense, "I preach" implies that this is what he preaches all the time.[121] It is the gospel he preached when he was with the Galatians and the one he is still preaching.

Paul's Purpose

Paul's purpose in conferring with the leaders in Jerusalem was *to be sure I was not running and had not been running my race in vain* (2:2c).[122] Some suggest that Paul wanted the leaders in Jerusalem to approve his mission and declare it valid.[123] But that does not fit the context. The opening chapter of this letter shows that Paul was certain of the validity of his gospel and confident that it had been assigned to him by God. His reason for visiting the leaders in Jerusalem was to ensure that they maintained unity in the midst of diversity. Fellowship with Jerusalem would be a blessing to his cause.

When I was growing up, there was a sharp divide between Protestants and Catholics. I was taught many reasons to beware of "them". Some of what I was told was true, but what I was not told was equally important: I was not told that a Roman Catholic who has exercised faith in Christ is one in Christ with the Protestant who has done the same. Today, I see the same thing happening between Pentecostal or charismatic church movements and the older more traditional churches. These divisions undermine the work of Christ. Faith in Christ unites us whether we are baptized by sprinkling or immersion, whether we dance as we sing or whether we stand still. We should never allow secondary matters to undermine our primary unity in Christ. This unity should be evidenced by leaders of different denominations having warm fellowship with one another. Ordinary believers will then have visible proof that Christ unites us.

Paul uses a sports metaphor when he describes what he does as "running my race". But we should not interpret this metaphor as implying that he was in competition with the believers in Jerusalem. They were all in the race together, like runners in a relay. He would be "running in vain" if they misunderstood what he was doing and hampered his work or tried to trip him up. We see such hampering today when one preacher criticizes another not because of some fundamental issue of doctrine but simply because of differences of opinion on minor secondary issues or some simple misunderstanding.

By laying his message before his fellow believers in Jerusalem and letting them understand his ministry, Paul showed his respect for them and his appreciation of the need for all believers to work together in the cause of truth.

The Outcome

The Judaizers in Galatia would be eager to interpret Paul's meetings in Jerusalem as proof that he was inferior to the apostles there. So Paul immediately spells out three important things achieved by this visit.

Recognition of equality

Paul seems to disparage the status of the leaders in Jerusalem. When he speaks of them, he uses a Greek word that expresses scepticism in the way we do when we speak of "so-called experts", implying that they are not as expert as they claim to be. However, the word can also mean "esteemed", that is, "influential and having a good reputation."[124] It is not automatically a bad term, which is why the TNIV translates it as *those esteemed as leaders* (2:2). But the way Paul uses it here does seem to lean towards the "so-called" meaning, so a more literal translation would be "those who seemed influential" (ESV). In 2:6, he repeats the word "seems" when he twice speaks of *those who seemed to be something* (NKJV), and in 2:9 he speaks of the people *who seemed to be pillars* (NKJV).[125] This last group are identified as *James, Cephas* (the Aramaic form of the name Peter) *and John*. This gives us a clue as to the core group Paul has in mind as he uses the word "seems" throughout this passage.[126] These were probably the people the Judaizers had singled out as the most important.

But if Paul is talking of the three leading apostles, why does he use language that almost denies their position of importance in the church? The best way to answer this question is to look at the context in which he is writing. These three men were the rightful leaders in Jerusalem. Paul acknowledged their status when he chose to meet with them. However, the false believers were probably exaggerating the status of the apostles in order to belittle Paul by implying that the other three were the only true leaders. Paul refuses to accept this assessment of their relative status. He acknowledges these men as leaders but not as his superiors, and he does not accept any suggestion that he himself is not a leader, particularly when it comes to ministry to the Gentiles. Bruce puts it well: "Paul does not question the Jerusalem leaders' personal status and prestige; what he does object to is the appeal made in some quarters to their status and prestige to diminish his own – in particular, the argument that their authority is so much superior to his that, if he acts or teaches in independence of them, his action and teaching lack all validity."[127]

This is also why Paul adds that *whatever they were makes no difference to me* (2:6b). His use of the past tense here shows that he is thinking of these leaders' past roles.[128] James was Jesus' brother and Peter and John had been his personal companions. Paul does not belittle the wonderful privilege James enjoyed in growing up in the same family as Jesus. Nor does he deny that Peter and John were privileged to be Jesus' companions for three years. But their past status is irrelevant to the fundamental issue that is at the heart of the conflict with the Judaizers in Galatia. These men's past experience does not make them Paul's superiors.[129]

Paul backs up his position by citing a proverb: *God does not show favouritism* (2:6c).[130] God does not base his judgment "on external and irrelevant considerations" and he cannot be bribed.[131] Thus he will not "favour companions or relatives of the historical Jesus over someone, like Paul, who received his apostolic commission later".[132] What matters to God, and thus to Paul, is that God commissioned him.

This is an important principle for those called to ministry. We come from many different backgrounds, but what matters is the Lord's calling. Some come to seminary from a Bible school, others from universities. Some have received professional training in fields like law and medicine, others have not. Some grew up in Christian homes, others did not. All of us, however, have been given the same message to pass on, namely, the message of justification by faith in Christ. It makes no difference whether we come to ministry after working as a fisherman like Peter or as a scholar and tentmaker like Paul, whether we have a PhD or only a college certificate. All of us are called to proclaim that Christ is the Saviour of the world. God may use our backgrounds to help us reach specific groups of people, but that affects only the way we present our message, not its content. This is the point Paul is making when he says that James, Peter and John *added nothing to my message* (2:6d).[133]

The false believers may have been arguing that Paul owed his gospel to the Jerusalem apostles; Paul strongly denies this. More likely, they were claiming that these leaders demanded that Paul modify some part of his teaching.[134] But the three apostles demanded no modification to Paul's message of justification by faith alone, with no need for circumcision. In view of this, how can the Judaizers in Galatia insist on circumcision? Their position is not supported by James, Peter or John, the pillars of the church in Jerusalem.

Mutual Acceptance

Rather than reproving Paul as the Judaizers expected, James, Peter and John gave Paul and Barnabas *the right hand of fellowship* (2:9). This act was "a common pledge of friendship or covenant".[135] It communicated "a formal agreement, clearly set out, and not simply a private arrangement or vague expression of good will".[136] This positive act is introduced with the words *on the contrary* to stress the point that they added nothing to Paul's message. All they did was bless what he was doing.

This was not an undiscriminating endorsement. It was shaped by their understanding of the circumstances, the theological basis of their fellowship, and their common purpose.

Based on circumstances

Before extending the hand of fellowship to Paul, the apostles recognized that Paul *had been entrusted with the task of preaching the gospel to the Gentiles* (literally, "the uncircumcised"), *just as Peter had been to the Jews* (literally, "the circumcised") (2:7). Paul does not say exactly what led to this recognition. It was probably a combination of factors, including Paul's statement of the content of his gospel, how he received it, and the results of his proclamation of it. The apostles could not deny "that Paul's missionary work was having precisely the same results among the Gentiles as Peter's among their fellow Jews".[137] In 2:9b, Paul summarizes it as *they recognized the grace given to* me (2:9). There could be no doubt that God had called him and blessed his work among the Gentiles. The apostles needed to be assured of this before they welcomed him as a colleague.[138]

The apostles recognized the need to affirm each other's ministries. We should not hesitate to do the same, even with those whose philosophies of ministry or teaching may differ from ours, provided we are in agreement on the essential content. Once it is clear that we are on the same team, we should offer sincere words of support and encouragement. It is always unfortunate when two Christians cannot demonstrate the love of Christ to each other simply because their styles of ministry differ. The uniting message about Christ should remove any such barriers. This is the will of God, the master of the vineyard into which he has called us as labourers.

The description of the Jews as "the circumcised" and Gentiles as "the uncircumcised" in 2:7 is both a mark of identification and a deliberate reference to the state of each of these two groups when they accepted the gospel. The Jews were circumcised, the Gentiles were not.[139] There is nothing rude about these terms. It is equivalent to identifying some people as "lake people" and others as "mountain people". The terms are neutral in themselves. However, when a term develops a negative connotation, believers should avoid using it. For example, in South Africa foreigners are sometimes referred to as *amakwerekwere*, implying that they are inferior and ignorant. Believers should not use such language.

The specific mention of Peter and Paul indicates that just as Paul was the missionary par excellence to the Gentiles, so Peter was to the Jews. This division was not absolute, for Paul preached to both Jews and Gentiles. Nor does it imply that there were two gospels, one for Jews and one for Gentiles. Rather, it was a matter of reaching different groups in different contexts. Both Paul and Peter had been entrusted with the responsibility of presenting the gospel wisely. This involves knowing whom one is preaching to. Preaching is always more effective when the preacher takes the time to analyze the audience. The content of the message may be the same, but the application and delivery of the message will be different for different audiences.

Both Peter and Paul "had been entrusted" with their message (2:7; see also 1 Cor 9:17; 1 Thess 2:4; 1 Tim 1:11; Titus 1:3). The verb here is passive, meaning that someone else has given it to them as a trust to be delivered to the groups to whom they were sent. Peter was sent to the Jews, Paul to the Gentiles. Who have you been sent to? God has entrusted us with the message of salvation and given us specific assignments. What he wants from us is faithfulness as stewards of his word in the area in which he has asked us to serve. Faithfulness is the only basis on which we can compare our ministries.

People in some mission fields are more responsive than others, and so there will be more converts in those fields. But the number of people converted has nothing to do with how faithful the worker has been in carrying out their assignment. A church that withdraws its support from a missionary simply because he or she has fewer converts than someone else is missing the point.

If we look at church history, we could argue that Paul's ministry was more successful than Peter's, because there were more Gentile believers than Jewish believers. But we should not judge by numbers. All factors must be considered, with the primary one being faithfulness. Luke presents Peter as a courageous steward of the gospel in Acts 1–12, before the focus of his book moves to Paul's ministry. Both men remained faithful in their respective missions. So should we.

Based on theology

What is implied in 2:7 is spelled out more specifically in 2:8: *God, who was at work in Peter as an apostle to the Jews, was also at work in me as an apostle to the Gentiles.* The past tense used here suggests that Paul is not speaking simply of the ministry he and Peter have been doing, but is instead thinking of the time when they were called to this ministry. Both had received a special call and commissioning, and both were carrying out the assignment they had been given.[140]

Though this statement occurs in the middle of Paul's wider statement of the circumstances which resulted in the three leaders of Jerusalem giving him their hand of fellowship, it is an independent theological interjection. It underscores the point that there is only one God, who is the God of both Peter and Paul. In the same way, there is only one gospel for both Jews and Gentiles. If the Judaizers in Galatia accept the ministry of Peter to the Jews, they also have to accept the ministry of Paul to the Gentiles. Both men serve a common master and there is no competition between them.

Based on a common purpose

By extending the hand of fellowship to Paul and Barnabas, the three leaders of Jerusalem signalled that they had reached an agreement.[141] Paul puts it like this: *they agreed that we should go to the Gentiles and they to the Jews* (2:9).[142] This was not a new assignment of responsibilities but recognition of an assignment God had already made.

The "we" stands for Paul and Barnabas and the "they" for James, Peter and John. As said earlier, this is not a geographical or racial division but a division for orderliness. Paul customarily went to the synagogues first (Acts 17:2, 10; 18:5; 19:8) even though his focus was on the Gentiles, and Peter's ministry and that of James were not limited to Jews or Jewish territories only (Acts 11:19–21; James 1:1; 1 Pet 1:1). The situation parallels that of someone who chooses to major in chemistry and minor in biology, while someone else chooses to major in biology and minor in chemistry. Their courses will overlap, but they do not conflict. It is only the focus that differs.

Governments appoint cabinet ministers, with one serving as the minister of health, another as the minister of agriculture and another as the minister of finance. It is foolish (and bad for the nation) if ministers are in competition. They are all there to serve the good of the same nation, and each should do his or her part. The same applies in churches. Both the senior pastor and the youth worker are called to minister to the same congregation. In a seminary, both the one who teaches biblical studies and the one who teaches missions are there to serve the same students. We are called to complementary ministries. If we refuse to recognize this, we miss the mark.

A Request

Paul has been stressing his independence of the leaders in Jerusalem and their acceptance of him. But now he adds that they did make one request of him: *All they asked was that we should continue to remember the poor* (2:10a).[143] The Greek verb translated "remember" has the idea of making a "diligent effort" to do something.[144] When they made this plea, the apostles were probably thinking particularly of the poor in Jerusalem. There was a famine in Palestine in AD 46, and the combination of famine and persecution (Acts 8:1) left the Jerusalem church financially impoverished. The situation may have been made worse by the fact that so many of the believers there had sold their possessions (Acts 2:45; 4:34).[145] Help was needed.

Christians have a social responsibility. The same James who was one of those making this request to Paul says that "religion that God our Father accepts as pure and faultless is this: to look after orphans and widows in their distress" (Jas 1:27). "Orphans and widows" represent all those who are in need. It is our Christian duty to respond to human need, no matter where it is felt nor by whom. We should not discriminate on the basis of ethnicity, colour or creed. The leaders in Jerusalem recognized different spheres of ministry, but the church was still one in essence and everyone should respond to the needs of the poor.

Help sometimes takes the form of financial assistance. This was what was needed by the Jerusalem church at the time.[146] If this visit is the one described in Acts 11:28, Paul and Barnabas had already brought some money to assist the impoverished believers. However, money is not the only form of help we can offer. It is only one aspect of brotherly affection and recognition of another's need.[147] Practical help can often be offered, and even the poorest of us can afford to pray for those who bless us, asking that they will find the Lord's favour in their lives and relationships.

Paul was delighted to accept this request from Peter, James and John, for it was *the very thing I had been eager to do all along* (2:10b). He was aware that the church of Christ is one body, no matter where it is located or what groups attend it. Every organ, whether the eye or the tongue or the little toe, has a role to play for the good of the whole (1 Cor 12:14–27) and "if one part suffers, every part suffers with it" (12:26). The needs of believer A are thus also the needs of believer B, and the needs of B are the needs of A, for there is a bond between them that crosses tribal, racial and status boundaries. Therefore Paul had no difficulty in acknowledging that the need of the Jewish believers was also the need of the Gentile believers.

When we share Paul's vision of the church, we will never offer help with an attitude of superiority, as if tossing coins to beggars. Instead, we will recognize that each believer and every region where believers are found makes a contribution to the whole body. Sometimes part of that contribution is providing an opportunity for those who have material wealth to give and by so doing grow in the Lord as they see him replenishing what they have. If we truly believed this, we would hear far more people saying, "How can I help?" and far fewer saying, "Help me!"

Some people have asked why Paul suddenly switches to the first person singular when he says "*I* had been eager", particularly when the request had used the plural "*we* should continue to remember". Does this mean that Paul is inconsistent when it comes to acknowledging what others contribute to his team?[148]

Probably not. There are other possible explanations for the change from singular to plural. The most likely one is that Paul uses the singular "I had been eager" because he is expressing his own attitude, which holds true regardless of the attitudes of the others in his team. It is quite acceptable to express one's own determination to do something within the context of a team. Moreover, it is likely that when it came to matters of policy, Paul was the leader of the group.[149]

A team may have many members, each of them equally important, but the executive director is the leader. He or she is the one who is responsible for keeping the vision clear and the mission going. If the team gets nowhere, others may have an excuse, but not the leader.

Some who speak of "servant leadership" act as if they are more servant than leader and fail to lead. More often, however, the problem is that the "leader" component overshadows the "servant" component. To be a leader does not mean that one dictates what others should do, but rather that one gets everyone to pull together. Paul as leader never lost sight of the fact that the needs of the Jews in Jerusalem were also the needs of the Gentiles in Antioch.

In good administration, the executive director takes the lead not by demanding respect and honour but by showing the direction in which everyone should be moving. In a local church, the pastor is the executive officer. If the senior pastor lacks vision, the youth pastor will be hindered, no matter how visionary he or she is. In a nation, if a president or prime minister lacks vision, the country suffers.

Sadly, although many leaders in Africa pay lip service to good principles of leadership, in practice they are little less than dictators, ordering their subordinates to do things. We see this type of behaviour at all levels of society, from local officials to presidents, from pastors to bishops. They think that being a dictatorial leader is a way of maintaining control, but that is a misconception. Their leadership style alienates others and breeds dissatisfaction.

In a local church, "leading" does not mean that the senior pastor tells the youth pastor how to conduct youth ministry. Nor does it mean ignoring Sunday school teachers or the youth pastor and letting them do things on their own, without any help from the senior pastor (which is what often happens if they refuse to do exactly as the pastor dictates). A true leader comes alongside and works with the youth pastor so that both pastors can achieve their visions for the congregation. The senior pastor then becomes part of the Sunday school or youth leadership – not to give instructions but to blend the zeal of the young into the vision of the church. This principle is applicable in all areas, from raising a family to building a nation. The young learn from their elders, but without the elders domineering over them. Yet, sadly, lions training their cubs to hunt and birds training their young to fly seem to do better than we do when it comes to watching over young ones while also training them to be in charge of their own destiny.

Paul's example as he pulls resources together to help believers in need is a model of someone who works as a member of a team and also provides leadership to achieve the team's vision. For Paul, the vision was to keep the church united in Christ even when the focus of ministry differed.

We all need to cultivate the ability to be both a team player and a good leader. Team members need to be able to answer in the affirmative when asked two questions: "Am I made to feel that I have an active role in what is going on?" and "Does our leader know where we need to go?" When the answer to both questions is "yes", there is a winning team.

Paul's team would have had no problems in answering "yes". In 1:2, his team members were reminded of their importance to his ministry, and in 2:10 Paul states his vision without ambiguity.

Questions for Discussion

1. Have you ever been in a situation where there was potential for misunderstanding and conflict about important issues? What were the issues, how did you handle the situation, and what were the results? How do your answers compare with the way Paul handled the situation he was in?
2. What motivates you to do good to others? Does it come from within or is it a response to the demands of others? What acts of goodness have you done in the last few months? Were some of them directed to people who are not part of your own group?
3. How would you and the members of your team answer the questions: "Am I made to feel that I have an active role in what is going on?" Discuss ways in which you can increase the likelihood that someone will reply "yes" to this question.
4. Team members need to be confident that the leader knows where they need to go. So where do you think your team is going?

RIVALRY INSTEAD OF TEAM SPIRIT

In Africa, areas of jurisdiction are jealousy guarded. There is strong resentment of any leader seen as interfering in another leader's constituency. In Kenya this attitude was especially pronounced in the early years of political independence. At that time there were two prominent political leaders in the Machakos district. I will call them Paul and William. Paul was a government minister who liked to brag that he had been in prison with Jomo Kenyatta, the founding president of the Republic of Kenya. He felt that this gave him the right to control every part of Machakos district, including William's constituency. William strongly resisted this. Instead of working together to promote the interests of Machakos, they put their energy into unnecessary fights.

I attended a large political rally in the area represented by William. Just before the meeting started, Paul arrived, intending to take control. The two leaders exchanged words. Then before my astonished eyes, they exchanged blows and fell to the ground, pummelling each other. Their behaviour was not only the main topic of conversation for weeks, but was also a clear indication that their desire for personal power outweighed their unity as members of the same political party. They were incapable of working together for the good of all.

When we focus on our own interests and lose sight of the broader ministry of Christ's church, we are becoming like William and Paul. We have become self-focused rather than Christ-focused. This applies whether we are preoccupied with our political constituency at the expense of the nation, with our denomination at the expense of the body of Christ, or with our own ambitions at the expense of our neighbour's needs.

The apostles Paul and Peter could also have been in competition, but instead they focused on the source of their assignments and their Saviour. What an example for us who allow minor issues to master us rather than our mastering them! Africa needs to unite to overcome its woes, while maintaining the autonomy of each nation. Each nation needs to unite to deal with its social, health, economic and other challenges, while respecting its varied ethnic inheritance. Every believer in Christ, local church and Christian denomination must focus on Christ, the founder of the church, even while protecting its traditional or liturgical interests. We need more people with the spirit of Paul and Peter, and fewer with that of Paul and William.

UNIT 6
GALATIANS 2:11–14

CLASH OF TWO GREAT MEN

To assume that our lives will proceed without conflict is to delude ourselves. Even if we do our best to avoid getting drawn into conflicts, those around us will bring them into our lives. On a daily basis, there are clashes of all kinds at all levels of relationship.

For proof of this, I scanned the newspaper headlines for two weeks in September 2004. Several clashes made the news:

- Minister X and the Honourable W "traded words" about an allegation that one of them was inciting his people to break the law.
- Guns drawn as Y "clashes with his rival", Z, about allegations regarding the politicizing of the disbursement of development funds.
- Ministers A and B "clash over sackings", with one alleging that the other had dismissed some officials without following the right procedure because of ethnic bias.

Such clashes are not unique to Kenya. Nor are they limited to the political arena. In fact, the church has seen many clashes – although fortunately few of them reach the headlines.

The question we need to ask ourselves is: Are all conflicts bad? If not, how do we distinguish bad ones from good ones? What do we make of the clash between Paul and Peter?

Background

Paul's account of his clash with Peter comes at the end of the biographical section that began in 1:13. He has been making the point that the gospel he preaches is neither derived from the apostles nor parallel to the gospel they preach but is the same gospel, deriving its authority from the same source as their gospel. He has given three items of historical information to back up this claim. Each of them introduced with the same Greek word translated as "then" or "later" (1:18, 21; 2:1):

1. Following his conversion, Paul did not consult the apostles in Jerusalem but went to Arabia and then returned to Damascus. It was several years before he met Peter, and his visit then lasted a mere fifteen days, during which he saw none of the other apostles, although he met James, the Lord's brother (1:18).
2. Thereafter he undertook a preaching ministry in Syria and Cilicia, which were far from Jerusalem (1:21).
3. Fourteen years later, he visited Jerusalem again. This time, he met with James, Peter and John who gave Paul and Barnabas the hand of fellowship. They supported his resistance to having Titus circumcised and supported his mission to the Gentiles just as they supported Peter's mission to the Jews.

The division of their ministries agreed to in Jerusalem was for the sake of orderliness and was not an absolute demarcation of territories. Thus there is nothing wrong with Peter later turning up in Antioch, which was technically in Paul's area of ministry.

Peter's Role

Some time after the meeting in Jerusalem, Peter arrived in Antioch, the capital of Syria, and a place that the ministry of Paul and Barnabas would transform into the centre of Gentile Christianity.[150]

At first, Peter shared meals (not just the Lord's Supper) with Gentile believers. He may have been doing this ever since his encounter with Cornelius (Acts 10–11) or he may only have started doing this after his arrival in Antioch, but it was certainly his regular practice.[151] But things changed when *certain people came from James* (12:12a).[152] These men must have come from Jerusalem where James, the Lord's brother, was probably the "leading administrative figure in the Jerusalem church from sometime in the late 40s until his martyrdom in AD 62".[153]

After their arrival, it became evident that Peter was becoming reluctant to share in meals: *He began to draw back and separate himself from the Gentiles* (2:12b).¹⁵⁴ His motive was that *he was afraid of those who belonged to the circumcision group*.¹⁵⁵ The "circumcision group (literally, "those of circumcision") simply means "Jews", just as "the uncircumcised" in 2:7–9 meant "Gentiles". Paul deliberately refers to them in this way to remind his readers that these people were proud of their circumcision and would have liked to require the Gentiles to be circumcised too. They do not seem to have raised this as an issue in Antioch, but what they did do was make it clear that they expected Peter and the other Jews there to obey the full Jewish law. Part of this law was that Jews would never share meals with Gentiles. Peter gave in to their pressure and began to avoid associating with Gentiles.

As a leader, Peter was influential, and other Jewish believers in Antioch started to copy his behaviour and avoid Gentile believers (2:13a). They became Peter's associates in dividing the church into Jewish and Gentile groups.¹⁵⁶ So strong was the peer pressure that even Barnabas, a Jew who was a close associate of Paul in his ministry to the Gentiles, followed suit (2:13b). Paul, however, uses a stronger term than "peer pressure" to describe this type of behaviour – he refers to it as *hypocrisy* (2:13b).¹⁵⁷ And he describes the effect on Barnabas as his being *led astray* (or "carried away", NASB). The verb suggests that Barnabas was acting irrationally on the basis of emotion, without taking time to think through the issues.

Barnabas' withdrawal and separation from the Gentiles, no matter how short-lived, was tantamount to a denial of all that he and Paul had been preaching in Southern Galatia during their first missionary journey.¹⁵⁸ Paul was amazed and horrified. The words *even Barnabas* imply that he was the last person Paul would have expected to act like this. In later years, Barnabas was probably embarrassed at how badly he had handled the situation.

What about us? Do we ever look back on our own behaviour with horror? Why did we do the thing that shocks us now? Did we take the time to think carefully, or did we allow ourselves to be swept along by the mob? Why would any believer join others in doing something that hurts others? For example, while a believer may take part in a strike or protest to express dissatisfaction about some situation, we should not allow ourselves to get caught up in looting or stoning motorists.

As soon as such behaviour starts, believers must disassociate themselves from the situation.

Barnabas failed to resist the tide and he and the believing Jews fell into sin, but their fall was ultimately Peter's responsibility. He had set them a bad example, which they had followed. As a leader he should have known that his example could build others up or cause them to stumble. This may be one of the reasons why James told his readers, "Not many of you should presume to be teachers, my brothers and sisters, because you know that we who teach will be judged more strictly" (Jas 3:1). Peter's followers were accountable for their own behaviour, but Peter carries a heavy responsibility for having led them astray.

Paul's Assessment

Given Peter's responsibility for the situation that was developing in Antioch, and for the many he had misled, Paul rebuked him. In fact he went so far as to say that Peter *stood condemned* (2:11).[159] By separating himself from the Gentile believers, Peter had put himself in a state of condemnation (that is, blameworthiness) and this state would continue as long as the grounds for the condemnation endured.

There is debate about who condemned Peter. Was it God? Was it all right-thinking people who recognized that his behaviour contradicted his own beliefs and misled others? Or was he enduring self-condemnation, in which he was judged by the inconsistency of his own actions, rather than by any external authority?

These options are not mutually exclusive, but the focus is on the last one. Paul did not initiate condemnation of Peter. He merely pointed out that Peter stood condemned by his inconsistency and violation of the very standards he was convinced were right.

When we deal with people who have sinned, we need to remember that it is not we who condemn them. Their own actions have condemned them. When they genuinely confess their sin, our role is to lead them out of guilt into an acceptance of God's forgiveness (1 John 1:9). If we have to excommunicate someone who refuses to confess, we must not do so with a condemnatory attitude but rather with grief that they do not want to change their own status from "condemned" to "forgiven".

At times we ourselves may need to accept discipline from others. When this happens, we must curb the temptation to assume that they are disciplining us because they do not like us. We need to set our egos aside and remember that our own acts have condemned us. May the Lord help us to freely confess our sins, for that is the only way of changing our status from "condemned" to "acceptable" before the Lord by way of the cleansing blood of his Son, Jesus Christ (1 John 1:9b).

Not only was Peter condemned, he was also hypocritical. Paul repeats the word twice in 2:13, where he says that the other Jews *joined him* [Peter] *in his hypocrisy* and adds that Barnabas was led astray by *their hypocrisy* (that is, the hypocrisy of Peter and the Jews who followed his example). The word "hypocrisy" carries with it the idea of playing a part on a stage. When used metaphorically, it means outward show by someone who is pretending to be something they are not. Peter's failure to remain true to his beliefs means that he is concealing his "true character, thoughts, or feelings under a guise implying something quite different".[160]

Finally, Paul saw Peter as *not acting in line with the truth of the gospel* (2:14a). The word translated "acting in line" means "walking straight or uprightly."[161] When used in the negative, as here, it has the connotation of not living up to the expected moral standard.

The standard Peter failed to live up to is "the truth of the gospel".[162] The gospel sets the standard for what constitutes truth. In withdrawing from the Gentiles, Peter was diverging from the gospel that both he and Paul had agreed must be preached to both Jews and Gentiles, namely justification on the basis of the work of Christ alone.

Some commentators prefer to interpret this phrase as meaning "the truth contained in the gospel".[163] This does not contradict the other interpretation, but whereas the former sees justification by faith alone as a general principle embedded in the gospel, the second interpretation assumes that this doctrine was already well-formulated and known to both Peter and those who followed his example. It seems more likely that at this time it was simply a general principle and not yet a propositional statement. But the principle was one with which all the believers in Antioch should have been familiar. By separating themselves from the Gentiles, Peter and those who followed him were not only failing to live up to this standard, but were actively contradicting it.

It is interesting to look at the verb tense Paul uses here. The TNIV translation reads, "were not acting" (past tense), but in the Greek Paul uses a present tense, "are not acting" or "are not straightforward" (NASB).[164] Paul writes as if this is the way Peter and those who followed him are still acting at the time he is writing to the Galatians. Yet this incident was definitely in the past, and Peter had repented of his behaviour. So why use the present tense? The answer is that Paul wants to get the attention of the Judaizers in Galatia and tell them that they are part of the same group as Peter and the Jews who followed him. They, too, are not walking according to the truth of the gospel.

This bears thinking about. What we do today puts us in the same category as others in the past. Either we are among those who are living in accordance with the will of God as spelled out in the Scriptures, or we are not. Every time we make a decision, we are deciding which group we wish to join. Peter, the Jews who withdrew with him, and the Judaizers in Galatia are all grouped together as those who have not lived up to the central truth of the gospel.

In Paul's day, one of the lines of division between people was whether they were Jews or Gentiles. Today, there are other lines of division such as race, clan, denomination, status and so forth. If we truly believe that God accepts people from all groups on the basis of their faith in Christ, we need to accept all our fellow believers without any discrimination. There is no excuse for refusing to accept them. You are either in the right or in the wrong. May the Lord help us to remove all the barriers the evil one attempts to place between brothers and sisters in the Lord.

Paul's Action

When Paul recognized that Peter had fallen into serious theological error, he did not ignore what was happening but instead *opposed him to his face* (2:11).[165] He did not send someone else to speak to Peter or discuss Peter's behaviour with someone else behind his back. He recognized that the issue was so serious that face-to-face talk was urgently needed.

Paul was not hostile to Peter, although this might be inferred from the words "I opposed". The Greek verb means "stand against somebody" (especially in battle), "withstand" and "resist".[166] It is not used of attacking somebody. From Paul's perspective, Peter was the aggressor because he was attacking the truth of the gospel by withdrawing from Gentiles.

Sometimes when we disagree with someone, we can decide just to let the matter go. At other times, we may need to send someone else to communicate our concerns. And at other times we must talk to the person ourselves because the issues are so important that they can only be dealt with through face-to-face interaction. It takes courage to set up such a meeting but, when handled well, it brings blessing as the person being challenged senses how much the one who disagrees with them cares for them.

We do not know how Peter responded to Paul's correction, but we can assume that the results were positive if Paul mentions it here. Paul is happy that he acted as he did, and the Galatians should learn from this incident.

We also do not know whether Paul met privately with Peter, as laid down in Matthew 18:15–20. Paul does not mention any such meeting.[167] It seems more likely that Paul decided to address the issue publicly because this was not a personal disagreement but one that involved the truth of the gospel and the unity of the body of Christ. Peter's act of withdrawal was a public message, and called for a public response. So Paul spoke to Peter *in front of them all* (2:14b). The "all" here is broader than just the group who followed Peter.[168] It is likely that Paul was speaking in the presence of all the members of the church in Antioch.[169]

His words were blunt: *You are a Jew, yet you live like a Gentile and not like a Jew. How is it, then, that you force Gentiles to follow Jewish customs?* (2:14). Peter's meeting with Cornelius in Acts 10 had convinced him that he should ignore his earlier belief that all Gentiles were unclean and should eat and drink freely with Gentile converts. In doing this, he was living like a Gentile, not a Jew. Now, however, he is abandoning his principles, not because he has decided that he was wrong but because he wants to remain in good standing with those who had come from Jerusalem! But the price he is paying for acceptance is the truth of the gospel.

To put Paul's question in other words: If Peter who is a Jew has come to believe that the Gentiles are acceptable to God and that he is not sinning if he freely mixes with them, how does he explain that he is now sending Gentile believers the message that they are only acceptable if they follow all the Jewish rules? He is being inconsistent. The believing Gentiles are either to be shunned completely or accepted completely – regardless of what anyone in Jerusalem thinks. Given Peter's experience when Cornelius' was converted, he has to accept the second option.

When Paul says that Peter is "forcing"[170] the Gentiles to follow Jewish customs, he is not saying that Peter was actively arguing the case of the Judaizers (the earlier agreement in 2:9–10 precludes that possibility). Rather, he was exercising moral force by setting an example which communicated that following Jewish customs was the only right way to live. This was hypocritical, for Peter was acting against his own principles.

It is very important that we maintain consistency between what we say we believe and how we actually live. We failed to do this in 2007–2008, for many Kenyan pastors did not condemn the post-election violence when it was perpetrated by their own people. We failed to do this when Tutsi believers did not rally round to protect the Hutus during the genocide in Rwanda. We fail to do this when we do not take a strong stand against racism in South Africa, the USA, and other places. If we believe that we are one in Christ, then we must demonstrate our unity in the way we respond to events. Our message must be rooted in our convictions, and our convictions must be reflected in the way we respond to social and political issues.

Questions for Discussion

1. Are all clashes bad? What role do the roots of a conflict and their consequences play in how we decide to respond?
2. Have you witnessed any conflict in your local church recently? How was the issue resolved? To what degree have any wounds caused been healed? Could anything have been handled differently?
3. Was Paul right in the manner in which he handled Peter? What can we learn to do or not do from what happened in Antioch?

UNIT 7
GALATIANS 2:15–21

JUSTIFICATION BY FAITH

Many years ago, when my youngest brother, Timothy, was about nine years old, he became angry with a woman who worked for our family. He decided to deal with the situation using a traditional technique that he must have learned from his playmates, for disagreements were certainly never handled this way by my parents. Looking at Lois, he picked up a clay pot and deliberately dropped it, shattering it. The action represented a curse: "May you be broken like this clay pot was broken." Lois was terrified. It did not matter that my brother was much younger than she – such curses are believed to be effective, unless something is done to ward them off.

My parents and I wanted to dismiss the incident. We saw it as a display of childish anger, and as Christians we had no need to fear magic and curses. But many people in our village did, and they were worried that Lois would suffer serious harm because of what my brother had done. They insisted that my brother undo the curse by bringing an animal to be slaughtered in a public ceremony. My brother could not afford to pay for an animal, but eventually Lois' grandfather, who was a village elder, found someone who would perform the cleansing ceremony using some small object that a child could afford to get. The cleansing was duly performed and Lois could feel safe again. The curse had been undone. It was now purely a matter of history, and no longer an active threat. Her faith in a very simple act before a village elder removed the curse imposed on her.

This incident throws vivid light on the truth Paul was defending to the Galatians. Lois, who had been very frightened, left the presence of the elder with the assurance that everything had been taken care of. In the same way, those who believe in Christ need no longer fear judgment but can have assurance that they are saved. However, their assurance is not based on the word of a village elder but on the word of God.

God's declaration that sin has been dealt with is what we call "justification". Faith in Christ is the only essential requirement for justification, regardless of whether we are Jews or Gentiles.

Areas of Agreement

The TNIV treats 2:15–21 as a continuation of what Paul said to Peter. This may or may not be the case – ancient Greek had no quotation marks, so we cannot tell exactly where the quotation ended. But regardless of whether these verses are a summary of what Paul said or an exact transcript, they are related to Peter's behaviour. Paul moves from the specific situation in Antioch to the universal principle involved. Then from 3:1 on, he will show the Galatians how this principle applies to them.

Paul begins with the things on which he and Peter agree: the difference between Jews and Gentiles, and the means of justification.

The difference between Jews and Gentiles

Paul and Peter both accept that people fall into two broad groups: Jews or Gentiles.[171] Using *we* Paul categorizes himself and Peter,[172] and possibly all the other Jewish Christians in Jerusalem, Antioch and Galatia,[173] as Jews. They are *Jews by birth* (or "by nature" – NASB). They "were born and bred, not proselytes, far less resident aliens or God-fearers".[174] Their ethnic identity was Jewish. They had been born into the nation with which God had made a covenant and to which he had given his law. To be born a Jew was thus a heritage and a privilege.

In today's terms, we could think of their situation in terms of the privilege of being born in a Christian home. A couple of stories from my own family illustrate what I mean. My young daughters were once given a ride by one of our American friends. As they got into her car, she asked them, "What is the first thing you must do when getting into a car?" She expected the reply, "Put on your seat belt." But our daughters answered in chorus, "Pray!" On another occasion, a doctor was trying to relax our second daughter before giving her an injection: "You have lovely eyes," he said. "Who did you get them from?" Katee knew the answer to that question: "Jesus". The doctor had expected "from my mom" or "from my dad". Our daughters' responses in these everyday situations are evidence of the privilege they enjoyed in being brought up by believing parents in a home where they were taught to love and honour God in all they did. They would not have thought of these answers if we had not been believers. This is the type of unavoidable difference that Paul has in mind when he contrasts Jews and the Gentiles.

The Gentiles, on the other hand, are labelled as *sinful* (2:15b).[175] From a Jewish perspective, Gentiles were sinners simply because they were Gentiles. They were outside the covenant and without God's law to guide them. Therefore they must be sinners.

We would be wrong to take this passage out of context and assert that it proves that Paul supported the ethnocentrism that asserts that our group is better than some other group. Paul is using a Jewish colloquialism[176] with gentle irony as he contrasts the Gentiles with the "perfect" Jews who have God's law.

Ethnocentrism (the "we" versus "them" mentality) destroys relationships and is wrong whether practised by the more privileged party that looks down on others or by the less privileged party in reaction to their oppression. I saw examples of both attitudes when I was a student in America. I saw racism among some white Christians, but I also saw some of my African American brothers speaking of our white brothers and sisters as "them". Their reaction was understandable given the sins that had been committed against their people, but that does not mean that their reaction was not sinful. Every people group has its own strengths and weaknesses. This was made clear to me when I was still a child through being told a story about two soldiers from two different people groups. These groups were quite closely related, but because of minor differences each looked down on the other. When the two soldiers met, each stood ramrod straight and proudly thought that he was the best qualified to be a soldier. "You don't look too bad," the one patronizingly told the other, "but your legs are bowed". "You can talk," replied the second, "you didn't look too bad either, until I saw your hunchback."

Paul is not being like those soldiers and running down the Gentiles when he calls them sinners. He is certainly not saying that the Jews are not sinners. Rather, he is acknowledging that the Jews have a privileged position in God's plan of salvation in that they are the people of the covenant. Yet by believing in the Saviour, the privileged Jews have shown that believing is the way of salvation for them, just as it is for the Gentiles. Both Jews and Gentiles need to accept Christ by faith.

The means of justification

The second matter on which both Paul and Peter and his followers can agree is the means of justification. But before Paul can state the general principles involved, he needs to clear the ground, stating which route does not lead to justification.

Not the law

Paul and the believing Jews are in agreement in that they *know that a person is not justified by observing the* law (2:16).[177] But what exactly does the word "justified" mean?

"Justified" and "justification" are among Paul's favourite words. Most of the forty-one uses of them in the New Testament are found in his letters.[178] It is easer to understand what they mean when we learn that the Greek word for justification (*dikaiōsis*) is closely related to the Greek word for righteousness (*dikaiosynē*). Justification is thus equivalent to making someone righteous. This is what God does for sinners on the basis of the work of Christ on the cross. To put it another way, justification involves God, the examiner, declaring that we are righteous and qualify for salvation.

Paul asserts that we cannot be justified by keeping the law.[179] Here "the law" may mean the whole legal system of statutes and ordinances imposed by the rabbis, which was the standard by which people were judged. There was no question of grace, passing or failing was determined solely by obedience. Alternatively, given the situation in Antioch and Galatia, Paul may be referring to specific laws, such as those on circumcision and food.[180] These specific laws may have become the standard by which people were judged. Or Paul may have meant the law that God gave to Moses, including both its ceremonial and moral aspects. That law as spelled out in the Scriptures became the standard for passing or failing, for being righteous or unrighteous.

The last of these options seems the most likely.[181] Paul, Peter and other Jews knew from their own experience that no matter how hard they tried to keep the law of Moses, they failed. This law could not justify them; it only condemned them.[182]

Faith in Christ

Having reminded his readers that observing the law does not result in justification, Paul now states what does.[183] We are justified *by faith in Jesus Christ* (2:16b) or "through faith in Jesus Christ" (NASB). We exercise faith and Jesus Christ is the object of our faith.[184]

However, the Greek word translated "faith" can mean either "faith" or "faithfulness", and so a few commentators have argued that what justifies us is Jesus' faith or the faithfulness Jesus showed in his life of obedience to God to the point of going to the cross. One could even interpret the faithfulness here as God's faithfulness to his covenant in Jesus Christ.[185]

While both translations are possible, the first one, which is the standard translation, is more likely. As George says, "While the faithfulness of Jesus Christ is a prominent theme in Paul's theology … what is being contrasted in Galatians is not divine fidelity versus human fickleness but rather God's free initiative in grace versus human efforts towards self-salvation."[186] In this context, it is we who exercise faith in Jesus and not Jesus who exercises faith in God.

After these two statements of what Paul, Peter and the other Christian Jews knew, Paul reminds them of a universal principle.

Universal principle

The universal principle that Paul cites at the end of 2:16 is, *by observing the law no one will be justified* (TNIV).[187] When it comes to keeping the law, no one can ever get high enough marks to get a passing grade from God. Paul is here giving a free quotation of the Septuagint translation of Psalm 143:2.[188] The psalm says that no one can ever claim to be sinless before God. Because the Jews accepted that the Old Testament was authoritative, Paul can use this verse as a proof-text for the doctrine of justification by faith (see also Rom 3:20).

The words translated "no one" in the TNIV could literally be translated as "no flesh". This is an example of metonymy, a figure of speech in which part of something represents the whole. Paul uses this word in order to focus attention on the extent to which we are bound by the limits of the flesh with all its "finitude, weakness and corruptibility".[189] Jews and Gentiles, rich and poor, we all share a common humanity. A car accident injures the flesh of the rich just as much as the flesh of the beggar. We all fail or overcome in the same manner when trials or temptations come. Given our common flesh, we have no excuse for boasting or for treating others badly on the assumption that we are superior to them.

Some people try to excuse their failings by saying, "I'm only human", but that is not how Paul sees things. He sees "we're only human" as a reality check, reminding us that we can never attain God's standard of holiness. But that is no reason to despair. Christ has attained the standard for us and we believe in him, in gratitude that he became our substitute. He has satisfied the demands of the law in our place. All we have to do is believe in him.

Evidence of Agreement

The principle that Paul has outlined applies to both Jews and Gentiles. Peter and the other Jewish Christians have indicated by their actions that they agree with it: *So we, too, have put our faith in Christ Jesus that we may be justified by faith in Christ and not by observing the law* (2:16c). The "so" and the "we too" ("even we" in the NASB) are emphatic, stressing the Jews' acceptance that they cannot be justified by observing the law.[190]

The verb translated "have put" is a past tense that brings out the idea of a "once-for-all response", made in the past and continuing into the present.[191] This was what Paul did when he committed himself to Christ on the Damascus road. Now he is asking Peter and other Jewish Christians to remember their conversion experiences. They put their trust in Christ not because they believed the law was unimportant, but because it was unable to justify them.

Paul does not actually say that they put their trust "in" Christ Jesus but more literally "into Christ Jesus". This way of putting things is "characteristic in the New Testament of that faith which implies union with its object, or consciously places calm confidence on it".[192] It is a total commitment "of one's self to Christ on the basis of the acceptance of the message concerning him".[193] The difference between putting one's faith "in" someone and "into" someone is well illustrated by the old story about the tightrope walker offering people the opportunity to cross Niagara Falls with him. Almost everyone in the crowd was prepared to accept that the man could safely push someone across in a wheelbarrow, but no one was prepared to volunteer to be that person. They had faith in his ability, but were not prepared to risk their lives by committing themselves into his hands. The faith the New Testament asks from us is to "believe into", a total surrender to Jesus. Sadly, there are many who are happy to believe in Jesus and his ability to save without being willing to take a step of moving "into" complete faith in him.

Paul and the other Jewish believers had turned to Christ for a specific purpose, "that we may be justified by faith in Christ". Faith in Christ was the means of justification even for the Jews, notwithstanding their privileges. Our own reflection on how we came to faith should lead us to say, "If it was not for God, I would still be lost."

Answering an Objection

Paul now raises a question and then answers it himself. He probably does so to respond to a point that his opponents were making. Their argument seems to have run something like: "If believing in Christ means ceasing to trust in the law, that means that we are abandoning the law and living a life of sin, just like the Gentiles (who never had the law). In that case, *Christ promotes sin* since he takes people away from the law" (2:17a). Paul totally dismisses this argument with the words, *Absolutely not!* (2:17b). There is no justification for drawing this conclusion. In chapters five and six of this letter, Paul will show clearly that faith in Christ results in love of the law as the will of God.

The Real Violation of the Law

Paul has been accused of breaking the law, but now he sets out to defend his own position in personal terms, beginning, *If I*. He may be using himself as a hypothetical example so that what he says is not misinterpreted as a direct attack on Peter's behaviour in Antioch, or he may actually be referring to his own experience. He uses a metaphor of destruction and reconstruction: *if I rebuild what I destroyed* (2:18a). Paul once lived behind the wall erected by Jewish legalism, but his experience on the Damascus road convinced him that this wall needed to be torn down because Christ alone is the means of salvation. Since then, his actions have made it clear that he thinks that the law no longer applies.

It is not clear whether the law he is referring to here is the whole of the Mosaic law[194] or "the food laws which were the occasion of division between Jew and Gentile at Antioch"[195], but ultimately it makes little difference. Paul's main point is that he has demolished the idea that keeping the law is a requirement for justification. He sees no need to rebuild that particular wall (which is what Peter was doing in Antioch).

But what does Paul mean when he says that if he were to rebuild this wall, he *really would be a lawbreaker"* (2:18c)? There are two possible answers. First, if Paul rebuilds a system that he once destroyed, he is acknowledging that he made a mistake, in which case he broke the law by destroying the law. Second, returning to the state of subjection to the law involves returning to the status of a lawbreaker, for everyone breaks the law and the law offers no hope of justification (Gal 3:24).[196]

The first view fits the flow of the argument here better. To go back to trying to be justified by keeping the law will indicate that he was wrong to have ever stopped doing so.

It is significant that the word Paul uses here is "lawbreaker" (or "transgressor" – NASB) rather than "sinner" which is the word he applied to the Gentiles in 2:15. While Gentiles are involuntarily sinners, Christian Jews who go back to erecting the wall of legalism as the basis for justification are conscious lawbreakers. They are deviating from the right path.

Our courts assert that ignorance of the law is no excuse for not obeying it. Scripture puts things the opposite way round: knowing the truth makes us even more accountable for obeying it. That is why when students ask me what God will do with our ancestors who died before they ever heard of Christ, I can say that "God is just and he will judge in light of what was known by those being judged." We cannot decide the case of our ancestors, for that is God's business, but we can be assured that God holds us accountable to what we know. We hear God's word on every street corner. How have we responded to it?

The Real Meaning of Justification by Faith

Pauls now sets out the heart of his convictions about the real meaning of justification by faith. In doing this, he repeatedly uses the emphatic first personal pronoun ("I" and "me" are used nine times in 2:19-20). In the previous verse he may have been using "I" hypothetically, in a situation where the speaker could be Paul, Barnabas, or any other Jewish Christian. But now Paul is speaking of his own experience of justification and spelling out what it means in four propositions:

1) Through the law I died to the law so that I might live for God

The law of Moses as a body of statutes revealed Paul's own "inability to meet its spiritual requirements and its own inability to make him righteous".[197] It demanded perfect obedience as a condition of justification; anything less automatically resulted in condemnation. Paul must have longed to look for life elsewhere. In fact it was his longing to obey the law, combined with the impossibility of doing so, that led to his death to the law. When Paul says *I died to the law* (2:19) he means that he turned away from it and "ceased to live in that world in which law was dominant".[198] The law ceased "to exercise the same hold over him; that which was his constant stimulus to action now failed to find any response in him; he became dead to what had previously been his primary motivating force".[199]

This death to law, however, was not an end in itself but the means to finding life elsewhere, namely, in God. To *live for God* (or "to God" – NKJV) has the idea of a "life under the control of God and for the honour of God".[200] Such a life contrasts with a life governed by mere obedience to a set of rules. Eadie puts this well when he says,

> To live to God is to be in Him – in union with Him, and to feel the assimilating influence of this divine fellowship – to give Him the first place in the soul, and to put all its powers at His sovereign disposal – to consult Him in everything, and to be ever guided by His counsel – to do His will, because it is His will, at all times – to regard every step in its bearing on His claims and service, and to further His glory as the one grand end of our lives."[201]

Living for God thus involves fellowship, obedience and friendship.

We can understand this better if we think in terms of the relationship between parents and children. Some parents only issue rules, and all that their children hear is "do this" or "don't do that". Their children's obedience is like that of the little boy who was running around causing trouble until his angry father said to him, "Sit down!" The child sat down, but as he did so he looked across at his father and said, "My body is sitting down, but in my heart I'm standing up!" His obedience is purely external and based on fear of punishment. Such obedience is almost meaningless. By contrast, think of a child whose loving father has taken him to work with him. If that child starts to run around near some machinery, his father will be concerned that the child will be injured. He, too, will say, "Sit down!" But this child is in a warm relationship with his father and trusts his father's judgment. The child may be reluctant to sit down, but he does so without complaining because he loves and trusts his father. This is an example of the type of relationship we should have with God.

The new life that Paul has found is definitely not a life of sin but a life of holiness. Now, however, he seeks "holiness in relationship with God" and not "holiness in order to establish a relationship with God". He has a relationship with God established through faith in Jesus Christ as Saviour and Lord. He no longer needs to struggle at the impossible task of keeping the law perfectly.

2) I have been crucified with Christ

When Paul says, *I have been crucified with Christ* (2:20a), he is thinking of a specific completed event.[202] His experience on the Damascus road turned a persecutor of Christians into a missionary for Christ. The persecutor was "crucified" and lives no more. This figurative language emphasizes "the finality of the death which has put an end to the old order."[203] Moreover this close identification with Christ's experience communicates Paul's "fellowship with Christ in being called upon to endure a similar spiritual crucifixion to self"[204]. Thus, far from justification by faith in Christ leading to a godless life, it leads to a life in which "self" has died. Just as the death to law gives way to life to God, so the death of self gives way to life.

3) I no longer live, but Christ lives in me

Because Paul's "self" was crucified with Christ, it is no longer alive. Instead it is Christ who lives in him (2:20b). Self has been replaced by Christ. Although Paul is the same person who once persecuted the church, he now serves a different master.

This experience is difficult to define, and so commentators speak of it using words like "mystical union" and "spiritual fellowship". But the meaning is clear. Christ so dominates Paul's whole experience that Christ-likeness is all that is seen in him. Burton puts it well:

> With this spiritual being (Christ) Paul feels himself to be living in such intimate fellowship, by him his whole life is so controlled, that he conceives him to be resident in him, imparting to him impulse and power, transforming him morally and working through him for and upon other men.[205]

Dunn describes this fellowship as "the awareness of a new focus of identity expressed in different goals and new inner dynamic, with Christ as the inspiration and Christ-likeness the paradigm".[206]

All who share in this experience have a totally different perspective on life. Everything centres in Christ and the desire to glorify him.

Thus Paul's teaching of "justification by faith" does not lead to a life without rules. But the rules now come from Christ himself, who is our master, and the believers' obedience is rooted in love for Christ.

4) The life I live in the body, I live by faith in the Son of God, who loved me, and gave himself for me

Although Paul is in a mystical union with Christ, this does not mean that he has ceased to have a physical existence. He still lives *in the body* (2:20c). He is still very much part of this world. We sometimes need to be reminded of this as believers, for it is possible for us to be "so heavenly minded that we are of no earthly good". We are here to bear witness to the world, not to hide from it. That is clear from Jesus' prayer for his disciples: "My prayer is not that you take them out of the world but that you protect them from the evil one" (John 17:15). Consequently believers should be the best politicians, business people, lawyers, civil servants, teachers, farmers and so on. We live in the world and must be involved in all spheres of life so as to be light and salt there. The problem is not with our being involved in "worldly matters", but with the devil destroying what we are supposed to be in the world – representatives of God, promoting his ideals of love, peace, justice and righteousness.

The life Paul now lives is lived *by faith* or "in faith".[207] Faith gives Paul the proper perspective on his life on earth. It is also the atmosphere of wholehearted trust within which he operates. He enjoys heart-to-heart fellowship with Jesus.

The object of Paul's faith is *the Son of God*. This is the title of the person Paul earlier referred to as "Jesus Christ" or "Christ" (meaning God's Chosen One or his Anointed One). God chose him to be the one we should trust. He is the object of Paul's faith.[208] The Son of God is the one *who loved me and gave himself for me.*[209] What Paul deserved (and what we deserve) was condemnation. Jesus took this away by his death in our place.

The Implications of Justification by Works

Paul has presented a magnificent description of what justification by faith means. This description has serious implications for those like the Judaizers, who insist on the need to obey the law in order to receive justification.

People who insist on the law can be said to *set aside the grace of God* (1:21a), that is, the grace God showed.[210] Grace is God's "sovereign kindness manifested in the death of His Son, spontaneous on His part and wholly unmerited on ours".[211] By fully surrendering to God's chosen path of salvation, Paul is magnifying the grace of God. Those who take pride in their good deeds as a means of meriting God's favour are acting as if God's grace is not particularly important. They are dismissing God's kindness as irrelevant.

Moreover, those who dismiss God's grace are implying that Christ died for nothing. If our own works can secure righteousness, as the Judaizers wanted the Galatians to believe, there was no need for him to die.

Summary

Paul began this section by declaring that justification by way of works of the law is impossible. The only way to achieve justification is by faith in Jesus Christ. Paul, Peter and all other Christians accepted and affirmed the truth of this statement by the very act of believing in Jesus Christ.

However, Peter at Antioch and every Jew who follows the Judaizers has failed to uphold this truth. So have the believers in Galatia to whom Paul is writing. Paul, however, has devoted his whole life to proclaiming justification by faith. His experience that the law can only bring condemnation is too vivid for him to believe anything else. What matters is life to God with Christ as master. That is the way of justification and sanctification.

What wonderful truths for proclamation! Christ loved me and gave his life for me. I have fellowship with him, and bear witness to the world.

Questions for Discussion

1. When you first heard the word "justification", what did you think it meant? What does it mean in the writings of Paul, specifically in this passage?
2. Do believers in your local church seem to think that something needs to be added to faith for them to be justified? What do they add? Give specific examples.
3. How could the preaching in your church be improved so that every believer will clearly understands what justification means?
4. What does Paul mean when he speaks of death through the law, to the law, for the purpose of living to God?

INTRODUCTION TO GALATIANS 3 AND 4

Some African traditional stories were intended to teach moral lessons while others were meant to explain why certain things happened. For example, why do dead people not come back to life? A number of stories explain this, but here is the basic outline of one common variant.

God originally intended people to wake from death just as they wake from sleep. He sent Chameleon to tell people this. But Chameleon dithered – just like chameleons today, it kept putting its foot forward and pulling it back several times before taking a step. Bird, who left God's presence several days after Chameleon, flew much faster. Bird reached human beings first, and told them that they would not return to life after they died. By the time Chameleon arrived, the wrong message was firmly entrenched.

This story explained why death is permanent, and taught a moral about the dangers of procrastination. But above all it taught that when someone you love dies and does not come back, you should blame the chameleon, not God. Today people might ask why God did not get the bird to deliver the message about resurrection since it could fly faster. But an older generation readily accepted "blame the chameleon, not God".

My reason for telling this story is to make the point that arguments and explanations that will convince one group may not convince another. Each argument has to be shaped to fit the world view of the group to be convinced. So does the way the argument is presented. The African explanation was presented as a story. Paul may have adopted the pattern of a typical Greek letter of rebuke when he wrote to the Galatians.[212] Such letters had three key parts:

1. A narrative laying out the background to the letter and the reasons for the rebuke. This is what Paul has done in 1:1–2:14.
2. A statement of the points of agreement and points of disagreement. Paul provides this in his discussion of the principle of justification by faith in 2:15–21.
3. Detailed proofs and arguments to support the letter writer's case. This is what Paul now presents in Galatians 3:1–4:11 as he offers seven arguments in support of his position that justification is by faith alone.

As we read Paul's arguments, we should remember that they are tailored to the people to whom Paul is writing. Not all the arguments he presents come across as very strong arguments today – but they would have convinced the Galatians that Paul's teaching is logical and has the backing of the Old Testament. These seven arguments that Paul uses are:

1. The Galatians' own experience (3:1–5)
2. The case of Abraham (3:6–9)
3. The available alternatives (3:10–14)
4. The relationship of law and promise (3:15–25)
5. The contrast between a young child and a grown child (3:26–4:11)
6. The Galatians' relationship to Paul (4:12–20)
7. The relationship of Hagar and Sarah (4:21–31)

We might not use all the same arguments today, but the central point that Paul is making stands firm. He makes it abundantly clear that the principle of justification by faith is at the heart of the gospel.

FATHER–CHILD RELATIONSHIPS

Paul saw himself as the spiritual father of the believers in Galatia. Reflecting on this, I was reminded of my own experience of the blessings and responsibilities of parenthood.

My first daughter, Mwende, was born early and small. An excited but anxious new father, I drove to my parents' home to tell them of her arrival. I desperately wanted them to say, "Yes, she will live; many other children have been born that small and have lived." They said that, but her grandmother also said, "I am coming back with you". So Mwende began her earthly journey rocked in the loving arms of her parents and her grandmother.

As a child, Mwende was allowed to cry herself to sleep when she was crying without a good cause, enjoy her favourite foods, and sit on my shoulders to watch soccer games. My wife and I loved her, prayed for her, and disciplined her – as we also did for our other much loved children as they arrived.

When Mwende was in high school, she began to question some of the truths of the Bible. My wife and I continued to pray for her. But I also did something else: I took her into my study and showed her the many books representing different faiths on my shelves. Then I told her, "Read them and decide what you want to be." Today, she joyously declares herself "strong in my faith in God, Jesus and the truths of the Bible!"

The small baby has grown into a responsible married woman. Along the way, she has experienced her mother's scolding and her father's discipline, all rooted in love and a desire for her to grow to healthy maturity.

In this letter, Paul speaks to the Galatians as a father. He scolds them for forgetting that they were reborn by God's grace. Though we have no record of how the Galatians responded, our hope is that they listened to Paul and continued to walk in the path of grace.

We, too, will have to deal with "Galatians" in our ministry and in our own families. There will be times when those we love are exposed to bad influences. When this happens, we must not only scold but also love. Our desire should always be that our spiritual and physical children will grow to be responsible people who will build the kingdom of God. This was Paul's prayer for the Galatians.

UNIT 8
GALATIANS 3:1–5

ARGUMENTS BASED ON THE GALATIANS' EXPERIENCE

Some memories last a long time. One of my daughters, who is now twenty-eight years old, still has vivid memories of the three days she spent with me on a farm when she was thirteen. For her, the highlights of that visit were learning to suck bamboo seeds and to ride the workers' bicycle. She now lives in California with all its paved streets, but when I told her that I was going to the farm again, memories of the good time she had there came flooding back.

Some of our memories are about far more significant things than bamboo seeds and bicycles, and can be a guide to aspects of truth. That is why Paul encourages the Galatians to remember their own spiritual experiences. He asks them a series of questions about how Jesus was presented to them, how they received the Holy Spirit, their starting point in their spiritual journey, their past suffering, and the miracles God has performed among them. He wants them to recognize that buying into the idea that "faith + works of the law" is required for salvation contradicts their own experience.

Their Understanding of Jesus Christ

Paul's first question is very blunt: *You foolish Galatians! Who has bewitched you?* (3:1). The message that Paul preached was so clear that the Galatians joyfully accepted it. But why, after doing that, would they want to move away from freedom in Christ and prefer a legalistic approach to justification? Such extraordinary behaviour must require some extraordinary explanation. This is what Paul means when he talks of their being "bewitched". He is not making any theological point about the existence of witches and witchcraft, but is simply using this metaphor to express his bewilderment at the change he is seeing in the Galatians.

What was it that had moved the Galatians to follow Christ? Paul puts it like this: *Before your very eyes Jesus Christ was clearly portrayed as crucified* (3:1).[213] In a world where there were no newspapers or radio news bulletins, important information was sometimes announced on placards posted in prominent places.[214] (The same approach is still used in some areas of Africa today.) Paul's preaching has been equivalent to his holding up a large placard for the Galatians to read.

The news on this "placard" is that Jesus Christ has been crucified.[215] This was not just a statement about a historical event, but about the long-term implications of that event, or in other words, about its ultimate significance. Paul preached that Jesus Christ made atonement by his obedience and suffering, and had thus provided a free and complete salvation received through faith in him.

Paul's words about his own preaching remind us that we, too, should present the gospel in a way that is clear and easy to remember. If we rush through it, we may give our listeners the wrong impression about its value and meaning. Once people have clearly understood it and enjoyed the benefits of being free from slavery to legalism, to vices, and even to some of the rituals of African traditional religion, we can be confident that any call to abandon that freedom and go back into bondage must be a trick of the devil, who is always eager to enslave us again.

Their Reception of the Holy Spirit

Paul's next question to the Galatians is, *Did you receive the Spirit by observing the law, or by believing what you heard?* (3:2).

There is a difference between taking, earning and receiving. When Paul says that the Galatians had received the Holy Spirit, he "does not refer to a self-prompted taking but rather to a grateful reception of that which is offered".[216] The gift was not offered because the Galatians had "earned" it by strict obedience to the law. It was given freely because they believed what they had heard.[217] Paul had proclaimed that Christ had been crucified for them, and they had accepted Christ as their Saviour and had been blessed with the gift of the Holy Spirit.

Paul's question here shows that he assumes that when the Galatians believed, they received the Holy Spirit. It is, therefore, erroneous to teach that the Holy Spirit is received some time after believing. Filling or control by the Holy Spirit may be gradual, and the gifts of the Spirit may follow later, but possession of the Holy Spirit is a privilege tied to believing and effected as the act of believing takes place.

Those who doubt this may ask why the lives of some who claim to have believed show no evidence of the fruit of the Holy Spirit (Gal 5:22) and why some lack power in their ministry. The first response to this question is to ask whether such people have truly believed. But assuming that they have, the problem may not be lack of the Holy Spirit but failure to allow him to have full control. We believed; we have the Holy Spirit. Let us allow him to take charge and we shall never go back to our old life of sin, allow ourselves to be dominated by legalistic thinking, or lack the power to serve effectively.

Their Starting Point in Their Spiritual Journey

Paul's third question is, *After beginning with the Spirit, are you now trying to finish by human effort?* (3:3b).

The Galatians started their spiritual journey relying on the Spirit,[218] but they are now attempting to finish it relying on their own power.[219] As far as Paul is concerned, the Christian life starts, continues and ends in dependence on the Holy Spirit. This is the natural order of things. The Galatians were following an unnatural order by starting the Christian life within a higher sphere (in the Spirit) and finishing within a lower one (in the flesh).

This backwards movement makes no sense. It is stupid. So Paul asks them, "Are you that foolish?" (3:3a). It is as if the Galatians had graduated from the elementary school level of belief, and moved on to high school, but are now being persuaded that they need to re-enrol in elementary school. Doing that shows a lack of common sense. They need to move on; not return where they came from (see also 4:3).

Their Suffering in the Past

Paul's next question to the Galatians is, *Have you suffered so much for nothing – if it really was for nothing?* (3:4, NIV).

The Greek verb translated "suffered" in the NIV can be used to refer to unpleasant experiences such as persecution or to pleasant experiences such as the blessing of the Holy Spirit spoken of in 3:3 and 3:5. It can also be neutral, allowing for both good and bad experiences.[220] Consequently there are several different translations of this verse, including the TNIV version, "Have you experienced so much in vain?"

Given that pleasant experiences are dealt with in 3:5, it seems likely that in 3:4 Paul is referring specifically to unpleasant experiences. We have no specific records of persecution of Christians in Galatia at that time, but it is likely that they had witnessed or endured the same type of harassment and even assaults as other early Christians (including Paul, Barnabas and Silas – Acts 13:50; 16:22–24).

When Paul says that they may have "suffered ... for nothing" (or "in vain"), he is not saying that they will lose their salvation. What he means is that they will stray from the right path. He had taught them that justification is by faith alone, and they had accepted that. They had probably also suffered for their decision to become Christians. For them now to get off course and think that they need to obey the law in order to be justified is tantamount to losing all the ground they have gained. There is something wrong with a farmer who endures the hardship involved in planting and caring for a crop and then cuts it down before it is ripe. The whole purpose of the hard labour was to harvest and enjoy the crop; it was not just a way to get some exercise! The Galatians are doing much the same thing as they fail to build on what they know.

We may say, "no farmer would cut down his or her crops before harvest," but that would be to take this metaphor too literally. A child or teenager who braves the cold and gets up early every Sunday to go to Sunday school, and then starts to live in a way that is at odds with the way he or she was taught is like a farmer cutting down the crop before harvest. The values taught to us, the memory verses we learn, and the love of God we show at a tender age are meant to bear fruit when we are adults and temptations crowd around us. If they do not, we can expect the question, "Did you suffer all that for nothing?"

Paul's addition – *if it really was in vain* (3:3b), suggests that he is still hopeful that it is not too late for the Galatians to turn back from the disastrous course they have embarked on.

The Miracles They Have Seen

Paul's final question to the Galatians is, *Does God give you his Spirit and work miracles among you by your observing the law, or by your believing what you heard?* (3:5).[221]

God gives his Holy Spirit to each believer when they believe, as the Galatians had experienced.[222] And he continues to work miracles in them and among them.[223] The word translated "miracles" is *dunameis*, which is the word from which we get the word "dynamite". It literally means "powers". Paul may be thinking of healings, exorcising evil spirits, speaking in tongues and prophesying, and other outward demonstrations of divine power.[224] The Galatians had witnessed God doing such things in their midst. They also knew that his power was at work in their own lives and was manifested in gifts like those referred to in 1 Corinthians 12:7–11.

Paul reminds them of what God has been doing even though the Galatians were not obeying the law of Moses. God showed his power among them simply because they had faith in him.

The situation has not changed. When God does wonders in our lives and ministries it is not because of what we do but because we believe in Christ. Belief is fundamental – deeds follow from it. By contrast, in African traditional religion, the deeds come first. When we needed rain, our main concern was to identify and perform the right ritual to bring the rain. But while rituals have their place (as the Old Testament shows), God's first requirement is that we have a relationship with him. This relationship is far more important than how much we serve the church or how consistently we tithe. And as Paul again and again reminds the Galatians, this relationship is based on faith in his son, Jesus Christ. He gave his life for us, and so in faith we give ourselves to him. Deeds follow faith, and cannot substitute for it.

Questions for Discussion

1. What message or circumstances marked your giving your life to Christ? What has been your experience in the walk of faith since then?

2. What key experiences have strengthened your faith over the years? What trials have you had to endure? How well did you endure the trials? Where did you fail in times of trial?

UNIT 9
GALATIANS 3:6–14

ARGUMENTS BASED ON SCRIPTURE

My father recently reminded me of something very important. He has been a leader all his life, in the home, in the schools where he taught and in the churches to which he has belonged. He has found it hard to give this up, even in his nineties. On one occasion, when my mother and I were trying to dissuade him from some course of action, his reaction was to get his Bible and challenge us, "Show me from the Bible where I am wrong". While the Bible was not necessarily directly relevant to the issue we were discussing, what struck me was the extent to which someone who does not like submitting to others was prepared to admit that there is one authority to which he will submit, even in his very old age – the Scriptures. Paul draws on this same source to bring the Galatians back to the right path. In doing this, he shows that his teaching is based on more than just experience. Moreover, it is not some idea that he has come up with. Justification by faith can be found in the Scriptures of the Old Testament and was experienced by the Jews' great ancestor, Abraham.

It is possible that Paul focuses on Abraham because his opponents were citing Moses, the giver of the law, as their authority. If so, Paul is responding by saying, "Wait a minute, there is an authority that goes many years back before Moses. What about Abraham, the father and founder of the Jewish race?"[225] Alternatively, Paul's opponents may have been arguing that Abraham was justified on the basis of what he did in Genesis 12 and 17:10–14. If so, Paul responds by saying, "You have got it all wrong!"

Paul refers his opponents to the ultimate authority, Scripture. Just as within African traditional practice a child would never contradict the authority of a parent, so for Jews the highest authority was the Scriptures, as interpreted by the rabbis. If Scripture said something, then it must be so.

Not everyone agrees with this position. I have seen situations where quoting Scripture to prove a point was viewed as manipulation. I have even witnessed a pastor get angry when someone cited a relevant passage of Scripture and shout, "Do not quote Scripture to me!" (I suspect that he was afraid that he would lose his case.)

Paul, however, presents his argument from Scripture in a way that allows any reasonable reader to weigh what he is saying. He models a way to apply Scripture or scriptural principles to issues that are not directly addressed in the text. We, too, should apply careful exegesis to determine what Scripture has to say not only about our personal lives but also about the academic controversies and social, economic and administrative issues in our societies.

The Case of Abraham

Paul begins his arguments with the words, *So also Abraham "believed God, and it was credited to him as righteousness"* (3:6). He is quoting Genesis 15:6, which follows God's promise that the childless Abraham will have as many offspring as there are stars in heaven.[226] Thus Abraham's act of believing may be his response to God's promise that he will have descendants.[227] However, it could also refer to his response when God first called him to leave his home (Gen 12:1–4) or to all the events in his life described in Genesis.[228]

In the context of Paul's letter to the Galatians, "righteousness" is equivalent to "acceptance by God". If so, it seems likely that the belief that is referred to here is Abraham's first response to God's call. All the other events in his life are examples of the process of sanctification, not justification, as Abraham's initial faith bears fruit in action. Abraham's faith was not in a promise but in the God who called him and made the promise.

When we speak of something being "credited" to someone, we normally think of a bank transaction or a business transaction. The person being given the credit has paid in something and that amount is credited to their account. In the Old Testament, we also see this word being used for someone who has earned something, as Phineas did (Ps 106:30–31). But that is not how the word is used here.[229] Abraham did nothing to earn his status except to believe what God revealed.[230]

Some people will argue that believing is actually a way of earning God's favour, and is thus a "work", but such thinking muddles different categories. If, for example, someone gives me an envelope containing money, and I ask them, "What do you want me to do?", the response may be "Take it, it's a gift" or "Please wash the car for me". The gift is clearly in a different category to the second request, which includes an element of works. The one needs only to be accepted; the other needs action. In the same way, Abraham's faith was a fact, not an act. It was through faith that he took hold of the promise. God offered a gift; Abraham accepted it.

That is what God still expects of us today. He does not ask us to do this, that or the other before we can receive salvation. He simply asks us to believe – to accept the envelope of salvation he offers us. Those who add other things make the matter more complicated than God does, and that is wrong.

It goes without saying that anyone who has opened the envelope of salvation and enjoyed the first contents (justification and adoption as God's child) will want to find out more about the rest of what is in the envelope! Our belief that Jesus died for us and our acceptance of him as our Saviour leads to our accepting him as our Lord. The more time we spend in his company, the more we want to be with him.

Our Relationship to Abraham

Some of the Galatian believers were Gentiles. They may have seen Abraham as the ancestor of their Jewish fellow-believers, but not as their ancestor. This point would have been driven home by the Judaizers, who insisted that the Gentiles needed to adopt the ritual of circumcision, which was the sign of God's covenant with Abraham (Gen 17). They would argue that only the circumcised are children of Abraham. So Paul confronts this issue: *Understand, then, that those who have faith are children of Abraham* (3:7).[231] These are the people who take God at his word. They may not be Abraham's genealogical children (that is, his physical descendants) but they are his spiritual and ethical descendants because they share a key characteristic with him.[232] To be Abraham's children is "to have what he had, and that is faith; and to be what he was, and that is justified."[233] Those who believe are "those whose identity is grounded in faith, and whose relationship with God grows out of faith, is characterized and determined by believing and trusting (the promise of God, the gospel of Jesus Christ), without reference to any 'works of the law'."[234]

"Those who believe" are contrasted with *those who rely on observing the law* (3:10), that is, the Judaizers. Paul is not being antiJewish or unJewish when he says this. Rather, he is identifying a specific group who have shifted the focus of Jewish identity from "its original focus in the grace of God"[235] and have come to insist "more on imitation of Abraham's circumcision than on the possession of Abraham's faith – thus misunderstanding the place, nature, and meaning of the seal and rite, and deluding their victims away from the Spirit to trust in externalism, and seek for perfection in the flesh."[236]

The logical conclusion of the fact that Abraham was justified by way of faith (3:6) is that anyone who desires to be identified with him (and that is what the Galatians, and especially the Judaizers, would want) must follow in his footsteps. His "children" are those who, like him, do not seek to be accepted by God by obeying some law but rely on faith. The object of this faith is the God of Abraham, who has provided the way of justification through his Son, Jesus Christ.

Many African groups have specific traditions that must be observed. For example, one group in Nigeria will never eat rabbit meat. It is taboo because many years ago a rabbit saved the life of their ancestor by diverting the attention of a snake that was about to strike at him. Other people groups have similar practices that characterize them and show whose descendants (or "children") they are. The people who are characterized by faith in the God of Abraham and the Father of the Lord Jesus Christ are the children of Abraham.

The Testimony of Scripture

Some of the Judaizers may say that Paul is twisting the Scriptures to make his point. So Paul goes on to show that his teaching about the place of the Gentiles is nothing new, but has been part of Scripture since Abraham's day. He does this using another quotation from the Old Testament: *The Scripture foresaw that God would justify the Gentiles by faith, and announced the gospel in advance to Abraham: "All nations will be blessed through you"* (3:8).

The passage Paul quotes is Genesis 12:3. The wording comes from the ancient Greek translation known as the Septuagint. But Paul makes one significant change to the verse he quotes. Instead of saying "all the tribes of the earth will be blessed through you", he substitutes the word "nations", which God uses when he repeats his promise to Abraham in Genesis 18:18. The two words are similar in meaning, but Paul chooses to use the word "nations" because by his day that was the word used for everyone who was not a Jew. Not only can Gentiles become fellow-believers with Abraham, they were also included in the original promise to Abraham. Paul's insistence that belief is the basis on which anyone can be accepted and justified by God is therefore not a new idea but was God's intention when he first made the promise.[237]

Paul insists that this idea was foreseen and proclaimed "in advance" to Abraham by the Scripture. In saying this, he is personifying Scripture and treating it as more or less "an extension of the divine personality".[238] He feels free to do this because he believes that Scripture "embodies the mind of God, and that God being omniscient, His Scripture foresees as well as narrates, glances into the future with the same eye as it sweeps round the present or looks back into the past."[239]

But what did God mean when he said that the nations would be blessed "through" Abraham?[240] Some understand the Greek as meaning "through your offspring" (referring to Christ) and others take it to mean "along with you" or "in the same way as you".[241] However, the best meaning seems to be "in you", meaning that Abraham is presented here as "the root and representative of all the faithful. They are in him as spiritual children in a spiritual ancestor or federal head, and are therefore included in his blessing – are blessed in him."[242] In other words, Abraham is the "spiritual progenitor" of all those who believe.[243]

In this context, it is clear that the blessing as Paul interprets it is justification, that is, being accepted by God.[244] But this does not mean that the blessing does not also include sanctification. Justification and sanctification go hand in hand: "God at one time both reckons a person righteous through faith and bestows on them the Spirit that transforms their lives."[245]

Faith and Blessing

On the basis of the facts that Abraham himself was justified by faith, and that it is God's plan from the very beginning to bless all nations in Abraham by way of faith, Paul draws the following conclusion: *those who rely on faith are blessed along with Abraham, the man of faith* (3:9). Some translations prefer "have faith" to "rely on faith", but the TNIV is right to focus on faith not as a possession but as part of the way one conducts oneself. One's faith is evident in one's day to day decision-making.

The blessings that come with faith are not pious hopes for the future but are already experienced in the present.[246] Those who believe are enjoying the same blessings that Abraham did – justification and all that goes with it.

Whereas previously Paul spoke of the blessings that came "through" Abraham or "in" Abraham (3:8), here he says that they will be enjoyed "along with" Abraham.[247] Those who believe are not just one with Abraham ("in you" implying "unity") but are also in fellowship with him ("along with" implying "company"). They are "one" with Abraham since he is the spiritual progenitor of all who believe, and "in his company" since just as it was faith that was the basis of his justification, so also it is for them.

Africans traditionally have a strong belief that nothing short of divine intervention can stop an elder's curse or blessing from taking effect. Abraham is our elder in matters of faith. As he is blessed, so are we all, whether as Galatian believers in the first century or African believers in the twenty-first century. The one doing the blessing is God, and when he blesses, there is no one above him who can intervene to prevent it.

The Only Alternative

Those who reject Paul's contention that we are saved by faith are left with the problem of explaining how we can be saved. Their only option is "rely on the law, or on their performance of the law, for their acceptance with God".[248] They cannot hope to live partly by faith and partly by law because, as Paul points out, *The law is not based on faith* (3:12). Faith and law are two different systems, so to speak. "The principles of legalism and of faith are mutually exclusive as bases of justification."[249] Paul underlines this point by quoting Leviticus 8:5: *whoever does these things will live by them* (3:12).

Those who choose to try to earn their salvation by obeying the law are free to do so. But they will face the problem that while those who come to God in faith are "blessed along with Abraham" (3:9), *all who rely on observing the law are under a curse* (3:10a).[250]

His readers may dispute this point, and so Paul carefully presents his argument in three steps:

1. Those who rely on keeping the law for their justification have to keep it perfectly. He backs this point up by quoting Deuteronomy 27:26: *Cursed is everyone who does not continue to do everything written in the Book of the Law* (3:10b). The words "continue to do" do not allow for any lapses in obedience.[251] The wording of the verse is all inclusive. No one is exempted, and every law is to be obeyed in every detail. Perfection is required.

2. Faith is the route to righteousness. Paul again refers to Scripture to show that faith is the means by which righteousness is attained, quoting Habakkuk 2:4: *The righteous will live by faith* (3:11). The future "shall live" is an assured fact.[252] That is the way things normally work. Those who seek righteousness in some other way are going against the tide.

3. Christ has already dealt with our sin. We are all under a curse because we have all failed to keep God's law. There is only one way to evade the effects of that curse, and that is Christ, who *redeemed us from the curse of the law by way of becoming a curse for us* (3:13a). As proof that Christ took on our curse, Paul quotes Deuteronomy 21:23: "Cursed is everyone who is hung on a pole" (3:13b). Unlike us, Christ had

never sinned and so was not cursed. But he allowed himself to be hung on the cross in order to take the curse we deserved on himself. The Galatians are free to choose whichever route to justification they want. But they must choose – they cannot try to follow both at once. Thus they must weigh their choice carefully. If they choose the route of works, they will soon find that they cannot possibly meet its demand for perfect obedience. On the other hand, there is the route of faith in the one who met the demands of the law for us. Jesus Christ opened the path to justification for both Jews and Gentiles. The effectiveness of his sacrifice is confirmed in everyone who believes by the presence of the Holy Spirit.

Our Redemption

In the course of his argument, Paul reveals some important facts about our redemption.

First, he explains what he was redeemed from, namely *the curse of the law* (3:13a). This curse is the result of Adam's disobedience, but he is not solely to blame. We, too, are all law-breakers, and thus we, too, are cursed (Deut 27:26, as quoted in 3:10). No matter how hard we try to obey God, we fail.

Second, Paul explains how we are redeemed. It was by Christ's *becoming a curse for us* (3:13b). There was some sort of exchange whereby he became cursed in order to redeem us from the curse. He was our substitute.[253] He took the curse that should have fallen on us in order to satisfy the demands of the law. From that moment on, the curse no longer applies to those who are in him by faith. We are hidden in Christ, and any element of the curse that comes our way simply bounces off him.

The result of our redemption is that we share in the blessing of Abraham, a point that Paul reiterates in 3:14a when he says that we are redeemed *in order that the blessing given to Abraham might come to the Gentiles through Christ Jesus.*[254] Abraham had received the blessing of being called by God, and through Christ's work this same blessing has now been extended to the Gentiles who have faith in Christ. Justification is no longer the exclusive privilege of Abraham's genetic descendants, the Jews.

The second result of our redemption is that *we ... receive the promise of the Spirit* (3:14b).[255] This blessing comes to each and every believer, whether Jew or Gentile. What is promised is the Holy Spirit himself.[256]

The Choice

If I want to send a parcel from Nairobi to New York, I have the option of sending it by air or by surface mail. If I send it by air, it will arrive within weeks; if I send it by sea, it will take two months. It makes better sense to send it by air so that it arrives in time.

In the same way, there are two paths to salvation. One is the "surface route", taken by those who want to follow the path of good works. They will achieve salvation – provided that they can survive the hazards of a long land journey and swim the ocean by obeying all the commandments and obeying each of them perfectly. But this is impossible. No one can swim the Atlantic.

Those who choose the path of faith will receive salvation instantly, the moment they put their faith in the Lord Jesus Christ. Why would they even want to consider the "surface" option, with all its hazards and the unlikelihood of success?

Everyone, however, must make his or her own decision. No evangelist can force you to choose the path of faith, but we can show you the implications of choosing another route.

The writer of Hebrews was right when he said, "without faith, it is impossible to please God" (Heb 11:6). The only reason we try to work for our salvation is that we have not comprehended how holy God is and how weak we are. May the Lord help us to choose the alternative that is guaranteed to bring blessings!

Questions for Discussion

1. Though not perfect in every way, Abraham is credited for responding to God in faith. In what specific areas in your life right now is God calling you to respond in faith?

2. One of the most essential tools for travellers is a compass. What do you think is the compass of the believer? To what extent do believers you are close to use this tool in their day-to-day activities and decisions?
3. Have you ever had to choose between two options, one of them impractical and the other with all costs paid? Which did you choose and why?
4. Have you ever had an experience where someone paid in full for you to do something you really wanted to do? How did you respond? How similar or different is that situation from Christ paying our debts and becoming a curse for us?

UNIT 10
GALATIANS 3:15–4:11

ARGUMENTS BASED ON EVERYDAY LIFE

Recently I had to undertake a long drive with a Kamba friend. Along the way, he told me about an incident in which a young goat jumped right into a car into which its mother was being loaded for transportation to another farm. I quoted the English proverb about blood being thicker than water. That led us into a long discussion of Kikamba proverbs like *mutinda na mukundu ndalea ukunduka* (one who keeps company with someone with an infectious skin disease will also get the disease) and *iui ya kiw'u itwaawa no kiw'u* (the banana plant carried to the edge of a farm by water will also be swept away by water). As we talked, we were reminded of how much truth is encapsulated in proverbs. We both knew of obedient children who had become corrupted by keeping bad company, and of people who had acquired wealth easily through corruption, but whose wealth had evaporated. We agreed that the Kamba people who crafted the proverbs were very observant. So were those who crafted the proverbs recorded in Scripture.

All proverbs draw from everyday life and teach lessons about something that is generally true. While a proverb may not apply to every single case without exception, it will generally elicit nods of agreement from those who hear it.

Paul uses the same approach here when he moves on from discussing the Galatians' experience and analysing Scripture and tells his beloved *brothers and sisters*[257] that he will use *an example from everyday life* (3:15a). He then presents two arguments based on familiar situations, one involving promises and contracts and the other involving the change from childhood to adulthood.

Promise and Law

Once you have signed your will and had it legally witnessed, no one else has the right to change it. Once you have bought a car and taken possession of it, you don't expect the car dealer to arrive on your doorstep and say, "I'm sorry, but we've decided to change the price." If that did happen, you would refuse to pay any more than you had agreed. This is the type of situation Paul has in mind when he says that *no one can set aside or add to a human covenant that has been duly established* (3:15). Once an agreement has been confirmed and every needed signature is in place, the agreement is permanent (unless of course, all the parties agree to change it). If one party does not honour the agreement, the other can take them to court and produce the signed agreement as evidence against them. The agreement is equivalent to a promise that something will be done.

We have to be very careful about whom we enter into covenants with. Some people feel free to disregard any agreement, even one that should be legally binding. There are people to whom you would never lend money, no matter what they promised, because you know that they will never repay the loan. There are people from whom you would never buy a car, because you would find that the car had all sorts of hidden problems that they had cleverly disguised. We only want to enter into covenants with people we can trust.

People are often unreliable and untrustworthy. But God is perfect in his faithfulness (1 John 1:9). We can confidently base our plans on any promise he gives. Moreover, God is eternal. Some of us fail to fulfil promises because our circumstances change or we die. But God has none of these limitations. His promises will be kept. And that includes his promise of an inheritance.

God's promise

Paul has been speaking about God's promise to Abraham that all nations will be blessed through him (3:8, 14). Now he zeros in on one word that is often repeated in God's promises to Abraham, the word "seed". For example, in Genesis 17:7 God says, "I will establish my covenant as an everlasting covenant between me and you and your descendants". The Hebrew word translated "descendants" in our translations can literally be translated "seed".

Paul points out that the word "seed" is singular, and says, *Scripture does not say "and to seeds" meaning many people, but "and to your seed", meaning one person, who is Christ* (3:16). This argument may strike us as odd, because grammatically the noun "seed" can be a collective noun. However, this type of reasoning was common among the rabbis in Paul's day, who felt free to draw from all kinds of Old Testament passages in order to make a point. So Paul's argument here would be quite acceptable to his readers.

Paul says that because the word "seed" is singular, it must refer to just one person, and that person must be Christ. When God chose Abraham in order to bless the world through him (Gen 12:3), this blessing was not limited to him as an individual but looked forward two thousand years to when Jesus would take on human flesh and be born of one of Abraham's descendants. The promise points to Jesus Christ, the Saviour of the world.

Paul presents this argument to underscore Christ's unique status. The Galatians were beginning to be persuaded that Moses, who received the law from God, was so important that he was Christ's equal. That is why they were starting to think that they needed to obey the law of Moses as well as having faith in Christ.

These days, we honour the theological and ethical teachings of many famous people. But just as Christ outranks Moses for the Jews, so he outranks everyone else who is honoured by other people groups. Christ is God. He took on human nature and as the God–man he satisfied the demands of God as a suitable representative of humanity. No other person can ever have that qualification. That is why we cannot shrink from proclaiming the uniqueness of Christ as we proclaim the good news of salvation.

A legally binding human agreement cannot be set aside, and it is unthinkable that a divine agreement can be broken. Thus there is no way in which God's revelation of himself to Moses can supersede his promise to Abraham: *The law, introduced 430 years later, does not set aside the covenant previously established by God and thus do away with the promise* (3:17).[258] God did not say, "Yes, I made you a promise, but I have changed my mind and now you have to earn the thing I freely promised four hundred years ago."

Paul reminds his readers that if getting their *inheritance depends on the law, then it no longer depends on the promise* (3:18a). The inheritance is either by way of the law or by way of promise. It is not a little of this and a little of the other. And the Scriptures are clear: *God in his grace gave it to Abraham through a promise* (3:18b).

The law is, therefore, excluded when it comes to inheriting God's blessing to Abraham. And that blessing is acceptance as one of God's people, or in other words, justification. It is thus the way of the promise, accepted by faith in Christ, which provides justification. We should not seek justification through obeying the law.

God's law

Paul's argument here naturally raises the matter of *the purpose of the law* (3:19a). If it is not needed for justification, why did God give it at all? Paul's answer is that it was needed *because of transgressions* (3:19b). By this he may mean that the law prevents people from sinning because they know what God commands. Or he may mean that the law increases sin because those who choose to disobey it cannot offer the excuse that they do not know what God wants. Or it may be that the law exposes sin by making us more aware of our failures. The last explanation seems to be the most likely one, although there is some overlap between all three possibilities.[259] Regardless of which interpretation we adopt, Paul's key point is that the law is associated with sin, not with justification.

The law did have a valid purpose, but it also had a time limit. It functioned only *until the Seed to whom the promise referred had come* (3:19b). Paul has identified this seed as Christ, who has already come (3:16). Therefore the Galatians no longer need to focus on the law as the basis for acceptance by God. The law never served as the basis for justification, and its time limit has expired. It has been replaced by faith in the Saviour of both Jews and Gentiles.

The time limit on the law indicates that it is inferior to God's unlimited promise. So does the fact that the law was given through a number of intermediaries. There was Moses, who passed it on to the Israelites, and there were the *angels*, whom Jewish tradition said were involved in the giving of the law (3:19c).²⁶⁰ By contrast, when God made the promise to Abraham, he was the only party involved (3:20).

But if the law is inferior to the promise, does that mean that they are in competition? Is the law actually *opposed to the promises of God*? Is there hostility between them? Paul's answer is a vehement, *Absolutely not!* (3:21a). He then goes on to explain the relationship between the law and the promise in more detail.

First, there is no competition because both the law and the promise share the same goal: righteousness. Where they differed was in their ability to give righteousness. As Paul says, *if a law had been given that could impart life, then righteousness would certainly have come by the law* (3:21b). But it could not. All that the law could do was expose sin, it could not remove it. In fact, it *locked up everything under the control of sin* (3:22a). It was like a doctor telling a patient, "You are sick, and I know what is wrong with you, but I don't have any medicine that can cure you."

The medicine that was needed was the coming of Christ. The helplessness induced by the law (a diagnosis but no cure) intensified the importance of the cure (faith in Christ), *so that what was promised, being given through faith in Jesus Christ, might be given to those who believe* (3:22b).²⁶¹

Changing the metaphor, Paul describes the law as our jailer. We were in protective custody, locked up and subject to strict rules to prevent us from wandering too far from God while we awaited the one who would set us free through faith in him (3:23).

Changing the metaphor yet again, Paul speaks of the law as being like someone who *was put in charge of us until Christ came* (3:24). It was like the pedagogue, who was both the bodyguard and babysitter of any upper-class Greek boy. His job was to escort the boy wherever he needed to go, to discipline him when necessary, and to teach him manners and the difference between right and wrong.²⁶² "During the boy's minority the *paidagogos* imposed a necessary restraint on his liberty until, with his coming of age, he could be trusted to use his liberty responsibly."²⁶³

In the same way, the law kept us safe from sinning – provided we obeyed it – and taught us the difference between right and wrong. Just as a child would outgrow the need for a pedagogue, so with Christ's coming, the need for the law as a pedagogue ended. Paul could thus say, *Now that this faith has come, we are no longer under the supervision of the law* (3:25).

Faith in Christ is the goal of God's plan of redemption. Those who have exercised this faith are mature and no longer need a pedagogue to escort them. There is no danger that they will run wild and do the things their pedagogue would not permit them to do. Rather, they have absorbed the lessons he taught and will now obey them naturally, without any need for external supervision.

Every society recognizes that there is an age at which a person is still a child and an age at which they become a responsible adult. In many African societies, there are specific initiation rites to mark the transition from the first stage of life to the next stage. A boy who has been initiated will no longer live in the same hut as his parents, but will seek to construct his own hut. Nor will he accept being referred to as a "boy" any more, for he has graduated from boyhood and is now a man. Paul is telling the Galatians that when one becomes a believer, one ceases to be a child. This does not mean that the values one was taught during childhood have become useless, but that they have become part of one's world view. One can now make correct judgments on one's own, without having to be told what to do. One now does what is right because it is right, and not because one is afraid of punishment. The law guided the child as an instructor. The law now guides the adult as a world view.

Paul's attitude to the law should also inform our own childrearing. Values, not punishment, should be our focus. When the cultivation of values in their lives has matured, we can trust that our children can be in Egypt like Joseph or in Babylon like Daniel and still say, "I have a God I love and must please". Why is it that so many of our young people are lost when they move to the cities where they are accountable only to themselves? Is it that they have matured physically but not morally, because they were told "do this" or "don't do that or else ..." rather than "do this because it is right" or "don't do this because it is wrong"?

In Christian terms, faith in Christ shows that we have reached the age of maturity. We please God because we love him, and we love him because he first loved us (1 John 4:10).

Son and Slave

Paul has been using the metaphor of childhood implicit in the idea of someone else being "in charge" or of our being under someone's "supervision". But the metaphor of childhood is such a rich one that he cannot refrain from exploring it further.

The blessings of membership in God's family

One of the great blessings of salvation is that *in Christ Jesus you are all children of God* (3:26a). This is our guaranteed status once we have met the condition of "faith in Jesus Christ".[264]

Our status as "children of God" signals both possession and a relationship.[265] The justified belong to God as his children and he is their Father (see 4:7). We were not born into this relationship but acquired it by being adopted as his children (see 4:5). Adoption focuses on the fact that we did not previously belong in this family, but have now gained the same rights as those who were born into it. It is as if we have been born again, as Jesus told Nicodemus (John 3:3–5).

Had it not been for Adam and Eve's sin, we would all have been born into his family and would have enjoyed God's fellowship forever (Gen 3:6). But their sin brought sin into the world (Rom 5:12), separating us from God (Rom 3:23). However, those who believe have this relationship restored. They are spiritually cleansed (John 3:5) and from then on they are part of God's family.

As members of God's family, we share a family relationship that can be described as Christ-likeness. Paul writes, *for all of you who were baptized into Christ have clothed yourselves with Christ* (3:27).[266] In the early church, baptism was a mark of entry into a new kind of life. Being baptised in someone's name meant that one identified with that person. The Galatians have identified themselves with Christ. Their relationship to him is now so close that it can be described as "being clothed with" or "putting on" Christ. To understand what this means, think about the role that clothes play today. Most African schoolchildren have to wear a uniform that tells the world which school they attend. We also see "uniforms" at weddings. The bridesmaids and groomsmen all wear similar dresses or suits to indicate that they are in a special relationship to the couple being married. In this same way, all believers have clothed themselves with the uniform of Christ-likeness. We are to take on "the characteristics, virtues, and/or intentions" of Christ.[267]

Sadly, at times our Christ-likeness is not clearly visible because of sin. It is as if the members of the wedding party have arrived with their clothes muddy and dirty. This is not the way they were intended to look! The church is Christ's bride (Eph 5:32), and no bride would dream of arriving for the wedding in a dirty dress. But Christ has made provision for cleansing our sins (1 John 1:9) and our clothes can be washed and restored to their original condition.

Our shared membership in God's family means that we are all united. Paul puts it this way: *There is neither Jew nor Gentile, neither slave nor free, neither male nor female, for you are all one in Christ Jesus* (3:28). These were the things that divided people in Paul's day. Race, tribe, social status, and gender still divide us today – but such things should cease to exist in Christ. Those who have put on Christ should no longer be seen as white or black, master or servant, man or woman. We have all put on Christ and we should thus all look alike – like Christ.

On many occasions, the church has failed to live up to this teaching. There are few countries in the world where some groups have not been discriminated against, and in many countries we still discriminate between men and women. There are also churches for the middle class and others for those living in the slums. Anything that divides believers into two groups is not of God. We, as sinful people, may maintain such distinctions, but God sees all of us as his children and so as one family.

Since we belong to the same family as Christ, and he is Abraham's descendant (3:16), we too are now Abraham's descendants. This is the point Paul is making when he writes, *If you belong to Christ, then you are Abraham's seed* (3:29a).[268] Belonging to Abraham was a very important matter to Jews (John 8:33, 39). The false teachers were telling the Galatians that they had to be circumcised and follow the Jewish law in order to be Abraham's descendants, but there is no need for this. Those who have faith in Christ are already part of Abraham's family.

In Africa, one of the greatest insults is to tell someone that he or she is not their mother or father's child. The person will usually respond by vigorously defending their membership in the family. After all, it is not the angry words of an aggrieved brother or sister that determine whether one is part of the family, it is the parent's decision. The parent's will takes precedence over everyone else's. The Judaizers can tell the Galatians that they are not part of God's family, but God is the one who makes the decision. He has made it plain that all those who have faith in Christ are part of his family.

Not only are they members of the family, but as such they are also entitled to an inheritance because they are now *heirs according to the promise* (3:29b). They are entitled to inherit all the blessings that were promised to Abraham and to his seed.

Paul's words make it clear that all believers are heirs of Christ – the only qualification required to become an heir is membership in God's family. If this is the pattern in God's family, should it not also be the pattern in our families? Why is it that we so often see that only sons are allowed to inherit their parents' property? Such discrimination against daughters is unjustified. Just as all believers are heirs of Abraham's and Christ's blessings, so all the sons and daughters in a family should be heirs of the family's wealth. Believers should set an example to their culture in this regard.

The final blessing that flows from our membership in God's family is that God sends *the Spirit of his Son into our hearts* (4:6a).[269] It is worth noting that Paul here says that the primary function of the Holy Spirit in a believer's life is not to produce demonstrations of power but to lead the believer to call God *Abba* (4:6b).[270] "Abba" is an Aramaic word that means *Father*, but which also suggests dependence, for it is equivalent to a small child's "Daddy" or "Papa". Those who cannot address God as *Abba* have not become believers (see also Rom 8:9b), or to use Jesus' words to Nicodemus, have not been born again (John 3:3).[271]

This filial relationship is fundamental, and only once it has been established can other gifts and blessings flow to the believer.

The life of an heir

Paul expands on what it means to be an heir, drawing on people's everyday understanding of the way an inheritance affects the life of a young child and of an adult.

Young children who inherit great wealth are not necessarily given great freedom. They cannot spend the wealth any way they want because their parents have specified that they are to be subject to *guardians and trustees* until they are mature enough to use their wealth responsibly.

Thus although in theory the child is the master, in practice he or she cannot give orders but has to obey the orders of the guardians. Thus the child is in much the same position as a slave (4:1–2).

In the past, the Galatians had been like this child, under supervision. Paul puts it like this: *So also, when we were underage, we were in slavery under the elemental spiritual forces of the world* (4:3). The words translated "elemental spiritual forces" can also be translated as "the basic principles of the world" (NIV).[272] These are the elementary things that one learns in one's first years of schooling. If you think in terms of maths, the elementary things are the times tables we had to learn: 2 x 2 = 4; 2 x 3 = 6; and so on. Once we knew these tables well, multiplication was easy. If we did not learn them, multiplication exercises were an uphill battle. Similarly, the alphabet is elementary knowledge when we start to learn a new language. The first step in learning Hebrew or Greek is to memorize the Hebrew or Greek alphabet.

What were "the elemental spiritual forces" that had ruled over the Galatians? Was it the Jewish law? Possibly, but the additional description of these as "forces of the world" makes this unlikely.[273] It seems more likely that Paul is talking in broad terms of the rituals of Gentile worship. By extension, these words also apply to the sacrifices of African traditional religion and of other religions. These systems do not represent the law as given and purposed by God but as misinterpreted and misapplied by human beings. This is what is being promoted in Galatia.

This elementary stuff is not useless or unethical, but it is insufficient. It has the "do's" and "don'ts" and gives some limited knowledge of God, but it provides no inner energy to move us towards maturity in obedience.

In their wills, parents often set a date when their children will be regarded as adults and allowed to exercise control over their inheritance. On that day, the child who has been the heir all along advances from being dependent on others to being governor of his or her inheritance (4:2). God, too, had set a time for humans who are still living under the elementary principles of religion to mature in their knowledge of his redemptive plan. He developed human thinking and human history to make sure that the time was right. The expectation of the Messiah among the Jews, the peace and security brought by Roman government, the widespread use of the Greek language promoted by the conquests of

Alexander, the excellent system of Roman roads, all were arranged to be in place *when the set time had fully come* (4:4a). At that time, *God sent his Son*. Good ideas within the world system governed human beings only as long as the Light of the world has not yet been revealed. Once that was done, all else became "elementary stuff" within God's revelation of his redemptive plan.

The Son whom God sent is described as *born of a woman, born under law* (4:4b). He could identify with human beings because he was himself human, being "born of a woman" (although he was also divine). Because he was also "born under law", he knew all about the obligations and demands of the law of Moses and of law in general, and satisfied them all perfectly. These characteristics fit him to be the one to *redeem those under law, that we might receive adoption to sonship* (4:5). It is faith in him that matters now. He gives those who believe the status of being sons and daughters of God.

The appeal

Having argued that believers are mature sons and daughters and should act their age, Paul makes an appeal to the Galatians. He reminds them that in the past they had no knowledge of God and served non-gods (4:8). Now they know God (or rather, God now knows them and acknowledges them as members of his family). But they are living as if they were still in the past! They are observing the religious rituals (*special days and months and seasons and years* – 4:10) that were part of their elementary knowledge, which could not save them and make them sons (4:9). This kind of behaviour suggests that Paul's efforts to bring them into knowledge of God through Christ and by faith have been wasted (4:11).

Let us think about the situation using an African example. Among the Akamba of Kenya, children used to have a strip of leather tied around their arm to protect them from anyone who might want to harm them. The Akamba also had an elementary knowledge of God through what they could see of him in creation. When the Christian message was brought to the Akamba, they acquired a fuller knowledge of God as revealed in the Scriptures. They learnt that God loved them and gave his Son to die on the cross for them. That Son, having risen from the dead, is now the companion and friend of those who believe. He is the one who defends them from the forces of evil, and there is no need to wear a strip of leather for protection. A Christian Akamba walks with Jesus, does business with Jesus, farms with Jesus, teaches with Jesus, and so on, and trusts Jesus to ward off malevolent attacks. They have truly moved beyond their "elementary" knowledge of God. If they now start relying on *majini* to protect them, this amounts to going back to elementary classes in the school of faith. Rather than going backwards, we should be continually growing in our knowledge of God.

Questions for discussion

1. Have you ever been appointed to a position in an acting capacity, say as an acting manager or academic dean? Or have you ever had to act for your parents when they were both away? What happens when the person you are filling in for returns or a permanent incumbent is appointed? How does this relate to what Paul is saying here? How does it apply to Jews in relation to the law and to Africans in relation to some traditional beliefs and practices?
2. Compare two experiences, one in which you were given a series of do's and don'ts and another in which you were allowed freedom within the bounds of your conscience. Which experience helped more in terms of developing your own value system? How does that relate to Paul's argument here?
3. Have you ever known someone related to someone who is important – for example a child of the president, a government minister, or a member of parliament? Did you attach some importance to the fact that your acquaintance was related to such a person? How does this throw light on the importance we need to attach to the fact that we are children of God?
4. Have you ever been treated differently (whether positively or negatively) because you were of a different gender, social status, level of education, or had some other differentiating characteristic? Is such treatment in accord with the way God treats us? How should we treat one another within the family of God?

WHAT MATTERS MOST?

I recently spent several hours with someone whom I had come to know in the course of a land transaction. He kept saying how happy he was to see me. I could not imagine why he felt so strongly about this, for we were only casual acquaintances.

As he showed me around his property, boasting about its size, I became aware that he was a little under the influence of alcohol. Noticing that I had noticed this, he remarked that even the local Roman Catholic priest drinks. Smiling, I asked him why he was saying this. He replied that he knew I would not approve of drinking since I was a pastor with the Africa Inland Church. I acknowledged that I did not drink and then asked him, "Why do you think I don't approve of drinking?" He again said, "Because you are a pastor with the Africa Inland Church, and that church preaches against drinking."

At this point in our conversation, I asked him who God is happiest with: someone who drinks, a priest who drinks, or me who does not drink. He immediately identified God's order of preference as "first you, since you do not drink; then the priest because though he drinks, he also preaches; and then me since I drink and am simply a layman". As if accepting his answer was correct, I asked him, "And why do you keep saying that you are always happy to see me?" He responded, "Because you accept me as I am."

I did not expect such a humbling response, but after giving thanks to God in my heart, I went on to show my friend that God accepts us as we are, whether we drink or not, and regardless of what denomination we belong to. I spoke to him about Galatians 3:23–29, and we concluded the day with a prayer for salvation. Money and land had brought us together, but what mattered most was that we were both accepted by God and given eternal life in his Son. Our status as believers counts for far more than our status as pastor or layman, abstainer or drinker. We are accepted simply because of our faith in Christ Jesus. Change of character and a call to service follow this free acceptance.

Every day, we are in contact with people and talk to them about all types of things including the economy, politics, the state of the crops and so on. There is nothing wrong with such talk, but there is someone else we should always introduce into our conversation. The God of economies, politics and crops is also and primarily the God of promise. He promises us justification (acceptance) through his Son, Jesus Christ. By grace, through faith in his Son, God is happy with us. In his presence, we can appreciate money, status, good harvests and other material blessings. This is the message of Galatians: The good life is not primarily a life of wealth or health but a life of acceptance by God.

UNIT 11
GALATIANS 4:12–31

ARGUMENTS FROM RELATIONSHIPS

Relationships change. They are always either growing or dying. I was reminded of this when my wife returned to Kenya in 2009 after a lengthy stay in the USA. On her return to our village, she was excitedly embraced by many relatives. But she was a little startled to be embraced by a woman she did not know, who was not a relative. My brother, who was present, was also surprised by this fervent greeting. Who was this woman?

Some time later, my brother discovered that she was one of three women who had made some African baskets as gifts for our first daughter when she was getting married in 2008. My mother told us that this woman "was so much moved by love that she felt a handshake would not do". Little things like the woman making a basket for our daughter and the appreciation with which the basket was received had built a relationship, even though the two women had never met.

If one of the relatives my wife did know had chosen to greet her with a handshake instead of a hug, my observant brother would also have noticed that. Our behaviour always signals the state of our relationships.

The same was true of the Galatians. So Paul appeals to them by reminding them of the relationship he and they had once enjoyed. He also uses the example of the competitive relationship between Hagar and Sarah to outline the options facing the Galatians.

The Galatians' Relationship to Paul

Paul's argument in this section is not as clear as his previous arguments. However, he seems to be saying something like this: "Remember how you treated me when I was with you? You must have believed that what I had for you was a treasure to be guarded. Keep on guarding it."

He again addresses the Galatians as his *brothers and sisters* and shows the seriousness with which he views the situation by saying *I plead with you* (4:12a). Usually he uses a milder verb that means "I exhort you".[274] The content of the appeal is *become like me, for I became like you* (4:12a). What exactly does Paul mean by this? For an answer it may be best to start by looking at the way in which the Galatians were not like him. Like him, they were children of God, but unlike him they were observing the Jewish calendar and dietary laws (4:10) and opening themselves up to the idea that circumcision is the way to attain acceptance before God. So Paul urges them to make the same change as he had done and become like him. He, too, had once been a strict observer of the Jewish law, but he had learned that the law brings condemnation and not salvation, and had wisely abandoned the way of works for the way of faith. He is urging the Galatians to adopt the same attitude to the place of law and faith in their lives. This appeal would touch the Jewish believers. At the same time, Paul was telling the Gentile believers, "I have taken no account of my own Jewish heritage and have fully identified with you."

Some commentators think that the way in which the Galatians differed from Paul is that whereas he still loved them, they were now hostile to him (4:16). If this is the case, then Paul is saying something like this: "Have the same goodwill and warmth of friendship towards me as I have towards you. I have shown my friendship by identifying with you, and I still have warm feelings for you. Please do not reject me and my message." Those who take this position stress the next phrase, *you have done me no wrong* (4:12b). The Galatians have not offended Paul, and he does not seek to offend them either. His motive for writing is love, and he is writing to people he cares about.

While it is not possible to be dogmatic about which interpretation of this verse is correct, the majority of commentators prefer the first view. On that interpretation, when Paul says "you have done me no wrong", what he means is that although the Galatians have not injured him in the past, he is hurt by their attitude in the present.

The relationship between Paul and the Galatians had been very warm. He had been ill when he first came to preach the gospel to them (4:13), but his sickness did not lead them to treat him *with contempt or scorn*. Instead, Paul says, *you welcomed me as if I were an angel of God, as if I were Christ Jesus himself* (4:14). In fact, they were so concerned about him that *if you could have done so, you would have torn out your eyes and given them to me* (4:15b).

This statement suggests that Paul's illness was some problem with his eyes. Clearly it caused him considerable difficulty and placed the burden of caring for him on the Galatians. They had acquitted themselves well.

The contrast between their attitude then and their attitude now leads Paul to ask, *What has happened to all your joy?* (4:15a) and *Have I now become your enemy by telling you the truth?* (4:16).

If the Galatians are now hostile to Paul, it is because some people are poisoning the relationship between them: *Those people are zealous to win you over, but for no good. What they want is to alienate you from us* (4:17). The Galatians had been zealous in caring for Paul and in their love of Christ, but the Judaizers' want them to *have zeal for them* instead. They want the Galatians to turn to them and not to Paul, for guidance.

Paul is not condemning zeal. He sees it as a good thing: *It is fine to be zealous, provided the purpose is good, and to be so always, not just when I am with you* (4:18). However, the Judaizers' purpose was selfish, whereas Paul was concerned for the Galatians' own good. This was the case when he was with them, and it is still the case now.

The Galatians, too, should maintain their zeal for the gospel he preached to them. "Out of sight, out of mind" should never apply in situations when zeal is for what is good. It should be there all the time. We should not be full of zeal when we go out on evangelistic campaigns, but allow our zeal to flag between campaigns. Rather, zeal for what is good should be an ongoing part of our lives. It should spring from our personal commitment to reach others for Christ and should not wait to be stirred up by some teacher or church leader.

The example of the Judaizers also reminds us that if we do not direct our zeal to reaching others, someone else will. Non-Christian religious groups have erected places of worship in many towns in Africa. These places are open to the destitute and children, and in times of famine they provide food. Underlying these acts of mercy is a strategy to turn the entire town to another religion. Some of the vulnerable towns are places where the church has been present for decades but has not affected people's lives at the social and material level. Unless Christians show more zeal for the gospel, these churches will not survive and these once Christian-oriented towns will become antagonistic to Christianity.

Paul is deeply concerned about the Galatians' attitude towards him. Their warmth in the past confirms that they had accepted him and his message, and he trusts that renewed warmth will make them hear what he has to say now. He is still filled with the same zeal he had for their good when he was with them as he writes to defend the message he preached to them. So deep is his love and concern for them that he addresses them as *my dear children* (4:19a).[275] He feels not only like a brother (4:12) but also like a mother towards them.

Paul evaluates the Galatians as having fallen so low that they need to begin all over again in their journey of being fully satisfied with Christ as their Saviour and Lord. They need to relearn that Christ is all they need (4:19b).

Paul's concern expresses itself in a longing to be with the Galatian believers. If he could see them, he would know that they are ready to grow in faith and are listening to him, and he would change his tone of voice accordingly (4:20).

Generally, when someone we love is not doing well, we want to be with them to monitor how they are doing and to look for every sign of improvement. That is how Paul feels about the Galatians. He is also perplexed by the contrast between their past and the present attitudes. Why have they changed? The Galatians need to look at the matter carefully and go back to the basics of justification by faith that Paul taught them.

The Relationship of Hagar and Sarah

Paul's final argument is addressed to *you who want to be under the law* (4:21a), that is, all those who want to insist on obedience to the law of Moses. This time, Paul bases his argument on an incident in Genesis.

Genesis 16 tells of Abraham and Sarah (or Abram and Sarai, at that point) not having children. Sarah suggests that Abraham sleep with her servant, Hagar, who conceives and gives birth to a son who is named Ishmael. Hagar was Sarah's Egyptian servant (Gen 16:3) and is *the slave woman* referred to in Galatians 4:22.

Later, in Genesis 21, we read that God enables Abraham's wife, Sarah, to give birth to a son, whom Abraham calls Isaac. Sarah is *the free woman* referred to in Galatians 4:22. Sarah then demands that Hagar and her son be sent away. With the Lord's permission, Abraham sends Hagar and Ishmael away to avoid further family fights. In giving Abraham permission to send Hagar away, God tells Abraham, "it is through Isaac that your offspring will be reckoned" (Gen 21:12b).

Paul uses this Old Testament story to draw a spiritual lesson (4:24a). He acknowledges that he is using the two women *figuratively*, not denying their historical reality, but using them to bring out a spiritual truth.[276]

This type of allegorization was acceptable in New Testament times. Later, some church fathers took this too far when they tried to find redemption-related facts in every detail in Scripture. For example, in preaching on the story of the good Samaritan (Luke 10:30–37), they would describe the man on the journey as a believer abandoning the place of salvation (Jerusalem) and pursuing the path of sin (Jericho), the thieves would be said to be demons who stripped him of all God-given graces, and so on.

But there is a difference between what Paul does here and such excessive allegorization. Paul acknowledges the historical setting of the story. He knows that Sarah and Hagar were real people, and that he is using an incident in their lives to illustrate a point in his argument. By contrast, some allegorical preachers seem to totally ignore the historical context. Thus in the case of the parable mentioned above, the church fathers would speak as if Jerusalem and Jericho were nothing more than two spheres of spirituality.

When we preach today, our listeners seldom like allegorization because they are schooled to pay attention to context and are concerned that every detail of the old context fits smoothly into the new context. So we would probably not use the type of example that Paul does here. But those to whom Paul was writing in New Testament times accepted this type of argument. What mattered to them was the relationship it illustrated and the act of redemption.

Paul's central argument is that Ishmael and Isaac represent the difference between the law and the promise that he spoke of in 3:16-21. Ishmael, the son of the slave woman, was born as a result of Sarah's suggestion, or in other words, *as the result of human effort* (4:23a). He was later driven out and did not share in the blessing (4:30). The path of inheritance is that of Sarah the free woman, whose son was born miraculously *as the result of divine promise* (4:23b; see Gen 17:16, 19a, 21).

Paul applies this story to the Galatians' situation, saying *Now you, brothers and sisters, like Isaac, are children of promise* (4:28). They are the beneficiaries of God's work of justification, which calls for faith and not good works as the basis for acceptance by the one who made the promise.

The mothers of the two sons *represent two covenants* (4:24). Hagar, who was driven into the wilderness, can be seen as representing the old covenant of law. That is why Paul describes her as representing *Mount Sinai*, where the law was given to Moses (Exod 19:20-20:17) and *the present city of Jerusalem*, the centre of Jewish faith (4:24b-25).

Sarah, on the other hand, represents the new covenant of grace. Paul describes her in terms of *the Jerusalem that is above*, that is, the future Jerusalem in which people of all nations will gather (Rev 21:2). Sarah is no slave but a free woman (4:26). She is as *our mother* in the same way that Abraham is our father, that is, the father of all those who believe (3:29). Because she is free, the Galatians are also free. They have no need to submit to slavery, that is, to the law the Judaizers want to impose.

In expanding the argument, Paul quotes Isaiah 54:1, which states that *more are children of the desolate [or barren] woman than of her who has a husband* (4:27). In Isaiah, the once barren woman represents the New Jerusalem that will re-emerge from the barren desolation of the ruins of old Jerusalem and surpass neighbouring cities that were never destroyed. She is like Sarah, who was also barren before she received God's miraculous gift of a child. She moves from a state of hopelessness to one of blessing.

Isaiah's message of hope and blessing was partially fulfilled when the exiles returned from Babylon and Jerusalem was rebuilt into the "present Jerusalem", the city of Paul's day. But that was not the only fulfilment of the prophecy.[277] Isaiah was, whether consciously or not, prophesying the coming of another New Jerusalem that would be a place of even greater hope and blessing. This city had not yet come in Paul's day, and today we still await the coming of the "Jerusalem that is above", which will belong not just to the Jews but to all the nations of the earth. Citizenship in the Jerusalem of Paul's day required that one be a Jew or live as a Jew, but citizenship in the spiritual Jerusalem is open to all who have faith.

Sarah, of course, did have a husband. There are also other places where the verse quoted is inconsistent with the details of the story of Abraham, Sarah and Hagar. This would not have concerned Paul. His focus was on Sarah who is now free and blessed. He was using the Old Testament quotation to make just one point, and had no intention of suggesting that every point in the quotation matched every detail of the allegory. He wants to use the story to remind the Galatian believers of their privileged status as free and blessed heirs of Abraham and Sarah and of the need to stay on the path of faith, not works. Each time they heard the story of Sarah and Hagar, they should remember this truth.

Paul acknowledges that the son of the free woman may be persecuted by the son born by human effort, following the pattern of Ishmael persecuting Isaac (Gen 21:9), but that does not mean that the one persecuted is not blessed. The Galatian believers can expect some persecution from those who want to enslave them to the law, but that does not take away their blessedness. Extending the analogy, Paul reminds the Galatians of the fate of the persecutor: he was sent away for he was not the heir (4:30; quoting Gen 21:10).

Paul wraps up his argument by telling the Galatians, *Therefore, brothers and sisters, we are not children of the slave woman, but of the free woman* (4:31). We are accepted by God, not on the basis of obedience to a set of laws, but by claiming the promise of God in the person of Jesus Christ.

We should be blessed by the reminder that our current hardships do not rob us of the status God gives us. God permitted the son of promise (Isaac) to be persecuted by the son of human effort (Ishmael), and he may permit those who believe in his Son to experience persecution. But our status as heirs with Christ (Rom 8:17) is rooted in the promise of God which never changes. Both Peter and James remind us of the positive things that persecution accomplished for us who are heirs of God's promise (1 Pet 1:3–8; Jas 1:2–4). We are blessed even if it does not always seem so to us.

Paul uses the allegory of Hagar and Sarah to convince the Galatians that justification is by faith and not by works or human effort. Their mother is Sarah, the free woman, and their pattern is Isaac, the son of promise and the heir to Abraham's blessings.

Questions for discussion

1. Have you ever sensed rejection from someone you expected to show gratitude? What was your response and why? What is the normal expectation when someone has benefited from our efforts or support? What causes abnormal reactions?
2. Is there room for giving people a failing grade? How do we balance honest evaluation and the need not to demoralize people who are not doing too well? How did Paul manage to maintain the balance here?
3. What duties for the kingdom of God are demanded by the fact that we are descendants of a promise and have an inheritance from God?
4. What are the dangers of focusing on law without taking note of the context of promise? From the allegory used here, what would that approach to God lack?

UNIT 12
GALATIANS 5:1–15

THREE CHOICES

Contrasts have been fascinating since the start of creation, when God first made light and darkness, day and night. Our bodies, too, are a study in contrast with differences between men and women and between the left hand and the right hand. We describe people in terms of contrasts, saying that they are tall or short, heavy or light, and so on. Contrasts have become part of our way of thinking about life.

While the things contrasted are often neutral in themselves (for they are all part of what God declared "very good" – Gen 1:31), we tend to imbue them with cultural significance. Thus light and dark are often used as symbols of the moral clash between good and evil. In some African cultures, giving something with the left hand signals an insult.

Contrasts are also sometimes used to justify discrimination. In Africa, boys may be treated better than girls. Members of one people group may be treated differently from members of another group. What justifies such treatment? Does anyone have any say about their sex or the group they are born into? I have no choice about being a man. I may pretend to be a woman, and even change my physical appearance so that I look like a woman, but in God's register, I remain a man. Similarly, the Galatian believers had no choice about whether they were born Jews or Gentiles.

There are, however, areas in which individuals can make choices. For example, I can choose to be kind or unkind to each person I meet. Paul deals with three very real choices when he writes to the Galatians. In each case, he encourages them – and us – to make the right choice, the choice approved by God, who treats us all alike when we come to him through Christ.[278]

Choice of Status: Slave or Free

At the end of chapter four, Paul contrasted Hagar and Sarah, the slave and free woman. He reminded the Galatians that they were descendants of the free woman and should prize their freedom. Now he reinforces this point by declaring, *It is for freedom that Christ has set us free* (5:1a).[279] Those of us whom Christ has set free from slavery to sin have been set on a course of freedom, and we should enjoy that freedom.

Christ had freed the Galatian Gentiles from their slavery to sin, but they were allowing themselves to be re-enslaved by another master – the law. But slavery is slavery, no matter who the master is. They were slipping back into the hopeless state from which Christ had freed them.

Paul urges them to *stand firm* (5:1b). He uses the same word in 1 Corinthians 16:13, where he tells the Corinthians to stand firm in the faith, and in Philippians 4:1, where he tells the Philippians to stand firm in the Lord.[280] Freedom, faith and the Lord are the firm ground that cannot be shaken in God's plan of salvation. The Lord is the only Saviour; faith is the only way of acceptance before God; freedom from sin and legalistic regulations is the purpose for which Christ died.

Standing firm is not a manifestation of foolish stubbornness, but a determined refusal to be moved from an assured conviction. The Galatians are already in the right position. They are free. They would be foolish to let themselves *be burdened again by a yoke of slavery* (5:1b).

A "yoke" is what Africans have traditionally used when harnessing oxen or donkeys to cultivate the fields or pull heavy loads. The animals do their work, but when the yoke is taken off at the end of the day, they enjoy their freedom. If the owner suddenly remembers some other job that he wants to do and tries to bring them under yoke again, they resist, particularly if the previous task was demanding. They will refuse to move, except when dodging any attempt to put the yoke across their necks. Paul's readers are to act in the same way and show the same determination. Why would a slave who has been freed ever want to become a slave again? To allow their position on this crucial matter to become shaky is to expose themselves to the danger of being thrown off their feet.

The symbol of this coming slavery is circumcision, not simply as a cultural rite but as a basis for justification (5:4).[281] It was being treated as a precondition for acceptance by God. But that is not the route to justification that Christ has provided. So Paul solemnly warns the Galatians, *Mark my words! I, Paul, tell you that if you let yourselves be circumcised, Christ will be of no value to you at all* (5:2). Those who choose that route are saying that they do not need Christ. The consequence is that they are *obligated to obey the whole law* (5:3b).

Paul made the same point in 3:12, where he asserted that when it comes to justification, the paths of faith and of the law diverge. Those who ignore Paul's teaching and still want to follow the path of law *have been alienated from Christ* and *have fallen away from grace* (5:4). Paul is writing to people who have already entered into the fellowship of Christ by accepting in faith his finished work on the cross as a sufficient basis for justification. When such people seek an alternate way of justification, they are turning their backs on Christ and on his grace. They were once saved by grace, but are now seeking to be justified by obedience to the law. But those who follow this law route have to recognize the implicit contract that they have signed: if salvation is earned by keeping the law, then every single law must be kept, and kept perfectly. This route is impossible! What a relief to know that Christ met all the demands of the law and all we need to do is to exercise faith in him!

Paul is not saying that they will lose their salvation as such. His focus is on how salvation is attained and maintained. The Galatians had already been saved within the sphere of grace (1:6). Now they are being told that they took the wrong path and need to start the journey all over again, this time with one foot on the path of faith and the other on the path of law. They will be like the hungry hyena who could not decide which way to go when he came to a fork in the path. Rather than making a decision about which path to follow, he tried to walk on both paths at once, with his left feet on one and his right feet on the other. But the paths diverged. All he achieved was to split himself in two. One has to choose a path and follow it.

Theoretically both the path of faith and the path of law can lead to justification. But the requirements for travelling each path are different. Those who follow the path of faith ride on the back of Christ, who has conquered all the challenges along the way. But those who follow the path of the law must face every obstacle on their own. They have to clamber over every law that stands in the way, and cannot progress until all the laws have been perfectly fulfilled.

It makes no sense for someone not to want to get on the back of Christ, by faith in him, and attain justification. Why suffer all the torture of the law without any assurance that one will be able to reach one's goal? This is why Paul does not hesitate to call any Galatians who choose to follow the path of law "foolish" (3:1). He exhorts them to be steady in the path of grace, the path of freedom from the demands of the law.

The "you" whom Paul addresses in 5:1–6 should not be interpreted as "all you Galatians", nor should the "we" in 5:5 be taken as referring only to Paul and his team. While it is fair to argue that the majority of Galatians may have belonged to the "you group", there were some in Galatia who belonged to the "we group", who identified with Paul's teachings. These are the two contrasting groups with two different ideologies.

Contrasting the "you group" with the "we group" in 5:5, Paul uses an emphatic personal pronoun (we ourselves).[282] The group to which he belongs operates by faith, not by law, and so he can say that *by faith we eagerly await through the Spirit the righteousness for which we hope* (5:5). This "hope" is an eager expectation, not merely of vague thought that something may or may not happen. Righteousness is an upward journey with a climax. There is righteousness at the beginning point (justification), righteousness all the way through the journey (sanctification) and righteousness at the peak (glorification). The righteousness Paul has in mind here is the righteousness of sanctification at the end of the climb. The "you group" are turning back before they reach the peak on this path of righteousness and are returning to the beginning to pursue another route.

Paul and the whole "we group" do not waver as they eagerly await the righteousness that is at the climax. They can do this because they are not undertaking the journey in their own power but are relying on the Holy Spirit.[283] To continue the earlier analogy, even though we are being carried along the route of faith on Jesus' back, there are strong winds that could blow us off his back. But the Holy Spirit helps us to cling. He enables us to remain in Jesus in all circumstances, producing in us what Paul will later refer to as the fruit of the Spirit (5:22).

Having opened this section with a reminder of the freedom Christ has provided for us, Paul closes with a statement on what has value within this sphere of Christ. *Neither circumcision nor uncircumcision* matters. The only thing that is really important is *faith expressing itself through love* (5:6).[284] Paul will bring this up again in 6:15 (see also 1 Cor 7:19).

There is a big difference between a relationship maintained by obedience to the law, which says "do this and that" and a relationship based on the love expressed by the one who says "see what I have done for you. In faith accept that it is enough, and in faith wait for me to come and complete the salvation process I have already begun in you." The latter relationship is based on an act of love (what I did for you), rests on a response of love (I love you too) and will be sealed in love (I am coming to complete the salvation process). Everything about it falls within the context of love. Within such a context, obedience to the will of the one who "did it all for me" is a natural thing. It is not perceived as a means to get something but as a response to the love that has been given. This way of justification by faith is open to both Jews (who are physically circumcised) and the Gentiles (who are physically uncircumcised).

The Christian rite corresponding to the Jewish practice of circumcision is baptism. Though we differ as to whether it should be done by sprinkling or by immersion, we agree that it symbolizes someone dying with Christ and living to please him. But we need to be careful not to imply that someone who has not been baptised is unacceptable before God. There is no need to rush to baptise people who are on their death beds. We are justified by faith, not by baptism. We should avoid doing anything that undermines this message. Baptism is simply our personal witness that we belong to Christ, but we gain acceptance by God simply by believing in him.

Choice of Leader: Consistent or Confusing?

Paul is fond of using a race as a metaphor for the Christian life (see Acts 20:24; 1 Cor 9.26; 2 Tim 4.7). The type of race he has in mind is a marathon, not a sprint. So he can tell the Galatians that they had been running well at the start (5:7a),[285] just like Paul, their example and coach. They may have been running at different speeds, but in a marathon it is not speed that counts but determination. It is better to run slowly but keep one's focus than it is to run fast at first and then get distracted, slow down and start looking around. I myself never won a medal in athletics, but my teachers in high school used to say that I never gave up a race until I finished.

It is the same in the Christian race. We may not all be moving at the same pace, but we must all be keeping on with the race on the same track. This is my prayer in my walk with the Lord. I want to stay in the race till the end, and pray that all my readers who have experienced the joy of becoming the children of God will do the same.

Paul would have had the same prayer for the Galatians. So he is horrified that someone has interfered with the race, and has *cut in on you to keep you from obeying the truth* (5:7b). The word translated "cut in on" also means "hinder" (NASB) or "prevent" (NRSV, HCSB).[286] The runners were doing well, until someone got in their way on the track and diverted them from the path of truth.[287] This is the worst thing anyone can do to an athlete. It will slow them down, and some may even trip and fall. That is exactly what had happened in Galatia. Paul had clearly taught them that justification was by way of faith in Christ, but some had been distracted from the race by the suggestion that they should rather be following the route of works.

Paul asks who the troublemaker was, not expecting an answer to his rhetorical question but trying to force the Galatians to reflect on what is happening (5:7b; compare 3:1). He asks this question as if he has a particular person in mind, but that does not mean he is thinking only of an individual. The Judaizers in general were responsible for interfering with the Galatians' growth on the path of grace. Behind them was the influence of Satan. But it is quite possible that one of the Judaizers had emerged as the leader of the group, and was Satan's key instrument in hindering the Galatians' growth.

One thing Paul does know about those who are disturbing them is that *this kind of persuasion does not come from the one who calls you* (5:8). Paul's words in 1:6 indicate that "the one who calls you" is God. So, whoever this person or group may be, he does not come from God, and consequently his attempts to persuade them to run the race differently do not come from God.

Using a common metaphor Paul likens the teachings of this person to *a little yeast* (5:9). A small amount of yeast worked into a *whole batch of dough* is sufficient to make the whole batch rise. In the same way, the false teachings will spread among the Christians in Galatia and lead many astray. That is why Paul writes to them so urgently.

Later in the letter, Paul describes the people who spread such teachings as *agitators* (5:12a). They are the type of people who like to stir up trouble and throw others *into confusion* (5:10b, also see 1:7). To understand what this means, think of a nest of ants. Ants are not only organized and hardworking (Prov 6:6) but also excel in job distribution, with each playing its role faithfully. If you throw something into the middle of a group of ants, they scatter in confusion and their work is disrupted. That is exactly what happens when a false preacher or teacher comes to a congregation. He or she begins to throw the members into confusion. The one doing this in Galatia has not been sent by God, nor by Paul or any of the other apostles. He is simply someone who is dissatisfied and wants to contradict the apostolic teaching.

One of Satan's strategies is to watch for a time when everything seems to be going smoothly in our personal lives or in a church and then throw in something that will disorient us and distract us from our calling. He can then take advantage of our actions (or reactions). For example, he may disrupt a Bible study group by introducing a person who always wants to discuss their own problems, or someone who always wants to argue about a controversial issue, not because they want to learn but because they enjoy debate. While it is not wrong to raise issues, these people become disruptive when they so dominate the group that there is no scope for others to carry on learning and growing in the Lord. Satan can use such people to frustrate the ministry in a local church and hinder others from developing a deeper relationship with God.

Before we leap to accuse others of doing this, we should stop and ask ourselves whether we ever allow ourselves to slip into a situation where we are the disruptive force. Are we helping or harming the spiritual growth of others? The question is a serious one, for Paul warns that if we do harm, we *will pay the penalty* (5:10b).

Paul does not tell us what this penalty will be, but he warns that it will come on the person who is confusing the Galatians *whoever that may be* (5:10b). This phrase suggests that Paul may have a particular individual in mind, who is probably a person of some influence and in good standing among the Galatians. If so, it is no wonder that many were being led astray.

While the Galatians are not absolved from their personal responsibility to remain true to the faith, Paul holds the false teacher accountable. His anger with such people becomes clear when he speaks of the agitators, and says, *I wish they would go the whole way and emasculate themselves!* (5:12). If these people think that removing their foreskin by circumcision will justify them, then why stop there? Why not remove the entire body part? Wouldn't that bring an even higher degree of justification? If they were prepared to go that far, Paul might be more convinced that they were teaching something they really believed and were not just trying to sow confusion and undermine his teaching.

Paul's harsh words may be prompted by his awareness of how much he has suffered for the gospel. He has been persecuted, and knows what it is to suffer for what he believes. Would his opponents be prepared to endure what he has endured? Are they prepared to make serious sacrifices? (5:12).

One of the reason he is suffering is that in his own teaching he preaches the cross and not circumcision. If he were preaching circumcision,[288] the Jews would not be persecuting him. But what he is called to preach is *the offence of the cross* (5:11). This "offence" is the truth that salvation and justification come through Christ's death for us.[289] This truth is foolishness to Gentiles and a stumbling block to Jews who want to cling to circumcision and the law as the paths to salvation (see also 1 Cor 1:22).

While acknowledging that the Galatians are endangered by the craftiness of the false teacher, Paul still gives them his vote of confidence: *I am confident in the Lord that you will take no other view* (5:10a). They will not accept the view that diverges from the truth Paul has taught them and in which they have walked thus far.

What an interesting way of encouraging a congregation who have been rebuked again and again! Yes, rebukes may be deserved, and delivered, but Paul still has high hopes for these people. He sets a good example for pastors who sometimes have to deal with people who are beginning to go the wrong way. While they need correction and even rebuke, they also need to be assured that we believe that they will choose what is right.

Paul expressed the same confidence when writing to the church at Thessalonica (2 Thess 3:4). It is an excellent pastoral practice. The same principle is also applicable when raising children. When children know that no matter what they have done, dad and mom have confidence that they can do better, they are encouraged to move on in the right course. When an employer does not just rebuke an employee but also expresses confidence in him or her, better performance can be expected. We should always mix rebuke and encouragement.

Choice of Lifestyle: Indulging or Serving

Paul returns to his emphasis that believers *were called to be free* (5:13a; see also 5:1). They are not to be legalists and live under slavery. But there are two possible approaches that believers can take to this freedom. One is wrong and the other is right.

One group will say "Hurrah for freedom", and go on to live as if they are free to do whatever they choose, without being accountable to anyone. In case any of the Galatians are tempted to do this, Paul admonishes them, *do not use your freedom to indulge the sinful nature* (5:13b).

The other group will use their freedom to *serve one another* (5:13c). This Christ-like approach to freedom is the right one – not just because Paul says so, but because it conforms to the law of love that summarizes those parts of the law of Moses that focus on human relationships (Matt 22:37–39; Mark 12:30–31; Luke 10:27). So Paul can say that *the entire law is fulfilled in keeping this one command, "love your neighbour as yourself"* (5:14).

The absence of a spirit of service and love for each other leads to the selfishness that is manifested in *biting and devouring each other* (5:15). Common sense tells us that such behaviour is destructive to both parties. A bites B, and B in return bites A. In the end, their constant biting leads to their devouring each other, destroyed not by any outside enemy but by themselves. The situation would have been quite different if they had settled their disagreement in a loving spirit.

The church in Africa has not been immune to this kind of biting and devouring (especially when it comes to elections). But this is not the spirit of Christ, who is the supreme example of service (Mark 10:45) and love (John 10:11, 14, 17–18). We are called not to think of ourselves as more deserving than others but to give ourselves so that others may be blessed.

We are not perfect, and will not always love and serve as we should. But the situation will not escalate to bring destruction if one of the parties can be mature enough to return love for hatred, give a pat on the back in response to a slap, and respond to selfishness with service. The devil will actively discourage such behaviour because he wants to have two warring parties at his service. But do not give in to him! If you are in a stressful relationship, take courage and extend love to the one you feel does not deserve it. If everyone could love their enemies just a little more, the world would change from being a place where war is all around us to a place where no one starves to death.

Questions for Discussion

1. How would you evaluate your own response to the choices presented in this passage? Do you live a life of faith in Christ or one in which you have to do certain things so that God will accept you? Do the preachers you like to listen to preach salvation in Christ or do they lead you away from him? Do you live for Christ and to serve others or do you live only for yourself?
2. Can you think of examples of people or groups in our day who are like those who were advising the Galatians to make bad choices? Explain why you think each group is leading people the wrong way.

UNIT 13
GALATIANS 5:16–26

THREE WAYS OF LIFE

Diseases can have external or internal causes. A rash, for example, may signal nothing more than a reaction to some component in a skin cream or detergent. However, it could also be a signal that your whole body has been infected by measles, chicken pox or some serious disease.

Something similar applies when it comes to behaviour. Some of the good and bad things we do may be superficial manifestations of vices or virtues, and have little to do with who we really are within. However, others may spring from deep within our character.

In this section of Galatians, Paul presents a list of the virtues that should and the vices that should not characterize those living in obedience to and in the power of the Holy Spirit. He does not suggest that a believer will never be guilty of some of these vices, or that an unbeliever will never show some of the virtues listed here. What is important, however, is the type of behaviour that characterises us deep down, and is produced not by our own desperate efforts to be good but through the enabling of the Holy Spirit who dwells in us as believers.

In 5:13, Paul urged believers not to use their freedom as an excuse to "indulge the sinful nature". He returns to this in 5:16 and goes on to discuss three ways of life: 1) life under the law, 2) life following the desires of the sinful nature, and 3) life led by the Spirit.[290]

Life under the Law

Paul does not spend long discussing life under the law because he has already dealt with this in depth earlier in the letter. However, he does refer to this type of life twice. He contrasts the spirit-led life with the legalistic life when he tells the Galatians, *if you are led by the Spirit, you are not under the law* (5:18). After listing the fruit of the Spirit he says, *against such things there is no law* (5:23b). His point is that the law, defined as the will of God, is fulfilled naturally in those led by the Spirit, because the Spirit will not lead them to act in any way that is contrary to the will of God. While the law does not produce justification, it is very much part of the way of life defined as life under the Spirit.

Life Led by the Sinful Nature

Our *sinful nature* (5:16) or "flesh" (KJV) is the part of us that is not in harmony with the Holy Spirit and leads us to desire things that are against the will of God.[291] Paul lists the types of vices this desire produces. Some of the vices he mentions could have been a natural part of the kind of life many Gentiles lived before their conversion into Christianity (some of them were already listed as vices by Greek philosophers living three and half centuries before Paul).[292] Others, particularly those involving social relationships, could easily have been triggered by differences of opinion resulting from the confusion brought by the false teachers.

Paul's list can be described as "disorderly, chaotic, and incomplete, corresponding to the random and compulsive character of sin itself".[293] However, it is possible to group the vices into four categories, namely sexual sins, religious sins, sins affecting relationships and sins of excess.

Sexual sins

- **Sexual immorality.** Greek and Roman culture tolerated some level of sexual relations outside marriage. But for Christians, just as for Old Testament believers, sex is only moral within marriage. It is a physical expression of an intimacy that can be compared to the relationship between God and Israel (Hos 2) and between Christ and the church (Eph 5:32).[294]

- ***Impurity.*** Paul is not referring to general impurity but to sexual impurity (see, for example, Rom 1:24; 6:19).[295] While the term covers sex outside of marriage, its scope is wide enough to include all kinds of sexual perversions, including homosexual sex.
- ***Debauchery.*** Debauchery involves living a life characterized by sensuality, licentiousness and promiscuity, with a total disregard for God and other people. Someone who is debauched has no sense of decency and does not care when, where and how sexual acts are performed.

Religious sins

- ***Idolatry.*** Idolatry is having something in one's life that takes precedence over the true God of the Bible. This may be a graven image, but it may also be possessions, for greed is a form of idolatry (Col 3:5). So is valuing a human relationship more than one's relationship to God.
- ***Witchcraft.*** The Greek word *pharmakeia* was once neutral, and referred to dispensing drugs (it is the source of the English word "pharmacy"). However, by Paul's time it meant using poison or sorcery to harm others.

Sins affecting relationships

- ***Hatred.*** Hatred may be expressed in actions or it may simply be an underlying hostility "between individuals, or between communities, on political, racial or religious grounds".[296] It is the opposite of love.
- ***Discord.*** Discord is the opposite of peace. It is the outward expression of hatred, the attempt to destroy those we dislike, as is clear from the fact that the Greek word Paul uses comes from the ancient name of the goddess of war and destruction.[297] Paul often mentions this evil in the New Testament and reminds believers that while it may have been part of their lives in the past, it has no place in their lives in the present. If it is still found among them, it is evidence that they are not being governed by God's Spirit of love. If their energy is consumed by fighting, they will be unable to move forward in the faith.

- **Jealousy.** A jealous person is "someone who wants what other people have" because he or she has a "basic posture of ingratitude to God, a failure to accept one's life as a gift from God".[298] Being satisfied with how God has made us and what he has given us is key to living peacefully with other people. While most of us would deny that we are ever jealous, a good test of our attitude is how we react when another student gets a better grade than we do, when another pastor's congregation grows faster than ours, when another teacher is more appreciated by students than we are, when another person's business or career is prospering more than our own, and so on. If we have a Christ-like attitude, we will honestly rejoice with those who are doing better than we are from a human perspective. Whatever we have from God is what is best for us at any given moment, and our hearts should be filled with gratitude rather than jealousy.
- **Fits of rage.** The type of behaviour Paul is referring to here is "a passionate outburst of anger and hostile feeling".[299] It is the type of behaviour that leads to attacking other people or to domestic violence in which men beat their wives and children. In its extreme form, it leads to the sad news reports of fathers killing their children, and sons killing their parents, and later being overwhelmed with remorse.
- **Selfish ambition.** The Greek word translated as "selfish ambition" initially referred to trying to get others to vote one into some political office. Eventually, it came to have the negative connotation of selfish devotion to one's own interests.[300] People with this attitude treat others as stepping stones to their goal and manipulate facts to benefit themselves. What was true of ancient Greek politicians is still true to today! But a Christian (and even a Christian politician – for there are such) must show love and care for truth.
- **Dissensions.** Like the previous word, this one also originated in the context of politics, referring to disagreements between political parties. But while it is healthy to have different opinions and debate them, there is a problem when those differences interfere with relationships. In the Christian church, believers are called to fellowship as one body in Christ and to work together to promote the kingdom of God. When there is division on ethnic, economic or ideological grounds, it becomes a vice. It results in what one commentator describes as

"the decided and violent taking of a side on selfish and unyielding grounds".[301]

- **Factions.** Factions arise when divisions become formalized and people make "intentional choices to walk in the way of selfish pride, envy, and bickering rather than the royal road of love, forgiveness, and magnanimity".[302] Paul uses the same word with reference to the party spirit in Corinth (1 Cor 11:19). Factions are detrimental to presenting a united front as we seek the truth of God and his will and pray for each other.
- **Envy.** There is a close link between envy and jealousy.[303] People who are envious rejoice when others face calamity because they cannot bear seeing others better off than themselves. They will even attempt to destroy what others have if they cannot have it for themselves. We see the effects of envy when we observe that many in Africa are afraid to succeed and grow rich. They know that the successful often face hostility from neighbours and become targets for robbers and murderers. The result is that the continent as a whole stays poor. It may be this link between envy and violence that resulted in some manuscripts including "murder" in the list between 'envy' and 'drunkenness', although this word is not included in the most ancient manuscripts of the New Testament.

Sins of excess

- **Drunkenness.** Excessive indulgence in wine is similar to gluttony, the term for excessive indulgence in food. But drunkenness does more harm, because it "weakens people's rational and moral control over their words and actions".[304] It takes over the whole person and controls their behaviour. It is impossible to be full of alcohol and full of the Holy Spirit at the same time (Eph 5:18).
- **Orgies.** Paul always uses the term translated "orgies" in the same context as drunkenness (Rom 13:13; Gal 5:21; 1 Pet 4:3). It refers to the type of behaviour that results from drunken carousing, including "marital infidelity, child and spouse abuse, the erosion of family life, and moral chaos in society"[305]. When one is controlled by wine, decency and consideration evaporate.

This list of fifteen vices is not meant to be exhaustive. The concluding words, *and the like* (5:21a), tell us that there are many more. What is important is that none of these vices should be part of a believer's life. Believers may sometimes slip and fall into sin, but it should never be said of us that we live like this. If we do, then, we must seriously question whether we have ever been saved for *those who live like this will not inherit the kingdom of God* (5:21b).[306]

These vices should not have been present in the church in Galatia and they should not be present in our churches today. Certainly, they are still prevalent in the society around us: morality is as low as ever, conflicts are frequent, and the fear of God is decreasing. The situation challenges the church to be even more vigorous in its witness.

Life Led by the Spirit

In contrast to the way of life controlled by our sinful nature, we should choose the way of life that Paul commends in 5:16a when he tells the Galatians to *walk by the Spirit* (that is, make it your habit to live under the control of the Spirit).[307] In 3:2 and 3:5, he said that the Galatians have already received the Holy Spirit, so he is not exhorting them to start doing something new but to continue doing something they have done before.

Those who "walk by the Spirit" are no longer obliged to obey the Old Testament law in order to please God (5:18), and they are also not given to self-indulgence. They enjoy freedom from the yoke of both law and sin. They follow the path of love, and their actions are not dictated by outside forces but by the inner compulsion of the Spirit. His grace is what makes it possible to love one's neighbour as oneself (Matt 22:39) and to love one's enemies (Matt 5:44; Luke 6:27–29), just as it was his grace that first brought the believer into the privilege of being in Christ.

Paul accompanies this exhortation with a strong promise that if they walk in the Spirit they *will not gratify the desires of the sinful nature* (5:16b).[308] To emphasize the certainty with which he says this, he uses a double negative, equivalent to saying, "you will not in no way do this". The Spirit expels our sinful desires. Where the Spirit is present, our sinful nature is not!

Paul is not saying that we can attain perfection now. There is still tension within us as our sinful nature fights a rearguard action against the invasion by the Spirit (5:17). And when there are areas where we do succeed in living by the Spirit, our sinful nature will be eager to pat us on the back and tempt us to take credit for our success, rather than acknowledging that it is God's work. It will also encourage us to make rules to ensure our continuing success, and so lure us back into legalism. So long as my sinful nature remains part of me, I cannot be perfect. I can only continue to surrender more and more of my life to the control of the Holy Spirit till the day I am glorified and my sinful nature is totally eradicated.

The idea that living ("walking") by the Spirit is not something that we can decide to do once and for all and then continue without any problems is underlined by Paul's second exhortation *Since we live by the Spirit, let us keep in step with the Spirit* (5:25).[309] We have to keep walking alongside him, not running ahead and getting into trouble or lagging behind and toying with sin.[310]

As someone walks in step with the Spirit, the Spirit will work in his or her life to produce a character that can be described as the fruit of the Spirit.[311] Note that Paul does not speak of the "fruits" (plural) of the Holy Spirit but only of one fruit – a holy character. That character will manifest itself in the specific virtues that Paul lists in 5:22–23.

For the sake of convenience, these nine virtues are divided into three groups.[312] Inevitably there is some overlapping between the groups, for "the nine qualities flow into one another, mutually enriching the process of sanctification in the life of the believer".[313]

Habits of mind

- *Love.* It is appropriate that love heads the list of virtues. Paul has already mentioned it three times in this chapter. In 5:6, he said that what matters is not circumcision or uncircumcision but "faith expressing itself through love" (a love that crosses all personal and ethnic boundaries); in 5:13 he urged us to "serve one another in love" (focusing on the manner in which we serve one other), and in 5:14 he quoted the words, "love your neighbour as yourself" as a summary of the law. It can be said that "judging by his highlighting of love in Galatians 5 as well as in 1 Corinthians 13, probably Paul saw all the other virtues of this list included in and springing from this first-listed virtue".[314] The type of love he is referring to is *agapē*, the love that does not seek its own but goes out of its way to serve others.[315] This is the type of love that God shows to us, and that we in turn should show to others. It says, "you deserve hatred but I will give you love; you have deprived me but I will feed you; you have attacked me but I will defend you." It is totally contrary to the philosophies of the world, but it is the will of God.[316]

- *Joy.* Outside the Christian faith, joy is closely tied to happiness and is dependent on pleasant circumstances. For Christians, however, it is associated more with hope than with circumstances. Yes, it is true that Christ has freed us from the bondage and condemnation of sin and that makes us rejoice (Rom 5:11). However, our joy also looks to the future, in expectation that one day he will come and make us like him (1 John 3:2). Thus even when we endure unpleasant circumstances, we are able to look beyond them to what we anticipate, and so still have joy in the present. Believers can rejoice even during times of tribulation in view of the ultimate victory that is ours in Christ.

- *Peace.* For the Greeks, peace involved physical health and an untroubled mind. For the Jews, however, the word "peace" is associated with the word *shalom,* and meant a condition of "wholeness and well-being that includes both a right relationship with God and loving harmony with one's fellow human beings"[317] The peace of God thus means freedom from anxiety due to the uncertainties of life (Phil 4:7), a harmonious relationship with God (5:1) and with fellow human beings at home (1 Cor 7:15), in church (Eph 4:3), and in society in general (Rom 12:18).

Habits in relationships

- *Patience.* The Greek word translated "patience" can also be translated "steadfastness" or "forbearance". It refers to someone who is long-suffering or "long-tempered" (the opposite of being short-tempered). When we have patience, we can put up with others even when their actions or words are deliberately meant to provoke anger or hurt us.[318] We will take time to think things through carefully before asking for an apology or compensation for a wrong done against us. God is patient ("slow to anger" – Exod 34:6; Ps 103:8) and his children must be like him (Eph 4:2; Col 1:11; 3:12). We need the Holy Spirit to give us the self-control that is part of patience, for this is a virtue we often have to practice. Even when we are with Christians, there will be some who will try our patience.

- **Kindness.** God is kind in that he blesses even those who do not deserve it (Rom 2:4; 11:22; Titus 3:4). His kindness combines with his patience as he gives sinners time to repent and carries believers along the path of spiritual growth without destroying them at the first sign of sin. Similar kindness should be manifested by God's children (2 Cor 6:6; Eph 4:32; Col 3:12). We must be kind not just to the people we like but also to the people who annoy us. For example, there are many people in our streets begging for financial help. When they bother us again and again, we may be tempted to respond harshly. But a patient and kind person will speak a word to bless the beggar even if not giving him money each time he asks. Kindness is not measured by the amount we give to others but by our attitude towards people. One person may give thousands of dollars without being kind; another may give very little but do so with great kindness.

- **Goodness.** There is considerable overlap between goodness and kindness.[319] Goodness involves "benevolence and generosity toward someone else, a going the second mile when such magnanimity is not required".[320] A good-hearted person will give assistance even when there are readily available excuses for not doing so. For example, in some cities in Africa, there are serious transport problems, especially at special seasons like Christmas or other holidays. As we drive by in our cars, we see people enduring long waits for buses or taxis, or setting out to walk long distances. We do not have to help such people, but it may be a mark of goodness to do so. Obviously, this goodness has to be practised with care. It would be irresponsible to indiscriminately offer rides to people who might be robbers or hijackers. But there are times when we know the people who are walking and still do not stop to help them. Even when we know that it is not safe to offer help and have to pass by, we should do so with a sense of reluctance.

Principles of conduct

- ***Faithfulness.*** There is nothing arbitrary about the fact that faithfulness is a fruit of the Spirit. God is faithful (Rom 3:3; 1 Cor 1:9; 1 Thess 5:24) and he expects his children to show the same quality of "being true, trustworthy and reliable in all one's dealings with others".[321] Sadly, we are all only too familiar with what it means to be unfaithful. Someone who had discovered that the officials in a society he belonged to had enriched themselves first, before distributing meagre profits to others, asked the despairing question, "Shall we ever find someone in Africa we can trust to handle our investments?" This deep longing for people who show faithfulness resounds across Africa. It is a call that needs to be heard by the leaders of the church, who should model faithfulness themselves and encourage other believers to do the same. While this can be hard to do in human strength, the Holy Spirit can enable believers to manifest faithfulness in all aspects of their lives.

- ***Gentleness.*** Those who are gentle are humble and considerate of others. Yet they do not allow themselves to be used as doormats, as if they have no personal goals, principles and convictions. The correct understanding of this virtue as found in the New Testament is that it is "strength under control, power harnessed in loving service and respectful actions".[322] It is the opposite of "an arrogant and self-assertive spirit".[323] The Greek philosopher Aristotle defined this quality as the mean between excessive anger and "the inability to be angry.[324] Those who are excessively angry seek to destroy, and those who are unable to be angry allow themselves to be destroyed. The gentle person balances the two impulses, and neither seeks to destroy nor accepts being destroyed. For an example of this type of behaviour, look at Jesus when he drove business people out of the temple. He was angry and took vigorous action, but could still be described as "gentle and humble in heart" (Matt 11:29) because of why and how he acted. The reason for his action was God's glory, not self-promotion. And the manner in which he acted did not destroy people's livelihoods. The sellers could come back and collect their goods from the floor or recapture their animals (note that he did not let the doves out of their cages – John 2:16). He was angry – but for the right reason and with consideration and good judgment. We need this kind of gentleness to deal with the many corrupt people in public service, the many vices in our own lives, and all that is evil that hinders Africa from moving ahead. We need people who combine driving power and good judgment. They should not be the type who shoot at anything that moves, for then there will be nothing to govern once all have been destroyed. But they should ensure that everything that moves for evil finds itself working against great restraining power, sometimes from the gun, but wherever possible from the law courts, where the case can be carefully considered. Leaders who are so gentle that they allow evil people to do what they want are not gentle in the New Testament sense. But a leader who destroys every evil person at first sight needs to learn what it means to be gentle. Both power and consideration for others are required.

- *Self-control.* The basic meaning of "self-control" is having mastery over one's desires, passions, wishes, wants and impulses.[325] In other words, someone who had self-control is in charge, rather than driven by their desires. These desires may be sexual (1 Cor. 7:9) but the concept should not be limited to sexual desire. Self-control is also needed when it comes to dealing with the emotions of greed or anger. It is also called for to avoid being among the more than one million Kenyan minors smoking their way to an early death, the majority of them addicted to tobacco.[326] It takes self-control to say "no" to the first cigarette, and to the next. It takes even greater self-control to say "no" once one has become addicted to them. Great harm has been done and is being done by failing to have self-control as a virtue. Believers, in the enabling of the Holy Spirit, should govern their lives no matter what temptations or situations come their way.

Looking at this long list of virtues, attaining them all may seem impossible. Thank God we do not have to cultivate them in our own strength. They are the fruit that the Holy Spirit produces in our lives as we yield to him. If only half of those who claim to be Christians showed these qualities, the wars, clashes and exchanges of bitter words that we have witnessed in Africa would be greatly reduced. If all those who claim to be Christians had these virtues, Africa would be a blessed continent.

But there is no point of our talking of Africa's woes as if Africa is "out there". We, individually and collectively, constitute Africa and it is we who will change its course for the better. Wear these virtues, practise them, and you will see the difference in the area where you live!

The Tension and the Cure

Why do we see so little of the fruit of the Spirit in believers? One reason is that there is a tug-of-war between our sinful nature and the Spirit: *For the sinful nature desires what is contrary to the Spirit, and the Spirit what is contrary to the sinful nature. They are in conflict with each other* (5:17a). The two pull in different directions and as a result, Paul tells the readers, *you do not do what you want* (5:17b, NIV).[327] Believers who want to live by the Spirit are pulled in the opposite direction by the sinful nature. Believers who want to indulge in sin feel the pull of the Holy Spirit, seeking to convict them of sin.[328]

The only solution to this tension is to kill one of the opposing parties. So Paul reminds believers that *those who belong to Christ Jesus have crucified the sinful nature with its passions and desires* (5:24). Admittedly, crucifixion is a slow death, and our sinful nature will not fully die before the day of glorification. Yet crucifixion does weaken it. Whenever it wants to take over, it must be reminded that it has been crucified.

This alone, however, is not sufficient to produce a godly life. Living by the Spirit must also be cultivated so that he controls more and more of our nature. In other words, there should be more and more subtraction of the sinful nature and more and more addition of life under the Spirit in a process that will not be complete until we come to the point of glorification.

We long to see African nations manifest justice, righteousness, integrity and love for one another. But if we desire only perfection, we are doomed to despair. A more helpful approach is to work towards seeing the vices reduced every day, while at the same time encouraging the practice of the virtues.

The change begins with one person at a time. It begins with you. And not tomorrow, but right now!

Questions for Discussion

1. What vices stand out in the places where you live and work? What virtues do you see there? What is your contribution to these vices and virtues?
2. How can we, individually or collectively, minimize the list of vices and maximize the list of virtues you identified in the previous question? Give some specific examples of how this has been done.
3. Have you ever had to choose between two alternatives and experienced the type of tension that Paul is talking about here? How did you deal with that situation then and what is your evaluation of your response now?

BALANCING THE BURDEN AND THE LOAD

A pastor was asked to provide funds to enable a young man to attend high school. The one requesting the funds was a single mother with very limited resources. She was staying with her parents and had recently given birth to her fifth child.

The pastor was uncertain about how to respond. On the one hand, his usual practice was to help where he could and he recognized the value of education. On the other hand, while he could sympathize with a single mother who had two or three children, it seemed unacceptable for a mother to have five children when she had almost no income. Were the school fees a burden he needed to help her carry, or were they a load that she should carry herself?

Paul's instructions in Galatians 6 did not supply an easy answer. The pastor's thoughts wandered to an earlier situation when a man who had six children and limited resources argued that he ought to be helped by a cousin who had only two children and a good job. Had that man been irresponsible in having six children when he knew he could not afford to educate and clothe them? Thinking even more widely, was this situation similar to that of poor countries demanding financial assistance from richer countries, even though their poverty is a result of poor governance? At what point should the one who is richer say, "Let the child reap the fruit of their irresponsible parent"? When can richer nations close their eyes and tell those impoverished by corrupt leaders, "Carry your own load"?

In all such situations, three parties are involved: the possible helper, the irresponsible parent or leader, and the victim. Is the suffering a load the child should bear or a burden the church should share? Should the load of a citizen of a poor country be a burden shared by the rest of the world? What relevance does Paul's teaching have to such situations?

In the end, the pastor did two things. First, he sent for the mother of the child. He talked to her at length about her irresponsibility and stressed that she should not have any more children. Then he moved on to do what he could to help supply the fees the child needed to go to high school.

The pastor saw the support of the five children as a burden the mother needed to be helped to carry, and the need for education as a burden the child needed to be helped to carry. Only history will tell whether the mother caught the lesson well. However, as far as the pastor was concerned, he did not balance the burden and the load in a way that neglected the victim.

By the same token, African nations should listen when richer nations call them to account. Any burden we impose on the world should not be due to irresponsible leadership but only to things we have no control of, like the earthquake in Haiti. In such circumstances, "their load" becomes "our load" and a crushing burden crushes none. This is the message of Galatians 6.

UNIT 14
GALATIANS 6:1–10

THREE KEY RELATIONSHIPS

A few years ago, I was shocked when a lady older than my mother asked me to greet her with *wakya* (a Kikamba greeting that I had always thought was reserved for those younger than the greeter). It was explained that because of a distant relation in our clan, I was technically defined as her father, and so was qualified to use this greeting when speaking to her.

African societies have always paid close attention to relationships, even very distant ones. But the modern generation pays less attention to relationships beyond uncles and cousins. In other words, times change. There are, however, some basic principles in relationships that are not affected by the times. These are what Paul looks at in terms of our relationship with others, with ourselves and with God.

Relationship with Others

Our relationships with others are multifaceted and so Paul presents several scenarios in which we are to manifest the fruit of the Spirit to others.

Relationship with people caught in a sin

We may be trying to "live by the Spirit" and keep in step with the Spirit, but Satan is always eager to break our stride. He will not leave us alone. There is thus always the possibility that some of us may fall into sin. It is comforting that Paul acknowledges this when he says, *If someone is caught in a sin* (6:1a).[329] The goal of Scripture is that believers will not sin (1 John 2:1) but the reality is that till glorification, even the holiest of believers may, and in fact do, find themselves in situations where they have sinned. An isolated act of sin should not lead us to despair of living the Christian life but to a greater determination to do so, with the support of those around us.

Paul's main concern here is how we should act when someone else has fallen and needs our support. The offender may have been caught in the act of sinning by someone or circumstances may have conspired to make them vulnerable, so that he or she slipped into sin.[330] This latter view suits the context better. Paul does not seem to be thinking of a habitual sinner who has been clever enough to hide his or her sinful acts until one day someone stumbled on them. Rather, he is expressing concern for committed believers whose sinful nature has lured them into some sin.[331]

What such a person needs is not condemnation but loving restoration or rehabilitation. The restorers should display the fruit of the Spirit as they *restore that person gently* (6:1b). The goal is to help a fallen soldier, not to give further blows.

Paul does not tell us what events have taken place before we arrive at this stage. It is possible that the one sinning has been convicted of sin by the Holy Spirit and has confessed it to the community. Alternatively, the sin may have been detected by someone else, and the community may have approached the sinner. If so, this should have been done in accordance with the principles Jesus laid down in Matthew 18:15–17 (private and personal admonition, admonition in the presence of two or three witnesses, bringing the matter to the whole community, and ultimately excommunication if the problem cannot be resolved). The situation Paul seems to have in mind here involves stage three of the process (although his words also apply to stages one and two). But however the matter has come to attention, the situation is that a fellow believer has sinned and needs help.

Our response should be characterized by humility, for it is only by the grace of God that we are not the ones sitting in the sinners' seat. In the past, this was a literal seat in which some missionaries to Kenya sat those who had sinned. While the practice may have had good intentions, it sent the wrong impression to those sitting on the ordinary seats. Were they any less sinful? Not in God's eyes. (It is also interesting

– and possibly indicative of a lack of humility – that no missionary was ever regarded as qualified to sit in the sinners' seat!)

When Paul talks about "those who live by the Spirit" or "the spiritual ones" (NIV), he is not referring to a permanent class of people within a congregation.[332] They are simply those who are currently living by the Spirit. The sinner being restored today may be the spiritual one tomorrow, restoring someone else. This is part of what it means to *carry each other's burden* (6:2a). Today I help someone else carry his or her burden, and tomorrow he or she helps me carry my burden. We are mutually sinners, and mutually each other's pastors.

The person who condemns others when they fail does not know himself or herself. The potential to fall is in all of us until we reach the point of glorification. That is why Paul exhorted the Corinthians, "if you think you are standing firm, be careful that you don't fall!" (1 Cor 10:12). This is not an excuse for us continuing to sin, but an acceptance of reality so that we can forgive ourselves once we have confessed and Jesus' blood has cleansed us (1 John 1:9) and so that we can support others who fall. We will stand by them as they go through the process of dealing with guilt, forgiveness, discipline and restoration. No matter how outrageous the sin was, we will not say, "How could you?" Nor will we impose such strict discipline that it crushes the sinner's spirit.

In the context of Galatians, the "burdens" we are to help others bear is the burden of sin. But we would be wrong to think that Paul would restrict the meaning only to sin. The word he uses refers literally to a heavy weight or stone someone has to carry for a long distance, while figuratively it means any ordeal or hardship that is difficult to bear.

> The term burdens may refer to all kinds of physical, emotional, mental, moral or spiritual burdens: for example, financial burdens, the consequences of cancer or the results of divorce. The list of burdens crushing fellow Christians could be extended indefinitely. And no doubt the command to carry each other's burdens covers every conceivable kind of burden and calls for us to be sensitive enough to perceive even the unseen burdens that our brothers and sisters try to hide.[333]

One of the burdens some have to bear today is being HIV positive. We must respond to those who bear this burden with love and understanding.

Not everyone who has AIDS or is HIV positive acquired the disease because they have loose morals. But even in cases where the disease is clearly associated with sexual sin, we should never have an attitude that communicates: "You are getting what you deserve."

Carrying each other's burdens is a way in which we *fulfil the law of Christ* (6:2b). In other words, it is a way in which we follow Christ's teaching and his example. He laid down principles for his disciples to follow in the Sermon on the Mountain (Matthew 5–7) and told us to love our neighbours, as Paul has just reminded the Galatians (5:14). While the "law of Christ" embraces more than just loving our neighbour, that command heads the list of what Christ requires of his followers. Coming alongside those who are in need and providing them with the support they need in the name of Christ is like doing this for Christ himself (Matt 25:45).

The directive to carry each other's burdens is later balanced by the statement *each of you should carry your own load* (6:5).[334] Helping someone is not the same as doing everything for them. The one who has sinned needs to take up his or her bed and walk.

In some situations, the community needs to surround us with help, and in others the community would spoil us if they did not allow us to carry our own load. It may help us to understand this distinction if we think of the way we treat young children. We train them to take care of their own rooms, but we do not expect them to be able to move the furniture around.

We need wisdom from the Lord to know what is a "burden" we must help someone carry and what are "loads" that they should carry themselves. A church that has found ways of drawing the line between the two has gone a long way in helping its members not to be crushed by hardship while at the same time not taking away each individual's responsibility. Too often, however, the problem is the opposite one. Believers are left on their own, carrying crushing burdens, because no one notices. Even when the burden bearer cries out, everyone is too busy to listen.

Ask yourself, when last you noticed that someone looked depressed, and tried to take them aside to find out whether there was something wrong? While we must not be busybodies, we need to reach out to others with more concern than seems to be the case at the moment.

After all, as the traditional African sense of community fades due to urbanization, the church becomes the believers' new community. Each individual believer must sense that he or she is a valued member of that community.

Relationships between instructors and instructed

We do not know what triggered Paul's switch from a discussion of relationships in general to a focus on the relationship between instructors and instructed. There was probably something going on in Galatia that Paul and his readers knew of but that we do not. Paul may have felt that his statement on each carrying their own load in 6:5 could be taken to mean that preachers of the word should carry their own load in terms of meeting their own financial needs. This would have fed into any reluctance on the part of the Galatian believers to support those who taught them the word. Thus Paul insists that *those who receive instruction in the word should share all good things with their instructor* (6:6).[335]

The "good things" that are to be shared may be "spiritual things",[336] but it makes better sense to interpret them as material things. The instructor shares spiritual things, and the instructed provides material things so that the instructor will have the needed energy and settled mind to instruct them in "the word", taken here to mean the Scriptures. Instructors should not be distracted by worries about how they are to meet basic needs.

In other places where Paul addresses this topic, he focuses on the right of the instructor to claim support from the instructed (1 Cor 9:3–14; 1 Tim 5:17–18). However, he also makes it clear that his own principle is to forego this right (1 Cor 9:11–18; 1 Thess 2:9) in order to avoid any dependence that could result in his having less courage to speak out and confront people when that became necessary. It is thus likely that Paul's words about sharing are not uttered on his own behalf but on behalf of those who are teaching his converts in the churches of Galatia. Paul was prepared to let go of his own right to be supported without implying that everyone else should do the same, or that it was wrong to be supported. He could say on behalf of others what he would not say for himself.

Each of us should take these words to heart. How have we supported our pastors and Bible teachers? Have we just accepted that those who do the work of the gospel (missionaries, pastors, evangelists, etc.) are poorly paid? I am afraid that this has been true in the past, as evidenced by the saying, "as empty as the preacher's pocket." May the Lord help us to give more so that our pastors are better supported! (Naturally, I am here talking about those pastors who are faithful in declaring the whole counsel of God and are still in need; not about pastors who are enriching themselves at the expense of the believers they constantly exhort to give more.)

Relationships with all

Paul speaks in inclusive terms when he says, *let us do good to all people* (6:10a). No boundary of any kind should be placed between the one in need and the one with the ability to assist. These words forbid all "ethnic, national, cultural, social, sexual, and even religious distinctions within the human community".[337]

However, Paul also speaks of a particular group when he says, *especially to those who belong to the family of believers* (6:10b). The beginning point is in the church. People of faith are to be in a close relationship and are to support each other. Paul is being quite logical when he says this. We do not pay the school fees for our neighbour's child while our own child stays home for lack of fees. However, if we still have money once we have paid our child's school fees, we should go ahead and pay for our neighbour's child's fees. In so doing, we will be obeying the law of Christ. Similarly, we may use half a loaf of bread to keep our child alive and use the other half to save the life of our neighbour's child. These types of situations call for special discernment and clear leading from Scripture. While our fellow-believers get first attention, we should not close our eyes to the needs of others outside the church.

We are to do this giving *as we have opportunity*. We should be ready to help at any time, recognizing the "divinely given and strategic nature of opportunities set before the Christian for good work".[338] Take, for example, financial assistance to those in need. We do not always have the money to help others. When we become aware of their financial needs, we can pray for them, but we cannot give since we do not have. But if we become aware of needs at a time when we do have money, then we have an opportunity to give assistance. The Lord of all lives and events knows how to coordinate things so that when one person lacks there is someone somewhere else who has and can help.

The reason that some lack basic necessities is not a failure of God's provision but selfish hoarding of what God has given us to share. We should ask ourselves, "Am I hoarding what God has given to me to pass on to someone in need?" This is not an easy question to answer, for we must save for tomorrow and for our children. In these areas of life we must seek a close walk with the Spirit so as to clearly discern the will of the Lord. If we lived like this, we would see the gap between the richest and the poorest person in Africa beginning to close.

Sometimes, the rich are heard to say, "I worked for all I have. Why should I give it away to people who have not worked hard enough to get themselves out of poverty?" Such a response prompts the counter-question: "Who gave you the strength and good health to be able to work hard and be rich?" It was the Lord, and he instructs us to do good to others as we become aware of genuine needs.

Sometimes, we hear African leaders calling on the West to give back what they "stole" from Africa in terms of minerals and other stuff. Of course, the West will never respond positively to such a demand. However, there is a higher demand right in this passage: the Lord who has blessed the West calls on Westerners to do good to others as God gives them opportunity.

While it would be wrong to deny that some Westerners are already giving, it is also important to note the way in which a gift is given. Believers should not give like the rich throwing alms to a beggar, but should give in obedience to the law of Christ. May the Lord help us who believe, no matter where we live or what our background, to see ourselves as one community, to meet needs among ourselves, and then to move out to help all others as we have resources.

Relationship with Self

It is very important that we have an accurate estimation of ourselves. That is why Paul warns those who are spiritual, *watch yourselves, or you also may be tempted* (6:1b). We are all vulnerable, particularly when we overestimate our strength. That type of pride provides a great opportunity to the evil one to attack us. Recognizing that we are vulnerable to the sins we see in others keeps us humble before the Lord, thanking him for the grace that has helped us stand thus far.

Paul adds, *If any of you thinks you are something when you are nothing, you deceive yourselves* (6:3). We have no grounds for spiritual pride. We are what we are not because of what we have done but by the grace of God. It is only by seeing our successes and failures within the context of grace that we will be able to counsel others when they fail, and get up again when we fall.

We should also beware of assessing our success in terms of what others do. Instead *each of you should test your own actions. Then you can take pride in yourself, without comparing yourself to somebody else* (6:4). When we succeed where others have failed, we may conclude that we are better than they are. Not so. If we reflect on our own actions, we will see the imperfections that are part of our own lives. It is only God's grace that has enabled us to succeed.

In 6:2, Paul told us to "carry each other's burdens", that is, to help when some problem is too big to be borne alone. But, as mentioned above, each of us is called to carry our *own load*, that is, our own metaphorical bag or backpack (6:5). When we compare ourselves to others, it is as if we are failing to see the content of our own pack because we are looking at what is in someone else's bag. Each of us has a bag of human weaknesses and failures. I need to know and deal with what is in my own bag; I should not be looking at my neighbour's bag as if that is what I need to bear.

Even though it may at times be necessary to confront those who fall into sin (6:1), we should not do so from a position of superiority, but should act gently to restore them, fully aware of our own vulnerability. And we should also note that even after we have helped the sinner by trying to share the burden that led them into sin, the sinner is still left with his or her personal load of responsibility. For example, someone who has confessed to stealing public funds and has been gently restored by those who live by the Spirit is still responsible for repaying those funds. Zacchaeus the tax collector is our example here. He saw his sin, Jesus gently restored him, and Zacchaeus took up his own responsibility, saying, "if I have cheated anybody out of anything, I will pay back four times the amount" (Luke 19:8).

We in Africa need to constantly ask ourselves what constitutes our "load" and what is a "burden" that richer nations need to help us with. When we are given development grants, why is it that others need to watch over our shoulders to ensure that we put the grants to good use? We need to pick up our own load of responsibility by dealing with issues like corruption, violence, lack of integrity, tribal pride, divisions on ethnic grounds and the like.

Relationship with God

Paul introduces the matter of our relationship with God, with the solemn words, *Do not be deceived* (6:7a). This phrase seems to be a formula to introduce a statement of warning (compare 1 Cor 6:9; 15:33; Jas 1:16). What we are being warned against is both a false sense of security and pretending to be very spiritual while indulging ourselves, assuming that God will not notice. But *God cannot be mocked* (6:7b) and he will judge deliberate disobedience. Whether now or in the future, he will reward each person according to how they have chosen to live (6:7b-8). Those who choose to indulge their sinful nature will reap destruction, while those who choose to please the Spirit will reap eternal life (6:8).

Paul urges the Galatians to choose to keep sowing with a view to reaping eternal life: *Let us not become weary in doing good, for at the proper time we will reap a harvest if we do not give up* (6:9). He is concerned that the Galatians who began well (3:2–5; 5:7) were losing the enthusiasm with which they started. They need to hang on to the end, and not be enticed into either legalism or libertinism. Legalism is judgmental and libertinism is self-centred. Neither requires much in the way of concern for others. But the Galatians are to hang on to the right route to salvation (justification by faith) and the right attitudes to others (love governing relationships).

It is possible that the exhortation not to "become weary in doing good" relates to the Galatians' losing enthusiasm for the collection that was being made for the needy believers in Jerusalem.[339] But the principle is broader than that. The one who sows and does not get tired of taking care of the crops eventually reaps a harvest. This is how God has made things work: sow, nurture, harvest. Anyone who neglects the crops, claiming to be too tired to remove the weeds, cannot expect a full harvest. Do the Galatians want a harvest? Then they must toil on. Do we want a harvest? Then we should never become tired. At the proper time, the time determined by God, we will receive our reward. It may come to us here on earth or it may only come once we are in heaven. But we can be certain that it will come.

Questions for Discussion

1. When was the last time you witnessed someone who had fallen into sin being corrected? Describe how it was done and evaluate what was done in light of Paul's words to the Galatians.
2. Have you been in a situation in which you felt you had done all the good you could do, and yet still more was expected from you? What was the situation and how did you respond?
3. What are some motives for doing good to others? Is the fact that we may need good done to us tomorrow an acceptable motive?

UNIT 15
GALATIANS 6:11–18

THE ESSENCE OF CHRISTIANITY

In the past, when an elderly African man wanted to meet with his whole family, he would ask his eldest son to summon everyone to a meeting on a particular date. The son would sometimes tell them what the meeting was to be about, but once the family had assembled, the son was no longer in charge. The old man would conduct the meeting. Not that he necessarily did all the talking. He might not do much of it if he was frail or on his deathbed. But even when the eldest son did most of the speaking, his words did not carry authority until the old man endorsed them by saying, "Do what your brother has told you" or making a gesture to that effect.

Very often, the father's closing words would be a summary of what has been said at the meeting so that as everyone leaves and goes back to their routine, they will remember the main point. In effect, the father says, "Many things have been said, and there have been some disagreements among you, but this is the essential point you need to remember."

Such a practice was not unique to the African context, for that it is what Paul is doing here. Many facts, arguments and exhortations have been given, but now here is the final statement, written with Paul's *own hand* (6:11). These closing paragraphs were not dictated to a scribe or secretary, but written by Paul himself. (The reason he prefers to have someone else do the rest of the writing may be clear from his reference to the *large letters I use,* which suggests that he had problems with his eyes – see also 4:15).

The points he wants to make about the essence of Christianity are so important that he wants to write them himself in order to ensure that the Galatians pay due attention to his words.

The Gospel

Paul reiterates the main point of this whole letter: the gospel is inward and not external, beginning in God's work for us and not in our good deeds to please him.

The Judaizers have failed to grasp this point. They *want to impress others by means of the flesh* and thus they are *trying to compel you [the Galatian believers] to be circumcised* (6:12a). But, Paul insists, *neither circumcision nor uncircumcision means anything* (6:15a). As far as our relationship with Christ is concerned, it makes no difference whether we are or are not circumcised. This is the point Paul argued at length in chapters 3 and 4 and summarized in 5:6.

What is important is *the new creation* (6:15b). In this new creation, it is not important whether someone is a Jew (circumcised) or a Gentile (uncircumcised). The old ethnic groupings have been abolished, as Paul told the Corinthians, "Therefore, if anyone is in Christ, the new creation has come: The old has gone, the new is here" (2 Cor 5:17). When we come to Christ by faith, it is not only our old sinful practices that change but also our old priorities. Before Paul's conversion, his number one priority was to defend what it meant to be a Jew. Now that he knows that means nothing, his number one priority is to preach Christ who removes all barriers.

This is a truth that some of us still struggle with. It is said of many people groups that they are Americans, or Tutsi, or Yoruba, or Kikuyu before they are Christians. Such people find it very difficult to cross their ethnic and tribal boundaries and associate with others in sincere brotherhood or sisterhood in Christ. But what we are by physical birth is irrelevant when we are in Christ. Being American, British, European, Asian or African, Igbo, Kamba, Yoruba, Kikuyu, Tutsi, Luo, Luyha or belonging to any other group does not mean anything for the kingdom of God. In Christ, there is a new race, in which we are all brothers and sisters.

This point does not mean that we cannot express our faith in worship in ways that are relevant to our particular cultures. That type of contextualization is needed. But regardless of how we worship, we must maintain the bond of unity in Christ.

Paul pronounces a special prayer of blessings on those who live out this truth: *Peace and mercy to all who follow this rule – to the Israel of God* (6:16). His singling out of the "Israel of God" (meaning here the Jews who believe in Jesus[340]) implies that he recognizes that the Jews found it especially difficult to cross their ethnic boundary and relate to the Gentiles as equals, and that those who have done so deserve to be acknowledged for it. Yes, the Jews had special privileges (the law given to Moses and God's special care) but these were in preparation for bringing in the new creation through the Messiah who died on the cross to reconcile us to God, whatever people group we belong to. Those who were in the formerly privileged group and have believed in Christ are certainly not left out of this blessing!

Paul's mention of "peace" and "mercy" may have been triggered by his personal reflection on what it means to live the kind of life he has been speaking about.[341] The physical marks or circumcision and uncircumcision are real and can be cause for not living in harmony. The saying "birds of a feather flock together" applies to people just as much as it does to birds. We find it easier to be close to people who are like us because they are of a similar race or clan, or have similar education or status. Since there will always be differences like these, peace is something we must deliberately cultivate in view of our oneness in Christ. Believers should be examples in showing that while diversity is real, unity is our way of life. This can best be achieved by constantly reminding ourselves that we are what we are solely because of God's mercy. If the millionaire believes that all that he or she has is a gift from God, then fellowship with beggars and street people is not impossible.

May Paul's prayer for the believers in Galatia be true in our times also – may we live in peace and keep before us the fact of God's mercy, as we also ask him for more of these blessings in our lives.

The Preacher

Paul finishes by again reminding the Galatians that it is important to determine whose message they can trust. He contrasts his own position as a true preacher with the misleading preaching of the Judaizers.

The Judaizers

The Judaizers had a hidden personal agenda. They knew that they would be more acceptable to other Jews if they had the Gentile believers circumcised, because that was the standard route for Gentiles proselytes who wished to convert to Judaism. The Judaizers would even be praised by conservative Jews for winning converts to Judaism, and would thus *avoid being persecuted for the cross of Christ* (6:12b).

Paul reminds the Galatians that what the Judaizers are insisting on is outward obedience to a law they cannot even keep themselves (6:13a). While they can carry out rituals like circumcision, that does not impress God, who knows what is happening in the hearts of men and women and also knows that it is impossible to keep the law perfectly (5:3; 3:10). God knows that the Judaizers are not acting in love towards the Gentiles, but are self-centred: *they want you to be circumcised that they may boast about your flesh* (6:13b). They were not concerned about the good of the Galatians but about the praise they themselves would be given by fellow Jews.

We may be happy to join Paul in condemning the Judaizers. But do we have similar motives to theirs? How do we define success? Is it just the number of people we can boast about having converted? As important as conversions are, the crucial question before God is how many people have really made an about-turn in their lives and placed their faith in the Lord Jesus Christ. Similarly, in pastoral ministry, do we attach more importance to how many people attend our churches than to how peoples' lives are being changed so that they become more Christ-like? A pastor who avoids preaching the whole counsel of God so as not to offend some may build numbers, but not lives. The prosperity gospel has tended to do this, as it has encouraged many to seek Christ in order to gain material possessions rather than a changed life.

The True Preacher of the Gospel

In contrast to the Judaizers, Paul does not seek to impress other people or to boast about his converts. Instead, he says, *May I never boast except in the cross of our Lord Jesus Christ, through which the world has been crucified to me, and I to the world* (6:14). "The world" is the sphere that Satan controls. It is no longer important to Paul. He has no fellowship with the world and the world has no fellowship with him. He operates within the sphere of the cross of Christ and its values, not within the sphere that opposes Christ.

When we view all that we have or are as given by God, it takes away any reason for boasting. God was the one who determined what race or clan we would be born into; he created the things that we use to classify ourselves as rich or poor; he provided the fees for our education; he gave us the gifts of beauty or strength. If God is the source of everything, then he is the only one worth boasting of. All that we boast of is the means by which we became what we are. Like Paul, I can boast in Christ by whose cross I have been made whole and brought into fellowship with God, my Creator. Careful reflection on these matters should make even unbelievers say "Thank you, God", let alone believers who have known God not just as Creator and Giver but also as Father.

Paul then says, *From now on, let no one cause me trouble, for I bear on my body the marks of Jesus* (6:17). Paul has settled where he came from and where he is going. He has been commissioned by Jesus to serve him and that is all that he is going to do. The Judaizers may want the Gentile believers to be circumcised, to mark their allegiance in their flesh, but Paul has no need for that. He bears the marks of Jesus on his body.

There is some debate about what exactly these marks were. There are three main possibilities:[342]

- The marks were metaphorical. Paul is saying that while others focus on the mark of circumcision on their bodies, he does not need that for he is marked by Christ. The same line of thought is found in 2 Corinthians 4:10a, where he says "we always carry around in our body the death of Jesus".
- The mark was some kind of tattoo or brand. The word translated "mark" was also used for the mark burnt onto an animal or a slave to show whom they belonged to. In Paul's day, it was not unknown for

people to be branded for religious purposes, to show they belonged to some god. Soldiers might also be branded with the name of the general they served under. So it is possible that Paul had chosen to be marked with something like a C (the first letter in the word "Christ" in Greek) to show that he belonged to Christ.

- The marks were the scars of persecution. Paul had acquired both physical and emotional scars during the years in which he preached Christ. Some of the Galatians may have witnessed this when Paul was stoned and left for dead at Lystra in Southern Galatia (Acts 14:19). And that was not the only time he endured physical abuse (2 Cor 6:4–6; 11:23–30).

This last possibility seems to be the most likely. Paul's body is scarred by persecution, and each scar testifies that Jesus owns him and that Paul has given himself to serve Jesus, whatever the cost. Others may seek to win human favour or look to the marks of circumcision to indicate that they are God's people but Paul has no need for this. It is pointless to bother him by telling him otherwise.

Here is someone who has personally experienced what he is writing about. Paul is like John the apostle, who wrote as a witness to what he had heard, seen and touched (1 John 1:1).

Personal faith backed up by personal experience is a weapon that can face any obstacle. Job was one who really suffered, yet clung to God because of what he personally knew of God. He lost all that he had, but could still say, "the Lord gave and the Lord has taken away (Job 1:21). Such faith goes beyond the wonderful intellectual truths we learn about God and becomes a childlike belief in God even when we cannot explain what is happening around us.

If Job had lived in our day, he would have been tempted to go to the most famous "witchdoctor" to find out the cause of his calamity. He would probably have been told that it was caused by his neighbour, whom he would then begin to hate. How deep is your faith? Can you tell the atheist, "Leave me alone, I know God exists"? Can you tell those who mock your faith in Christ, "Mind your own business; I know what Jesus means to me"? Can you tell anyone who advocates blessings from sources other than a life led by the Spirit, "I know what virtues he has brought into my life and I am satisfied"? Paul could. He knew Christ personally and all the marks of his suffering for Christ's cause spoke loud and clear.

It is not because Paul was physically fit in every way that he put himself totally in the service of Jesus. He had his physical struggles, as he mentions in 4:13–15. He did not wait until God gave him the perfect circumstances before he gave himself to dedicated service. Neither should we. Some of us may struggle in the area of health, others in the area of finances, and others in the area of relationships, just as Paul did with the Galatians. But we should be able to forget our hardships and focus on the joy the gospel brings to those who accept it.

It is not that we will not take personal responsibility for our circumstances. We are called to eat a balanced diet, exercise for the sake of our health, plan and follow a budget that stays within our means, and do our best to get on with others. But once we have done our best, and there is still some lack of health, finances and relationships, we should be content in our state and continue to serve God joyfully.

Concluding Prayer

Paul closes the letter with a prayer, *The grace of our Lord Jesus Christ be with your spirit, brothers and sisters. Amen* (6:18). He has been hard on the Galatians at times but they are still his brothers and sisters.

He refers to the believer's "spirit" here, just as he does in Philippians 4:23, 2 Timothy 4:22, and Philemon 25. In each of these cases, he is not referring to some disembodied spirit but to the whole person. The prayer has the same meaning as the "grace be with you" that he uses in Romans 15:33; 1 Corinthians 16:23; 2 Corinthians 13:11, 14; and 1 Thessalonians 5:28). Paul wishes them well, with God's grace, provided in and through Jesus Christ,[343] abounding in their lives.

This is a beautiful ending to a letter that has been very direct as Paul has reproved and rebuked the Galatians.

We can learn a lesson from Paul. Even when we go through conflicts in our relationships, the love of Christ should still be evident. It is all too easy for pastors who are experiencing conflict with their congregations to fail to maintain this love dimension in what they say and do. A stern word said in love may have a positive effect, but when said without love, it only drives the hearer further away. May the Lord help us as we serve others. Conflicts there will be, but may love never cease.

Questions for Discussion

1. What do others see reflected in your life? Do they see Christ? Or do they see self? What qualities affect what they see? What is your goal? Ask others to support you in prayer as you strive to achieve it.
2. What sort of relationship do you have with others who are different from you in their likes, background, and even faith?
3. What in the book of Galatians spoke to you in a personal way? How do you plan to make that part of your life?

NOTES

1. Martin Luther wrote an influential commentary on Galatians in which he expounded the centrality of faith in salvation. The nineteenth-century liberal scholar F. C. Baur of the University of Tübingen viewed Galatians as one of the four letters (the others being Romans and 1 & 2 Corinthians) that form the cream of Paul's teaching and constitute the touchstone by which all other letters bearing Paul's name must be tested.
2. For more information about the North Galatian theory, see Alan Cole, *The Letter of Paul to the Galatians* (Tyndale New Testament Commentaries; Grand Rapids: Eerdmans, 1965), 15–18.
3. For more information about the South Galatian theory, see F. F. Bruce, *Commentary on Galatians* (New International Greek Testament Commentary; Grand Rapids: Eerdmans, 1982), 3–18; Timothy George, *Galatians: An Exegetical and Theological Exposition of Holy Scripture – NIV Text* (New American Commentary; Nashville: Broadman & Holman, 1994), 38–46; Richard N. Longenecker, *Galatians* (Word Biblical Commentary; Dallas: Word, 1990), lxiii–lxx.
4. Longenecker (lviii) lists the few who dispute this attribution.
5. It appears that Paul only introduces himself by the title of "apostle" in situations where some of those reading his letters might dispute his authority (see 2 Corinthians, Ephesians, Colossians, 1 & 2 Timothy). He also introduces himself as "Paul, a prisoner" in Philemon 1:1.
6. The root *apostellō* (send) is used 131 times as a verb and 79 times as a noun in the New Testament.
7. Donald Guthrie describes the *shaliach*'s status as "clearly conditioned by the status of the one who sent him" (*Galatians* [New Century Bible; London: Oliphants, 1969], 56). As an apostle of Jesus Christ, Paul speaks with the authority of Christ.
8. Paul uses *ap' anthrōpōn*, using the plural "men", not the singular *ap' anthrōpou*. In the phrase which follows, the singular *anthrōpou* is used. The NIV captures the change well with its translation, "not from men nor by man". However, the term is generic and includes both men and women, and thus the TNIV's "human" is an acceptable translation. The preposition *apo* communicates "from beside" or "originating from" and focuses on the source that determines his authority.
9. The first preposition is *apo* (from) and the second is *dia*. When followed by an accusative, *dia* means "because"; when followed by a genitive, it means "through". When used in proximity to *apo*, as here, *dia* communicates the idea that the ultimate source used an agent. The TNIV translation "by" captures this idea well enough, but "through", which is used in the NASB, leaves no ambiguity in its focus on the agent (channel, medium, or instrument) through whom Paul came to be an apostle.
10. Paul introduces this statement with the word *alla*. He could have chosen to use *de*, but that word could also be translated as "and" and "even". *Alla* only means "but". Paul wants to be sure there is no ambiguity about the contrast.
11. It is possible that Paul was originally known by the Hebrew name Saul and received the Latin name Paul after his conversion. However, it is more likely that he had both names since childhood. When being Jewish was the focus of his life, he went by the name Saul. But when the Lord changed his life and he was called to reach out to the Gentiles, he preferred to use the name they would be more familiar with, Paul.

12. The same incident is described in Acts 9:5-20. There the call to apostleship is not mentioned, but Jesus gives Saul specific instructions that he obeys. Immediately thereafter he begins to preach that Jesus is the Son of God. Paul was thus called into salvation and commissioned into ministry by his encounter with Jesus.
13. He uses only one preposition, "by", or "through" (NASB), to link Jesus Christ and God the Father together as one agent.
14. The term "brothers" covers all those working alongside Paul at that time. Their exact identity depends on whether Galatians was written to southern churches following the first missionary journey or to northern churches at a later date. If it was written to the southern churches, then someone like Barnabas would likely have been one of the brothers. Some commentators make much of the fact that Paul here deviates from his usual practice of identifying his companions by name (1 Cor 1:1; 2 Cor 1:1; Phil 1:1; Col 1:1; 1 Thess 1:1; Phlm 1). They suggest that he uses the general term "brothers" in Galatians to obscure the fact that no one else supports his position. But this hypothesis seems highly unlikely. Paul was writing to defend his credibility, and any deceitfulness on his part would have provided his critics with a weapon they could use against him.
15. *Eirēnē* is simply a literal translation of the Hebrew *shalom*. Paul uses the same combination in Rom 1:7; 1 Cor 1:3; 2 Cor 1:2; Eph 1:2; and Phil 1:2.
16. Taking the aorist *dontos* (giving) in the phrase *tou dontos eauton* as constative.
17. The verse uses the common word for sin in the New Testament, *harmatia*, which carries the idea of missing the mark. Forms of the word *harmatia* are used 227 times in the NT. This word is more inclusive than *parabasis* (Gal 3:19), which means crossing a line or the act of transgression, and *paraptōma* (Gal 6:1), which means falling from where one is supposed to stand.
18. In 1:4, however, the meaning of "for" is likely limited to "concerning" or "with reference to".
19. The verb *exelētai* is an aorist subjunctive middle from *exaireō*. In Galatians, it is used only in 1:4, but it is also found in Matthew (5:29; 18:9) and Acts (7:10, 34; 12:11; 23:27; 26:17). In the middle voice, as here, it means to set free, deliver, rescue and remove from some impending danger. When used in a context of rescue from sin, it carries the idea of justification.
20. John Eadie, *Galatians* (John Eadie Greek Text Commentaries; Grand Rapids: Baker, 1979), 4.
21. Romans 6:23.
22. This construction is an example of the Granville Sharp theory: *theou* and *patros* are both in the genitive case, are connected by *kai*, and have only one article, attached to the *theou*. Thus they both refer to the same person.
23. See also the discussion of the recipients in the Introduction.
24. The verb is *euēngelisametha*, the first person plural from *euangelizō* (I preach). It is a constative aorist in the indicative mood and the middle voice.
25. The simple past *parelabete* (from *paralambanō* – I receive) focuses on the results of the act of accepting. The idea would be that the Galatians heard, appreciated and accepted the gospel. While the simple past does not necessarily limit their acceptance of the gospel to the past, the context suggests that Paul is referring to the specific period when he and others preached to them.
26. The verb *thaumazō* is a pictorial present that Paul uses to describe his astonishment.
27. Assuming that this letter was written to the churches of southern Galatia in AD 49, shortly after Paul's first missionary journey, two years is the maximum period of time that can be involved (see the Introduction for more details).
28. The Greek word is *metatithesthe* from *metatithēmi* (I turn away).
29. Taking the present tense verb *metatithesthe* as a durative present.
30. We here have a first class condition.

31 The Greek verb form is *tarassontes* from *tarassō* (I stir up, throw into confusion). In addition to the uses cited in the text, it is also used of the troubling of the water at the pool of Bethesda (John 5:4).
32 The aorist verb *metastrepsai* is taken to be tendential/conative, indicating that this was an attempt, not something that was accomplished.
33 Taking *tou Christou* as a subjective genitive, also involving the notion of a genitive of source.
34 Taking *tou Christou* as a genitive of content.
35 The Greek reads *en chariti Christou*. When the preposition *en* is followed by a dative it can mean "by" or "in". If we take this to be a dative of means, then the "by grace" refers to the means by which God called the Galatians, in which case "grace" stands for the whole work of Christ that Paul describes in terms of Christ giving himself "for our sins" (1:4). Alternatively, this may be dative of sphere, referring to the sphere of grace within which God called the Galatians. In other words, the context of God's calling is grace, not works as the Judaizers were teaching them. The correct translation for this phrase would then be "in grace". Finally, if we take the phrase as a dative of manner, it refers to the manner in which God called the Galatians. This interpretation overlaps with the dative of means above, but goes beyond it. It includes both what Christ did and the state of the Galatians. They were undeserving of any goodness but God in his bountiful mercy called them out of their helpless situation. If we adopt this translation, the phrase could be translated as "graciously". While these three ideas are not mutually exclusive, the focus seems to fall more on the last one. The genitive "of Christ", which qualifies the grace, is probably subjective, indicating that it is Christ who exercises the grace.
36 We are meant to strive to be like God as regards his holiness and righteousness (which are known as his communicable attributes). However we cannot share attributes that are uniquely his, like being everywhere at the same time (omnipresence) and knowing all things (omniscience).
37 The two Greek words are *heteros* and *allos*. For a discussion of them, see J. W. Wenham, *The Elements of New Testament Greek* (based on an earlier work by H. P. V. Nunn; Cambridge: Cambridge University Press, 1965), 62.
38 The combination of *ean* and a present subjunctive, *euangelizētai*, in 1:8 represents a third class conditional statement in which the premise is probable, but is not a fact.
39 Longenecker, 18.
40 In this conditional statement, Paul uses *ei* plus *euangelizetai* (a present indicative). This is a first class condition and assumes the premise as a fact.
41 This interpretation of the meaning of *anathema* in the New Testament is supported by Acts 23:14, Romans 9:3, and 1 Corinthians 12:3 and 16:22.
42 Henry George Liddell and Robert Scott, *A Greek-English Lexicon* (new edition; Oxford: Clarendon, 1940), 1354.
43 The use of the imperfect tense in both the premise clause and the conclusion clause (*ēreskon* and *ēmēn*, respectively) strengthens the point that Paul is thinking of the present. See H. E. Dana and Julius R. Mantey, *A Manual of the Greek New Testament* (Toronto: Macmillan, 1927), 289; Daniel B. Wallace, *Greek Grammar Beyond the Basics: An Exegetical Syntax of the New Testament with Scripture, Subject, and Greek Word Indexes* (Grand Rapids: Zondervan, 1996), 695.
44 Paul here uses a second class conditional construction (with *ei* in the protasis and *an* in the apodosis) which literally means "If I were, and I am not". The premise clause assumes what it represents is not fact. Paul is not trying to please human beings. The TNIV rightly supplies the word "trying", given that the present tense verbs *peithō* (win approval) and *areskein* (to please) are tendential, as also the imperfect *ēreskon*.
45 The repetition of the article before gospel and before the verb "I preached" is for emphasis. See Dana and Mantey, 148.
46 Bruce, 88.
47 Longenecker, 23.

48 The debate hinges on whether the genitive *Iēsou Christou* in the phrase *di' apokalupseōs Iēsou Christou* is a subjective genitive, in which case Jesus is the source who revealed the content of the gospel to Paul (compare 1:1), or whether it is an objective genitive, in which case Jesus is the one revealed by someone else, presumably God the Father (see 1:16). Supporters of the subjective genitive position include J. B. Lightfoot (*The Epistle of Paul to the Galatians*, 80), Eadie (36), William Hendriksen (*Galatians and Ephesians*, The New Testament Commentary; Grand Rapids: Baker Book House, 1968, 48); Longenecker, 24. Supporters of the objective genitive position include Ernest De Witt Burton (*The Epistle to the Galatians* [1920; International Critical Commentary; Edinburgh: T & T Clark, repr. 1980], 43); Bruce, 89; James G. Dunn *The Epistle to the Galatians* (Black New Testament Commentaries; Peabody: Hendrickson, 1995), 55.

49 The Greek *en tō Ioudaismō* is a dative phrase best taken as dative of sphere.

50 The TNIV's translation of the aorist *ēkousate* as "have heard" (and not just "heard") is appropriate here. It is a resultative aorist, with the focus on the current state of the Galatians. They are well informed on this matter.

51 Though the term "traditional healer" may be preferred by some, I have used "witchdoctor" here in order to bring out the point that such people use the spiritual sphere to bring about "healing", make "predictions" and the like. I am not attacking all elements of African traditional religion. Some aspects of it do not contradict Scripture and may be retained, but those aspects that do contradict Scripture must be discarded.

52 The imperfect tense of the verb *ediōkon* is best taken as iterative, representing a constantly repeated action in the past. The intensity with which this was done is expressed by *kath' huperbolēn*, which has the notion of "beyond all measure and proportion (compare its use in Romans 7:13; 1 Corinthians 12:31; 2 Corinthians 1:8; 4:17).

53 In *ekklēsian tou theou*, the words *tou theou* are best taken as a genitive of possession.

54 The imperfect tense *eporthoun* (from *portheō* – "I destroy") is best treated as tendential.

55 The imperfect verb *proekopton* (from *prokoptō*) is best taken as a durative imperfect.

56 Dunn, 60.

57 Longenecker, 29; see also Dunn, 60. The view that Paul is comparing himself to all others of his age is supported by Burton (47) and Lightfoot (81).

58 In Judaism at this time, there were at least four main parties: the Pharisees, the Sadducees, the Essenes and the Zealots. Lightfoot (81–82) says that "St. Paul seems to have belonged to the extreme party of the Pharisees ... whose pride it was to call themselves zealots of law, zealots of God. To this party also had belonged Simon, one of the Twelve, thus surnamed the Zealot. ... A portion of these extreme partisans, forming into a separate sect under Judas of Galilee, took the name 'zealot' par excellence, and distinguished themselves by their furious opposition to the Romans." However, Burton (47), Eadie (40), Bruce (91), and Longenecker (30) all argue for the more generic use of the word.

59 Joshua's zeal is seen both in his agony after the Israelites were defeated by Ai and in his confronting of Achan, whose sin had brought the displeasure of the Lord, and consequently defeat.

60 1 Maccabees 2:19–27; Josephus, *Antiquities* XII, 270–271.

61 Bruce, 91.

62 Dunn, 61.

63 Jewish interpreters of the Scriptures compiled the Talmud, part of which, the Mishnah, dealt with the *halakha* (legal concepts), while the other part, called the Gemara, dealt with the *haggada* (non-legal matters). Given the context of Galatians, it was the legal part that Paul was zealous to obey. He was determined to live by the letter of the law.

64 The Greek *ho aphorisas* ("the one who set apart") involves an adjectival use of a participle, here functioning substantively. "Me", that is, Paul, is its object.

65 George, 117.

66 Eadie, 43.

67 Guthrie, 68. However, viewing this passage in the context of eternal predestination (George, 117) may be reading a little too much into Paul's words here, though it is correct theologically on the basis of other passages such as Ephesians 1:4 "For he [God] chose us in him [Christ] before the creation of the world."

68 The Greek has *dia tēs charitos autou*. For the translation of *dia* with genitive as "by", see Dana and Mantey, 102. Here it is the equivalent of a dative of means, indicating the means by which God's acts of setting apart and calling are done (although it may be best to relate it only to the calling). The setting apart is qualified by a time indicator (from birth) and the calling is qualified by stating the divine instrument that brought about its realization (God's grace).

69 The demarcation between Paul's conversion and his commissioning is very narrow. Both happened at the same event, when Paul became both a believer and an apostle. Dunn (63) rightly says, "Paul always speaks of his entry into Christianity as a call or commissioning; he never speaks of it as a conversion". But Dunn exaggerates when he goes on to say that Paul "would almost certainly have disputed the use of that word (in the modern sense) in reference to his Damascus road experience, since he saw it not as conversion from one religion to another, but as a recall to a proper understanding of the grace-character of Israel's calling". Paul does not speak of his conversion because it is assumed or contained within his call. Thus Bruce (93) is correct to say, "The purpose of the revelation, that Paul should proclaim the Gospel of Christ among the Gentiles, was part of the revelation itself: conversion and commission came together."

70 Bruce, 92; Burton, 51; Longenecker, 31; Dunn, 64.

71 The Greek has *apokalupsai ton huion autou en emoi* (literally, "to reveal his son in me"). The *en emoi* is a dative, which a few commentators treat as a simple dative allowing for such possibilities as "to me" or "for me". However, this approach ignores the presence of the preposition *en* whose meaning is "in" or "by". For more discussion of this point, see Eadie, 43–44.

72 This approach treats *en emoi* as a straightforward dative of sphere, so that the translation could be "within me" (that is, a subjective revelation). Bruce (93) says that the phrase "probably points to the inwardness of the experience ... For Paul the outward vision and the inward illumination coincided: Jesus, whom he persecuted, was revealed as the Son of God, and the revelation was the act of God himself". According to this line of thought, the import of the revelation was "a transformation not so much of person as of purpose and commitment" (Dunn, 64).

73 This approach treats *en emoi* as a dative of agent, referring to an objective rather than a subjective manifestation of Christ. The focus is on the revelation Paul passed on to others. George (120), for example, says, "On balance it seems better to interpret *en emoi* as 'through me', linking the revelation of Christ in Paul to the divine purpose and mission God had planned for him, to preach the gospel among the Gentiles, rather than backward to his conversion and call, which has already been alluded to. See also Lightfoot, 83.

74 Daniel C. Arichea, Jr. and Eugene A. Nida, *A Translator's Handbook on Paul's Letter to the Galatians*. (New York: United Bible Societies, 1975), 22.

75 Commentators who think that Jesus himself was revealed include Longenecker, 31; Eadie, 44; John R. W. Stott, *The Message of Galatians* (The Bible Speaks Today; London: Inter-Varsity Press, 1968), 32–33; and Bruce, 93.

76 George, 120.

77 George, 122.

78 Longenecker, 32. See also Bruce, 93.

79 The aorist tenses in *aphorisas* (set apart) and *kalesas* (called) focus on definite action in the past. Now, however, he uses *euangelizōmai*, a present middle subjunctive from *euangelizō* (I preach). As a present tense, it is best taken as durative, indicating that this is to be Paul's ongoing task.

80 The Greek term *ethnē* (singular, *ethnos*) is used in the Septuagint to translate the Hebrew term *goyim*, which referred to nations other than Israel. This usage is clear from such New Testament passages as Acts 14:5; 21:11, 21; Romans 3:29; 9:24; 1 Corinthians 1:23; and

Galatians 2:15. Though Paul's ministry focused on the Gentiles (Rom 1:5, 13; 11:13; 15:16; Eph 3:8; 1 Tim 2:7), it should not be viewed as excluding Jews but rather as freeing the gospel from previous limitations. See Dunn, 66.

[81] Guthrie, 65; see also Bruce 88; Longenecker, 23.

[82] Paul uses the preposition *para* in stating the not-human (generic use of *anthrōpos*) origin of his gospel. There are debates about whether there is a difference between this preposition and *apo*, the other preposition he could have used, with some arguing that *apo* denotes the ultimate source and *para* the more immediate source. However, I agree with Longenecker, (23) that "the preposition *para* is often used in the New Testament in the sense of the ultimate source, with *apo* and *para* appearing indistinguishably in parallel accounts". For more on this debate, see Burton, 39-40; Eadie, 35; Lightfoot, 80.

[83] The phrase *sarki kai haimati* is an example of metonymy. The phrase was commonly used to denote human beings as distinct from God (Guthrie, 69). Longenecker (33) says that it denotes "'mankind in its finitude and frailty' or 'humanity as temporarily and corporeally conditioned'" in contrast to beings of a higher order, especially God". Jesus used the same words in Matthew 16:17 when he told Peter that flesh and blood had not revealed Jesus' true identity to him.

[84] Dunn, 67. See also Eadie, 46. Note that there are differences of opinion as to what the word translated "immediate" in 1:16 relates to. The TNIV, NASB, NKJV and HCSB relate it to consulting a human being, whereas the NIV translation reads, "I went immediately into Arabia". Both translations make it clear that Paul did not immediately go to Jerusalem, where he could have met with apostles like Peter and John.

[85] The idea is literally, "and I was still or remained (note the periphrastic imperfect, emphasizing the continuity of the action) unknown by sight to the churches of Judea which were in Christ."

[86] Lightfoot, 88.

[87] This region was ruled by Aretas IV from 9 BC to AD 40 (2 Cor 11:32). Herod Antipas married and later divorced Aretas' daughter in order to marry Herodias, which led to enmity between the two kings. See Bo Reicke, *The New Testament Era: The World of the Bible from 500 BC to AD 100* (Philadelphia: Fortress Press, 1964), 192–193; Emil Schürer, *A History of the Jewish People in the Time of Jesus Christ* (Part 1, vol. 2; Peabody: Hendriksen, 1994), 356–359.

[88] See Longenecker, 34. If Paul's conversion is dated to AD 36, the Damascus incident would be about three years later, in about AD 39. That was ten years before Galatians was written in AD 49 and during that time some political boundary changes could have taken place.

[89] Dunn, 70. Bruce (96) argues that "it is possible that in 'Arabia' Paul communed with God in the wilderness where Moses and Elijah had communed with him centuries before; but in the present context the primary purpose of his Arabian visit appears to have been the immediate fulfillment of his commission to preach the Son of God 'among the Gentiles'."

[90] Arichea and Nida, 23. See also Hendriksen (56) who says that Paul used this time for "rest, prayer and meditation"; Eadie (49) says that he set out "to enjoy solitary thought and preparation, sounding the depth of his conviction, forecasting possibilities, receiving revelations and lessons"; Lightfoot (90) says that he went there "to commune with God and his own soul ... to gather strength in solitude for his active labours".

[91] Burton, 55.

[92] Paul seems to be focusing on how his conversion/commission was separated from Jerusalem both in terms of distance and time, and so there is good reason to see his use of "after ... years (1:18; 2:1) as beginning at conversion. See the discussion of this earlier in this unit.

[93] The verb *historēsai* (the aorist infinitive form of *historeō*) occurs only here in the New Testament and is translated in various ways: "become [or "get"] acquainted with" – NASB, NIV and TNIV: "see" – KJV. Bruce (98) translates it as "interview", Dunn (73) as "get to know", Burton (59) as "visit", Eadie (50) and Longenecker (37) as "make acquaintance of". These interpretations are based on the use of this word in extrabiblical literature, especially the writings of Josephus, who like Paul uses it when speaking of people. Most other uses (in Herodotus, Aristotle, Plutarch and others) are used with reference to places.

94 Bruce, 98.
95 Eadie, 50.
96 Dunn, 74.
97 Understanding this brief stay in Jerusalem as the one recorded in Acts 9:26-29, Peter and James are the apostles to whom Barnabas introduced Paul (Acts 9:27).
98 Though *graphō* (I write) could be an aoristic present (see NIV), it may also be a durative present, referring to what Paul has written before, that is, in the earlier verses, and what he is writing now.
99 Longenecker, 40.
100 The function of *idou* ("behold" – an imperative, probably functioning as an entreaty) is that Paul beseeches them to give attention to the matter and not ignore it.
101 Syria and Cilicia were administered as one Roman province from 25 BC to AD 72.
102 The book of Acts implies that Paul made five visits to Jerusalem:
   - Acts 9:26–28   visit following his conversion
   - Acts 11:27–30; 12:25   visit associated with famine relief
   - Acts 15:1–31   visit focusing on the issue of Gentile circumcision
   - Acts 18:22   visit implied by "he went up (from Caesarea) and greeted the church"
   - Acts 21:17–25:12   final visit during which he was arrested

   Galatians mentions only two of these visits: In 1:18 Paul refers to a visit three years after his conversion, and in 2:1 he mentions another visit "after fourteen years". He was probably counting from the date of his conversion, not from the date of his previous visit (though Dunn, 87, would not agree). Given Paul's stress that he stayed away from Jerusalem (1:17), it seems likely that the visit mentioned in 1:18 was his first visit there, the one mentioned in Acts 9:26–28. It is difficult to be certain exactly which visit he is referring to in 2:1. Scholars are divided as to whether it was the visit associated with famine relief (Acts 11) or with the meeting of the Jerusalem Council (Acts 15). Given that circumcision does not seem to have been the main topic on the agenda, as it was in Acts 15, the visit is probably the one referred to in Acts 11. Its primary purpose was to deliver money raised for famine relief, but the presence of Titus among Paul's companions meant that issues of circumcision came up. For more discussion, see R. H. Stein, "Jerusalem", in *Dictionary of Paul and His Letters* (edited by Gerald F. Hawthorne, Ralph P. Martin and Daniel G. Reid; Downers Grove: InterVarsity Press, 1993), 463–474.
103 This is the first mention of Barnabas in Paul's letters. Paul later mentions him in his letter to the Corinthians (1 Cor 9:6).
104 The continuous use of the first person singular indicates that Paul was in charge and that Barnabas was accompanying him.
105 Those who read these words as affirming that Titus was not circumcised emphasise the *oude* and link it to "Titus", giving the reading "not even Titus" (Lightfoot, 105; Burton, 76; Bruce, 112; Eadie, 111–112). Those who read these words as implying that Titus voluntarily agreed to be circumcised link the *oude* and "compelled", giving the reading, "Titus was not even compelled" (J. N. Sanders, "Galatians", in *Peake's Commentary on the Bible* (eds. Matthew Black and H. H. Rowley; London: Nelson, 1962), 975.
106 Longenecker, 47; Cole, 62.
107 Bruce, 108; Dunn, 91.
108 Eadie, 105; Dunn, 91.
109 This interpretation is endorsed by Bruce, 109; Dunn, 93.
110 Longenecker, 47; Eadie, 105.
111 The Greek suggests the plausibility of there having been two distinct meetings. The indirect object of "set before" (*anethemēn* – 2:2b) is *autois* (them – 2:2b) and this is tied to going to Jerusalem. After that, Paul says "but privately to those who matter" (2:2c). The "them" and "those who matter" seem to be two groups, one larger and the other smaller.
112 The Greek word *dia* is translated "because of" in the TNIV, implying that the false brothers made the demand. However, when *dia* is used with an accusative, as here, it may mean "for the

sake of". If it is translated in this way, Paul is saying that the false brothers are the beneficiaries of a demand made by some other party anxious to avoid offending them. The "other party" could have been the apostles. However, the context seems to demand that the false brothers are the cause and not the beneficiaries.

113 The adjective *pareisaktos* means "secretly smuggled, brought in, smuggled in, sneaked in" and the verb *pareiserchoma* describes the action of bringing something in "with the connotation that it is done secretly or maliciously". Walter Bauer, William F. Arndt and F. Wilbur Gingrich. *Greek–English Lexicon of the New Testament and Other Early Christian Literature* (BAG) (Chicago: University of Chicago Press, 1957), 630.

114 Those who choose Antioch argue either that people from Jerusalem were sent to Antioch to interfere with Paul's work there, or that people from Antioch (or some other Gentile city) followed Paul to Jerusalem to undermine his report to the leaders (Bruce, 115–117; Burton, 78–79; Albert Barnes, "Galatians", in *Barnes' Notes on the New Testament: Complete and Unabridged in One Volume* (Grand Rapids: Kregel, 1962), 927). The movement could have been either way; the answer depends in part on how many people knew that Paul would be going to Jerusalem.

115 Dunn, 99.

116 The word *kataskopeō* (or *kataskopeuō*) is used only here in the New Testament. In the Septuagint, it is also used in a good sense when referring to the way Miriam kept watch over the baby Moses (Exod 2:4). However, elsewhere it is used with the negative meaning found in Galatians 2:4.

117 Here both shades of the dative ("means" and "sphere") apply simultaneously.

118 The words translated "for a moment" literally mean "for an hour", as in the NASB, indicating a very short time span.

119 Burton (86) agrees that what we have here is a genitive of possession (i.e., the truth belonged to the gospel). Lightfoot, however, takes it as a qualitative genitive (107).

120 The Acts passage is the only other place where this verb occurs in the New Testament. It is, however, also found in the Septuagint translation of passages like Micah 7:5 and 2 Maccabees 3:9. The verb can be used for communication between friends, from a superior to a subordinate, or from a subordinate to a superior. In itself, it does not reveal the relationship between the two parties. This has to be determined from the context.

121 The verb *kērussō* is a durative present tense.

122 Paul uses the present tense *trechō*, which can be indicative, meaning "I run, am running", or subjunctive, meaning "I should run" and also the aorist indicative *edramon* which can be rendered as "I ran" or "have run" on the basis of its being a resultative aorist. He is, therefore, thinking of both what he is now doing and what he has been doing.

123 For example, Longenecker quotes H. Schlier (*Der Brief an die Galater*, Gottingen: Vandenhoeck & Ruprecht, 1965, p 67–69) as saying that this passages shows Paul recognizing "the decisive authority of the earlier apostolate at Jerusalem and wishing to validate the genuineness of his mission by their acknowledgment" (Longenecker, 49).

124 BAG, 201.

125 In 2:2 we have *tois dokousin* (those seeming), in 2:6 we have *tōn dokountōn einai ti*, and in 2:9 we have *hoi dokountes stuloi einai*. The verb *dokeō* may simply mean "recognized" and so when used as a participle functioning as substantive it may mean "the one(s) recognized". When translated as "seem", however, it has the idea of only seeming important.

126 Burton (71) says, "Those who are here (2:2) designated as *tois dokousin* are evidently the same who in v. 6 are called *hoi dokountes* and *hoi dokountes einai ti*, and in v. 9 *hoi dokountes stuloi einai*, and in v. 9 are also identified as James and Cephas and John." This is also the view of Bruce (109), Guthrie (77), Cole (67), George (138), Stott (44), and Longenecker (48). I agree with this position, but like Dunn (92) would argue that while it must include these three, it could also include a larger group.

127 Bruce, 117.

128 This interpretation is supported by the use of the imperfect *ēsan* (they were), which "signals a particular past period of time", together with *pote* (then), which "points the reader back to an earlier time" (Longenecker, 53). If Paul had in mind what the three were at the time of the visit, we would expect *tote* (at that time) rather than *pote* (see also Dunn, 102; Bruce, 117; Lightfoot, 108).

129 The present tense (*diapherei*) can be viewed as durative present. This is Paul's position as he writes to the Galatians, and has been his position in the past.

130 A literal translation of the Greek is "God does not accept the face of a man". Longenecker (54) identifies this as a proverb. Several passages in the Septuagint shed light on its meaning (see the Septuagint translations of Lev 19:15; Deut 1:17, 16:19; 2 Chr 19:7; Job 13:10; Ps 81:2; Prov 18:5; Mal 2:9).

131 Burton, 88; see also Dunn, 103.

132 Bruce, 118.

133 The Greek simply says "nothing to me", with the "to me" in the emphatic position at the beginning of the statement. The addition of the words "my message" is defensible because what Paul is talking about is his gospel and his authority, which he defended so vigorously in chapter 1.

134 The idea of refuting some demand fits the context better in light of the strong adversative particle translated "on the contrary" at the beginning of 2:7. However, the "instruction" and "demand" notions are not mutually exclusive. Burton (89) may be right when he puts it as follows: "The Jerusalem apostles imposed on him no burden (of doctrine or practice), or imparted nothing to him in addition to what he already knew."

135 Eadie, 127.

136 Dunn, 110.

137 Dunn, 106.

138 The aorist tense of the participles "seeing" and "recognizing" indicates that these theological perceptions preceded the action of the main verb, namely, "gave ... the right hand of fellowship" in 2:9 (Dunn, 106). There can be debate about whether this is purely an indication of a sequence in time (so that the welcoming occurs *after* the recognition) or whether there is a causal relationship (so that the welcoming occurs *because of* the recognition). Probably both factors are at work. It is both because of and after the seeing and the recognizing that the three extended their hand of fellowship.

139 Both *tēs akrobustias* (of the uncircumcision) and *tēs peritomēs* (of the circumcision) are objective genitives (that is, they name the recipients of the action of proclaiming the gospel). This is an example of metonymy, a figure of speech in which something is identified by naming one of its attributes.

140 The simple past tense verbs *energēsas* and *enērgēsen* of 2:8, which the NASB translates as "effectually worked", are inceptive aorists focusing on how Peter and Paul's missions began and how they have continued. How the assignments are being done is the natural outcome of how they were given. Because God gave them, they cannot be less than God-approved. It would thus be right, but as a derived meaning, to translate the two aorist tenses as gnomic, referring to the "God who works"– enabling, confirming, and giving victory. As Bruce puts it, "the demarcation of the Jewish and Gentile mission-fields was based on the recognition that his [Paul's] own Gentile mission and Peter's Jewish mission were equally attended by signs of divine power which set the seal of divine approval on the one as on the other" (Bruce, 119).

141 The *hina* here is an equivalent to the classical *ephi hote* which has the idea of "on condition that", "on the understanding that" (Longenecker, 58; Bruce, 124).

142 In the Greek, this statement of understanding is elliptic in that the verb is omitted. But the context makes it clear that the required verb is either "we might go" or "we might preach".

143 The statement does not have a verb, but "they asked" can be supplied from the context. It appears that this request came from James, Peter, and John.

144 Burton (99), taking the present tense "remember" as durative.

145 Dunn, 112.

146 Bruce, 126; Dunn, 112.
147 Longenecker, 60.
148 See commentary on 1:2.
149 Longenecker, 61.
150 The aorist tense *ēlthen* (came) in 2:11 is resultative, with its focus on the fact that the event took place after Peter had arrived at Antioch.
151 The verb *sunēsthien* (was eating with) in 2:12 is an iterative imperfect, implying that he did this regularly.
152 The adverbial infinitive clause, *pros* (before) and *elthein* (literally, "to come"; here with the article it means, "the coming") tells us that the action of the main verb (*sunēsthein* – "was eating") took place prior to these people's arrival.
153 Longenecker, 72.
154 The verbs *hupestellen* and *aphōrizen* are also in the imperfect tense translated "used to eat". Here, however, the aspect is not iterative but inceptive, focusing on the start of the withdrawal and separation.
155 The participle *phoboumenos* is in the present tense to indicate the close connection in time between Peter's state of fear and his withdrawal and separation. The participle is circumstantial, with focus on the cause of the action of the main verb.
156 The dative *autō* here is a dative of association, while the word translated "joined him" means "to act a part along with" (Eadie, 154).
157 Taking *tē hupokrisei* as an instrumental dative, referring to the instrument that carries him away.
158 Assuming that this incident took place after Paul's first missionary journey, on which he was accompanied by Barnabas.
159 The use of *kategnōsmenos ēn*, a periphrastic pluperfect construction, stresses the state of affairs.
160 Longenecker, 76.
161 Liddell and Scott, 1249.
162 Taking *tou euangeliou* as a qualitative genitive, attributing a quality to the truth and making the gospel the determining factor of what the truth is.
163 Taking *tou euangeliou* as a genitive of content. Eadie (156) says, "'The truth of the gospel' is not the true gospel, but the truth which it contains or embodies – evidently the great doctrine of justification by faith, implying the non-obligation of the ceremonial law on Gentile converts and the cessation of that exclusiveness which the chosen people had so long cherished."
164 Burton (110) regards this use of the present tense in *orthopodousin* as "the present of the direct form retained in indirect discourse". He argues that Paul is quoting his exact words to Peter and his followers, "You are not walking uprightly". However, Burton does not explain why Paul uses the present tense here, while using the past tense for all the other verbs (except where Paul clearly intends to be quoting direct speech in 2:14). It seems simpler to interpret the verb here as an example of the historical present tense, which reports a past action as though it is still happening at the time of writing. It is clearly not to be read as a durative present, indicating that Peter and his followers are still acting in this way.
165 The Greek idiom is literally "to the face". It carries the idea of a direct encounter, as in Acts 25:16 and 2 Corinthians 10:1.
166 Liddell and Scott, 140.
167 George (179) assumes that a private meeting had been held. Most commentators disagree. They argue that if there had been such a meeting, there would have been no need for a public confrontation unless Peter had refused to listen to Paul. That possibility seems more unlikely than assuming that this was their first discussion of this issue.
168 The anarthrous position of *pantōn* supports this (see Burton, 111). Note that the TNIV's "them" before "all" is not in the Greek.

169 Dunn (127) describes it as "one of the larger (representative?) gatherings of Jewish and Gentiles believers in Antioch", and Longenecker (77) asserts that it most likely involved "all the members of the Antioch church in open session".

170 The verb *anankazeis* may be taken as a conative present, that is, "you are attempting to force".

171 Verse 2:15 lacks a verb and translators have to supply one. Some suggest an indicative verb, giving the translation, "We are Jews by nature, and not sinners from among the Gentiles" – NASB. This rendering with "are" is endorsed by Dunn (131), Bruce (136), George (186), Longenecker (83) and Eadie (*esmen* – 162), and is found in the TNIV, NKJV and RSV. Other translators prefer to add a participle, specifically *ontes*, the present active participle plural form of *eimi*. If this participle is viewed as concessive, the phrase is translated as "though we are" (Burton, 111); if it is viewed as causal, it is translated as "because we are".

Translators also have to decide whether 2:15 should be treated as a complete sentence (as in the NASB and HCSB) or as simply a clause, as in the TNIV, where 2:15 is completed in 2:16. Treating it as incomplete leads to the further question: What verb is this clause the subject of? If we translate the participle *eidotes* at the beginning of 2:16 as an independent verb, we get the TNIV translation, "We who are Jews ... know that" (see also George, 89). Alternatively, *eidotes* may be taken as dependent on a main verb *episteusamen* in the middle of verse 16, with the whole clause as the subject of this verb "believed". This gives a reading like "We who are Jews ..., knowing that a man is not justified, ... we believed" (NKJV, RSV; see also Longenecker, 89; Bruce, 136).

172 Dunn (152) says, "The readers of the letter could hardly understand the 'we' of 2:15 as other than a reference to Peter and Paul." See also, Eadie, 162.

173 Longenecker, 88; Bruce, 137.

174 Dunn, 133. See also Longenecker, 83, and Eadie, 162.

175 Literally "sinners out of the Gentiles"; *ethnōn* in 2:15b is taken to be a genitive of source.

176 Longenecker (83).

177 In the TNIV the word translated "know" is treated as an independent verb standing on its own with "we" as the subject. However, a more accurate translation takes the participle translated "knowing" as dependant on another main verb, in this case "believed". Thus the NASB translates verses 15 and 16 like this: "We are Jews by nature and not sinners from among the Gentiles; nevertheless knowing that a man is not justified by the works of the Law ... even we have believed in Christ Jesus". The participle is then either circumstantial, that is, "being in these circumstances or state of knowledge, we believed" (Longenecker, 83), or causal, that is, giving the reason why they believed (Eadie, 163). It is because the Jews knew that the law could not save them that they believed.

178 The noun "justification" (*dikaiōsis*) occurs only twice in the New Testament (Romans 4:25; 5:18) but the verb form (*dikaioō*) occurs thirty-nine times, mostly in Pauline writings.

179 Scholars disagree about how this phrase, which is literally "the works of the law", should be interpreted. Some treat *nomou* (law) as a subjective genitive and suggest that the works are the things one does under the guidance of the law; others treat it as a qualitative genitive and suggest that Paul is speaking of good works that meet the standards set by the law; still others treat *nomou* as an objective genitive and suggest that they are works that fulfil the law. In other words, Paul may be talking of the act of obedience, the measure of obedience, or the object of obedience. The TNIV translation "by observing the law" adopt the second interpretation. However there is considerable overlap between these positions. Those who perform good works view the law as their guide and the fulfilment of the law is the objective of the one seeking merit.

180 Dunn, 136.

181 Longenecker (85–86) states that Paul "directs his attack not just against legalism, which the Old Testament prophets and a number of rabbis of Judaism denounced as well, but against even the Mosaic religious system, for he saw all of that as a preparatory for and superseded by the relationship of being 'in Christ'".

[182] For a fuller discussion of the function of the law in God's redemptive plan, see the commentary on chapters 3 and 4 of this letter.

[183] In translating the following phrase, it is important to avoid a rendering that will make the *ean mē* (except) qualify "works of the law" and not the word "justified". Such a translation (for example, "a person is not justified by works of the law except ....") is correct linguistically but wrong contextually. Paul is stating that it is not "works of law" but "faith in Jesus Christ" that brings justification. The major English translations use paraphrasing in order to avoid the translation "except".

[184] This translation takes *Iēsou Christou* (literally, "of Jesus Christ") as an objective genitive. This position is supported by the major English translations (TNIV, NASB, NKJV, HSCB, NRSV) and many commentators, including Eadie, 166; Bruce, 138; George, 195–196; Burton, 121.

[185] Longenecker (87–88) gives a list of those who agree with him in treating *Iēsou Christou* as a subjective genitive. See also Bruce, 138–139.

[186] George, 195. See also Dunn (138–139) for additional arguments in support of the traditional translation as an objective genitive.

[187] The verb translated "shall be justified" (preceded by the negating particle "not") is best taken as customary future tense. That is what happens or does not happen as a matter of fact.

[188] LXX 142:2.

[189] Dunn, 140. See also Bruce, 140; Burton, 124.

[190] The conjunction *kai* is here treated as ascensive in function, meaning "even". The personal pronoun is *hēmeis* (we).

[191] Longenecker, 88; treating the verb as a historical aorist.

[192] Eadie, 168.

[193] Burton, 123. See also Longenecker, 88; Dunn, 139.

[194] Longenecker, 90–91.

[195] Dunn, 142.

[196] Eadie (181) says: "If, after Christ has come, you re-enact it [law], you not only confess that you were wrong in holding it to be abrogated, but you also prove yourself a transgressor of its inner principles, and a contravener of its spirit and purpose."

[197] Burton, 133.

[198] Guthrie, 89. In Romans, Paul uses a similar metaphor when he talks about "death to law" (Rom 7:4–6) and "death to sin" (Rom 6:2).

[199] Dunn, 145.

[200] Guthrie, 89–90.

[201] Eadie, 185.

[202] Taking *sunestaurōmai* as an extensive or consummative perfect.

[203] Bruce, 144.

[204] Guthrie, 90.

[205] Burton, 137.

[206] Dunn, 145.

[207] Eadie (190) and those who prefer "in faith" focus on the sphere in which the living is done. But "by faith" does not exclude the idea of "in faith".

[208] Taking *tou huiou theou* as objective genitive.

[209] One article links the two phrases "*who loved me*" and "*who gave himself for me*". The same person is performing both actions.

[210] Taking *theou* here as a subjective genitive.

[211] Eadie, 194–195.

[212] For more information about this approach to Galatians, see Hans Dieter Betz, "The Literary Composition of Paul's Letter to the Galatians", *NTS* 21 (1975): 353–379. He distinguishes the *narratio* (narrative), *propositio* (propositional statement) and *probatio* (proof).

213 The word translated "clearly portrayed" is *proegraphē*, a second aorist in the passive, indicative form. This word is used in three ways in Greek literature:
- with a temporal focus, meaning "to write beforehand"
- with a priority focus, meaning "write at the head of a list"
- with a locative focus, meaning "to write publicly"

This last meaning seems to be the one that applies here (and possibly in Jude 4). The priority focus is not found in the New Testament. The temporal focus is found in Romans 15:4 and Ephesians 3:3, but is unlikely here given the problem of locating the "beforehand" period when Christ was presented to the Galatians.

214 Guthrie, 92.

215 The perfect passive participle *estaurōmenos* seems to be intensive, focusing on the lasting effects of a past event. Longenecker (101) states that it emphasizes "the crucifixion as an accomplished fact with present results, and so should be translated 'having been crucified'."

216 George, 211. The verb "receive" is an inceptive aorist, focusing on the beginning of the Holy Spirit's indwelling in the Galatians' lives.

217 The phrase *akoēs pisteōs* is translated in a number of ways, in part because the noun *akoē* can mean the faculty of hearing, the act of hearing (as in the NASB, KJV, and NKJV), or the content of what is heard (as in the NIV, Philips and NEB). The relationship between *akoē* and *pisteōs* is also a matter of debate. The NASB, RSV, and NKJV treat *pisteōs* as genitive of association and translate, "hearing with faith" as equivalent to "hearing and believing" (Cole, 89) except that the NKJV retains both words as nouns ("the hearing of faith"), whereas the NASB and RSV treat one of the nouns as a verb ("by hearing with faith"). J. B. Philips and the NEB treat *pisteōs* as genitive of manner, and thus translate it as "by believing the message of the Gospel". The NIV takes it as an objective genitive and thus translates it as "by believing what you heard" (or even a qualitative genitive, indicating what kind of believing is involved, in other words, the kind of hearing that results in believing). In this commentary, *akoē* is taken as focusing on the act of hearing and *pisteōs* is treated as an objective genitive (or even a qualitative genitive), with the idea that they heard the gospel that focused on Christ crucified for them and their hearing resulted in their exercising faith to appropriate Christ as their Saviour.

218 The datives *pneumati* and *sarki* may be treated as datives of sphere. The Galatians started in the sphere of "the Spirit", but now want to finish being in the sphere of "the flesh", that is, of human effort. Alternatively, these may be datives of manner, indicating that they began by being led by the Spirit, but now want to finish by being guided by the flesh (see NASB). The dative may even be instrumental, that is, they began with the Spirit working in their lives, but now want to finish by leaning on the flesh (see TNIV). There is considerable overlap between these positions.

219 The verb *epiteleisthe* is best taken as a tendential present.

220 The verb *epathete* (second aorist indicative active from *paskō*) is here taken as a resultative aorist. The "persecution" translation is favoured by George (213), Guthrie (93), and Eadie (234); the "blessings" translation is favoured by Longenecker (104) and Cole (91); and the neutral interpretation is favoured by Dunn (156–157), and Burton (150).

221 In the Greek, the giver is not specified as God. However, the present participles *epichorēgōn* (who gives or supplies) and *energōn* (who works) are used substantively and are governed by the same article to communicate that one person is in view (Granville Sharp rule). This person is definitely God. The main point here is not who gives the Spirit (the giver is assumed to be known by the Galatians) but "the principle on which He usually acts, or the instrumentality which He usually employs, in the bestowment of such gifts" (Eadie, 226).

222 Taking the present tense *epichorēgōn* as an iterative present tense.

223 Taking *energōn* as a durative present tense. The dative *en humin* (among you) can also be translated "in you" (see 1 Cor 12:6; Phil 2:13). While the "in" translation makes the miracles more personal, the context suggests that a better translation is "among you", for Paul mentions the miracles as things that can be recorded as evidence. See Guthrie, 93; George, 214; Dunn, 158; Eadie, 225.

224 Longenecker, 105; Dunn, 58.
225 Gen 12–24; Isa 51:2; Matt 3:9.
226 In Romans 4, Paul also bases an argument on Genesis 15:1–6.
227 Dunn, 162.
228 Those who take it as referring to his initial response see *episteusen* as an inceptive aorist, while those who apply it to his whole life take it to be constative aorist.
229 The word in question is *elogisthē*, a first aorist, passive, indicative from *logizomai*.
230 Bruce, 153.
231 The mood of the verb *ginoskete* (understand) can be either indicative or imperative. If indicative, then Paul is indicating that the Galatians already know what he is about to say, namely, "those who believe are sons of Abraham". If it is taken as imperative, then Paul is telling the Galatians to "know", "consider", "recognize", "be sure" who are sons of Abraham. Given the tone of the letter, the imperative translation is preferable. Paul is writing to instruct, not to negotiate. See Bruce, 155; Dunn, 165; Eadie, 235; Hansen, 88.
232 Burton, 155. Bruce (155) refers to this as "an instance of the idiomatic Hebrew use of 'sons' (*bene*) with a following genitive to denote character". See also Dunn, 162.
233 Eadie, 236.
234 Dunn, 163. See also Burton (155) who states that the phrase expresses "character, standing, and existence governed by faith"; Lightfoot (137) says that they are those "whose starting point, whose fundamental principle is faith".
235 Dunn, 163.
236 Eadie, 236.
237 The verb *dikaioi* is gnomic present indicative active from *dikaioō*, indicating that this is God's habitual practice.
238 Bruce, 156.
239 Eadie, 237.
240 For discussion of the debate on this issue, see Eadie, 238–239; Ben Witherington III, *Grace in Galatia: A Commentary on Paul's Letter to the Galatians* (Grand Rapids: Eerdmans, 1998), 228.
241 Taking *soi* to be either a dative of possession or a dative of association.
242 Eadie, 238. This interpretation treats *soi* as a dative of sphere.
243 Lightfoot, 137.
244 Commentators also debate whether the verb *eneulogēthēsontai* (from *eneulogeō*) should be rendered as "will bless themselves" (middle voice) or "will be blessed" (passive voice). The problem arises because the Hebrew verb in Genesis 12:3 and 18:18 (the passages Paul quotes) has niphal, which is reflexive. However, as Bruce (156) points out, the niphal can also be taken as passive, as in the LXX, which is the version that Paul is quoting here. Dunn (165) comments: "Since Paul is citing the LXX the greater ambiguity of the underlying Hebrew (see e.g. Bruce, 156) is irrelevant."
245 Witherington, 229.
246 *Eulogountai* is present indicative passive from *eulogeō*. As a perfective present, it expresses the believer's current state.
247 In 3:9, the Greek is *sun tō pistō*, whereas in 3:8 is it *en soi*.
248 Bruce, 157.
249 Burton, 167.
250 The NASB translation brings out the presence of two are's in this sentence: "For as many as are of the works of the Law are under a curse." The first *eisin* is descriptive of their chosen path, while the second is gnomic, describing the status that automatically follows.
251 Taking *emmenei* as a durative present tense.
252 The verb is a gnomic future tense.
253 The Greek preposition *huper*, translated "for", means more than simply "on behalf of". It certainly includes the notion of substitution.

254 The phrase "given to Abraham" translates a genitive, *tou Abraam*, whose literal meaning would be "of Abraham". Taking the genitive as objective is in line with the context.
255 The TNIV renders the first *hina* as "in order that" (3:14a) and the second as "so that" (3:14b) because it sees the focus of the first as purpose and of the second as result.
256 Taking the genitive *tou pneumatos* (of the Spirit) as epexegetical.
257 The Greek *adelphoi* is an inclusive word that can accurately be translated "brothers and sisters", rather than just "brothers", as it is in many translations.
258 The figure of 430 years is for the period separating Abraham (or all the Patriarchs) from Moses. Genesis 15:13 and Acts 7:6 give 400 years for the sojourn in Egypt (from Jacob to Moses). These are simply rounded off figures.
259 If *charin* is taken as causal, the idea is that the law is intended to be preventative, minimizing or checking transgression (see George, 253); if *charin* is taken as telic, the law is intended to provoke sin (see Bruce, 175); if *charin* is taken as cognitive, the law is intended to expose our failures (see Longenecker, 138).
260 This tradition is reflected in the LXX translation of Deuteronomy 33:2 and Psalms 68:18. See Longenecker, 139; George, 256; Burton, 189.
261 The Greek phrase translated "faith in Jesus Christ" (*Iēsou Christou*) literally means "faith of Jesus Christ". Since the word translated "faith" may also be rendered "faithfulness" some, like Longenecker (145), have chosen to see the phrase as a subjective genitive meaning "the faithfulness of Jesus Christ". However, most commentators regard it as an objective genitive, with Jesus as the object towards whom faith is exercised. See Guthrie, 108; Hansen, 105; Dunn, 195-196; Burton, 196; Bruce, 181; Hendriksen, 144; and Eadie, 278.
262 Scholars disagree on the exact role of the pedagogue in instruction. Guthrie (109) says, "The educative idea (cf. AV 'schoolmaster') was not dominant, and was probably not present at all." Hansen (107-108) says, "the pedagogue supervised, controlled and disciplined the child; the teacher instructed and educated him." There is, however, general agreement that if the pedagogue did give instruction, it was only in the realm of morals. Dunn (198-199) refers to his duties as instruction "in good manners". When we apply this role to the law, it seems to limit its function to telling us what is right and what is wrong.
263 Bruce, 182.
264 Taking *este* as a gnomic present.
265 *Theou* here combines elements of a genitive of possession and of relationship. The believer is drawn into a new relationship with God, which amounts to belonging to God as one of his special people.
266 The verbs *ebaptisthēte* (baptized) and *enedusasthe* (clothed yourselves) are both resultative aorists, focusing on the status believers attain. They are a baptized people and as a result also Christ-clothed. The first, however, is passive and the latter middle in voice (although it can also be taken as passive – see the NIV). God baptizes those who believe into Christ, but the believer is then responsible to live like Christ.
267 Longenecker, 156.
268 "If you belong" is a first class condition that assumes the reality of belonging. Thus it can even be translated "since you belong".
269 Some manuscripts read "into your hearts", which makes the passage easier to follow. However, the manuscripts that support "our" (*hēmōn*) are more reliable than those which read "your" (*humōn*). This is also the only place in Scripture where the Holy Spirit is referred to as the "Spirit of his Son", although elsewhere he is described as the "Spirit of the Lord" or the "Spirit of Christ" (2 Cor 3:17; Rom 8:9; Phil 1:19).
270 The one who cries "Abba, Father" is the Holy Spirit in the believer, and by implication the believer possesses that Spirit.
271 It is interesting to note that in 4:6 all three persons of the Trinity cooperate in the believer's interest. Of course, it can be debated whether "Spirit" here has reference to the Third Person of the Trinity or needs to be understood as spirit (with small s). Most commentators take it as a reference to the Holy Spirit (see Dunn, 219; Guthrie, 115; Burton, 223; Bruce, 199).

272 For a discussion of the various interpretations of *stoicheion*, see Burton, 510–518.
273 *Tou kosmou* seems to be a qualitative genitive.
274 Paul only uses the verb *deomai* (I plead) here and in Romans 1:10 and 2 Corinthians 5:20; 8:4; 10:2. He usually prefers the word *parakaleō* (I exhort), as in Romans 12:1; 1 Corinthians 4:16; 2 Corinthians 10:1; 1 Thessalonians 5:11.
275 Greek has several words for child, including *paidion* and *teknion*. The form Paul uses here, *tekna mou*, is used with regard to people for whom the writer cares deeply.
276 Paul's guarded allegorization does not directly support the allegorical method of interpretation practised by some early church fathers, especially in Alexandria. Paul accepts the historicity of Abraham, Sarah, Hagar, Ishmael, Isaac and Jerusalem, whereas the early church fathers gave no regard to the historicity of the characters or places named as they drew spiritual lessons from them.
277 Double fulfilment is a common feature in the prophecy of Isaiah. For example, the prophecy in Isaiah 9:6–7 gave immediate hope to the Jews of Isaiah's day, but its use in Luke 1:32–33 shows that it also applies to the birth of Christ.
278 There is debate about where the theological section of Galatians ends and the ethical section begins. Do the theological arguments end at the end of chapter four, or do they continue up to 5:12? If 5:1–12 is seen as a continuation of the theological arguments, then it constitutes the conclusion of those arguments and 5:13 begins the conclusion of the epistle in general. Interesting as this debate is, it is not a major issue when it comes to understanding Galatians. Dunn (261) rightly says, "since the exposition leads into the conclusion and the conclusion has the character of exhortation, the disagreement does not amount to much".
279 Regardless of whether *tē eleutheria* is taken as a dative of indirect object and rendered as "for freedom" (NIV, NASB, NRSV) or as a dative of sphere and translated "into freedom" (HCSB), the point is clear: Christ has set us free.
280 In Galatians 5:1, we have *stēkete*, with the sphere (freedom) on which the standing is to be done implied in the context. In 1 Corinthians 16:13 we have *stēkete en tē pistei* (stand firm in the faith), and in Philippians 4:1 *stēkete en kuriō* (stand firm in the Lord).
281 The NIV and HCSB rightly treat the verb *dikaiousthe* in the phrase *hoitines en nomō dikaiousthe* as a tendential present, giving the translation "you who are trying to be justified". See also the NASB "who are seeking to be justified" and the NRSV "who want to be justified". Those who take this route do not find justification, no matter how much they try.
282 The Greek *hēmeis gar* is commonly translated as "for we" (NASB, NRSV, HCSB), but in a few contexts it can also mean "but". The TNIV translators have deemed that to be the case here.
283 The Greek word is simply *pneumati* (dative singular of *pneuma*), which can refer to either the human spirit (as opposed to the flesh, in this context), or the Holy Spirit who indwells and enables the believer. The translation "through the spirit" also reflects the translator's decision on the meaning of the dative here, for there is no preposition with *pneumati* in the Greek. Most translations agree that Paul is referring to the Holy Spirit and thus use a capital "S" for Spirit. There is also general agreement that the dative *pneumati* has an instrumental function here, meaning "by" (HCSB) or "through". A number of commentators prefer to translate the verse using "by the Spirit" and "through faith" (*ek pisteōs*) (Longenecker, 228; George, 360). Dunn (269) prefers "by the Spirit" and "from faith"; the NRSV has "through the Spirit and by faith"; Burton (277) has "by the Spirit, by faith". Regardless of the exact translation, the point is clear: Paul is contrasting the path of circumcision advocated by the Judaizers with the path of faith and reliance on the Holy Spirit.
284 The Greek has *pistis di' agapēs energoumenē*. The usual meaning of *energein* is "to work". Thus the literal rendering is "faith working through love" (NASB, NRSV, HCSB).
285 In the phrase *etrechete kalōs*, the verb is a durative imperfect. For some time (most likely from the time of their conversion until the arrival of the false teacher) they had kept on running on course. The adverb *kalōs* (good) does not so much describe the race (although it is a good race – see the TNIV) but rather how they were running.

286 The word *enekopsen* is a first aorist from the verb *egkoptō*, whose general meaning is "hinder" or "thwart" but which can also mean "delay" or "detain" (BAG, 215). This is a resultative aorist, indicating that the focus is on the result of the cutting in, which is that some of the Galatians are beginning to be shaken

287 The aorist tense *enekopsen*, translated "cut in" (5:7) is taken here as resultative. The act of cutting in is at the results level and some of the Galatians are beginning to be shaken.

288 Paul's exact words are, "if I am still preaching circumcision" (5:11). This way of putting things raises the question of when he preached circumcision. From what we know, he never preached this as a way of acceptance before God after his encounter with Jesus on his way to Damascus (Acts 9). It seems likely that he is here using the word "preach" to refer not so much to proclamation as to practising a way of life that could be interpreted as promoting circumcision. That has definitely been his way of life prior to conversion. After conversion, his principle was to let the Jews remain Jews and the Gentiles be Gentiles in such matters as circumcision, for the rite of circumcision was no longer important. Christ was for all and faith was the route for all who desired to be in right relationship with God. However, it is possible that he is here responding to some statement by his opponents in Galatia, who may have accused him of inconsistency for allowing circumcision for cultural reasons, as part of people's Jewish heritage, while opposing its being forced on the Gentiles. What Paul is saying here is that he never preached circumcision for any ethnic groups. For a fuller discussion of this issue, see Dunn, 278–290.

289 Taking the genitive *tou staurou* in the phrase *to skandalon tou staurou* as subjective, that is, the offence the cross causes.

290 The TNIV puts 5:13–15 together with 5:16–22 under the heading "Life by the Spirit", presumably because serving one another humbly and loving our neighbours are part of what we do when we walk in the Spirit. In this commentary, however, I have chosen to link 5:13–15 with the section beginning in 5:1 because that section then opens and closes with teaching about our freedom in Christ. When preaching on these passages, the best approach is to use verses 13 to 15 as a bridge, relating what precedes it to what follows it.

291 *Epithumian sarkos* literally means "desire (singular) of flesh". Flesh (*sarkos*) is singular and is probably a subjective genitive. This wording implies that the sinful nature has a will, a desire, a goal it wants to reach. This goal is expressed in the "passions and desires" (plural) referred to in 5:24. However, the translators of the TNIV regard the singular "desire" of 5:16 as a collective noun, and so render it in the plural "desires".

292 The founder of the Stoic philosophy in Athens, Zeno, prepared a clear and formal catalogue of virtues and vices that may be dated as early as 308 BC, See Longenecker, 249–252.

293 George, 399.

294 Bruce (247) translates *porneia* as "sexual irregularity in general"; Dunn (303) translates it as "unlawful sexual intercourse".

295 The word *akatharsia* can be morally neutral in some contexts, but here it is clearly related to *porneia*, and thus to sexual sin.

296 Bruce, 248.

297 The Greek word translated "discord", "strife" or "contention" is *eris*. In both Homer and Hesiod, this is the name of the goddess of war and destruction (Bruce, 248). This word is used nine times in the New Testament, always by Paul (the other instances are Rom 1:29; 13:13; 1 Cor 1:11; 3:3; 2 Cor 12:20; Phil 1:15; 1 Tim 6:4; Tit 3:9). In Romans 13:13, Paul exhorts us not to walk in "strife and envy" (NKJV). In 1 Corinthians 1:11 he says that he has been told that "there are contentions" (NKJV) at Corinth and in 1 Corinthians 3:3 he states that such discord is proof of their being worldly. In Titus 3:9 *eris* is mentioned as part of the past of the believer.

298 George, 395. *Zēlos* is itself neutral. However, when it is found in a list of vices, it is negative.

299 George, 395. The word *thymos* can have both a positive and negative connotation depending on context. Here, it is used negatively. In the New Testament, it is used closely with and even interchangeably with "wrath" (*orgē*) in places like Romans 2:8 and Revelation 16:19; 19:15. The difference is in the expression of the feelings. Someone prone to *thymos* will express their negative feelings in violent outbursts; someone filled with *orgē* may have the same feelings but not express them.

300 In the New Testament, *eritheiai* is always used with negative connotations (see Rom 2:8; 2 Cor 12:20; Phil 1:17; 2:3; Jas 3:14, 16).
301 Eadie, 418.
302 George, 396, quoting H. Schlier. Note that the word *aireseis*, translated "factions", is the same word from which we get "heresy".
303 The Greek word, *phthonoi*, translated "envy" refers to "the grudging spirit that cannot bear to contemplate someone else's prosperity" (Bruce, 249). It is closely related to "jealousy" (*zēlos*) already discussed above. Eadie (p. 419) defines it as "desire to appropriate what another possesses".
304 Bruce, 250.
305 George, 397.
306 Given the whole tone of the book of Galatians, this statement is not to be understood as teaching that not practising these vices qualifies one to inherit the kingdom of God. Paul's point is that those who are God's children do not do these things as a habit. John makes the same point in 1 John 3:6, 9 when he says that those who are born of God do not make a practice of sinning. They may commit a sin (1 John 2:1) but when they recognize what they have done, they are filled with remorse, confess their sin and are forgiven (1 John 1:9).
307 The Greek uses the present imperative tense, *peripateite*, denoting that this is to be their continual practice or way of life.
308 The Greek contains a double negative (ou and mē).
309 Where the TNIV has "since" other translations have "if". The meaning is the same, for what we have here is a first class condition, meaning "if we live by the Spirit (and we do)".
310 The word translated "keep in step with" conveys the idea of being in line with someone, standing beside them, or following in their footsteps.
311 The genitive *tou pneumatos* is subjective, implying that it is the Spirit who produces the fruit.
312 In the UBS *Greek New Testament* and in the Nestle-Aland *Novum Testamentum*, the virtues are arranged in three groups, separated by commas after "peace" and after "goodness". However, the Majority Text, which is followed by the King James Version, and the *Modern Greek New Testament* place a comma after every virtue. The significance of the grouping is open to debate. George (399) says that, unlike the list of vices, the list of virtues is "in beautiful harmony, balanced and symmetrical, corresponding to the purposeful design and equilibrium of a life filled with the Spirit and lived out in the beauty of holiness... Paul grouped these nine graces into three triads that give a sense of order and completion, although here too there is no attempt to produce an exhaustive list of the Christian virtues". On the other hand, Longenecker (260) says, "As with the catalogue of vices of vv. 19–21, so also here in vv. 22–23 the list of virtues is given without any necessary order or system." Most translations have not provided any punctuation to show that these are grouped into triads, thereby implying that the issue is not important. For further discussion, see Lightfoot, 212; Longenecker, 260. While agreeing with Burton (314), who says, "whether the terms listed in vv. 22, 23 fell in the apostle's mind into definite classes is not altogether clear", we will here, follow the arrangement found in Lightfoot.
313 George, 399.
314 Longenecker, 260. In 1 Corinthians 13:13, Paul describes love as greater than faith and hope.
315 Ancient Greek had four words that could be translated as love. They are *agapē*, *philia* or friendship, *eros* or physical love as expressed in sexual relationships, and *storge* or love for relatives. *Eros* and *storge* are not used in the New Testament. The noun *agapē* is not found in Greek classical writings, although Josephus uses the verb form, *agapaō*. The noun is, however, found 75 times in Paul's writings (in addition to 34 occurrences of the verb form *agapaō*).
316 In the New Testament, *agapē* dominates all discussions of personal relationships, whether between God and humanity or between human beings (Longenecker, 260). But it is seldom used of our love for God. The only place where this usage definitely occurs is Romans 8:28. In other passages that refer to the "love of God" (for example, 2 Thess 3:5; 1 John 2:15) it is

not clear whether God exercises or receives the love (in other words, the genitive *tou theou* may be either subjective or objective). However in Galatians 5:22 the focus is clearly on the love human beings show towards other human beings.

[317] George, 402.

[318] Eadie (423) says that it "enables us to bear injury without at once avenging ourselves". The expression "bearing with one another" in Ephesians 4:2 further explains what being patient means.

[319] Paul is the only New Testament writer to use the word *agathōsunē* (goodness). See Rom 15:14; Eph 5:9; 2 Thess 1:11.

[320] George, 403.

[321] Ibid. The Greek word *pistis* is used with three different meanings in the New Testament:
- The content of belief, as equivalent to doctrine or the gospel message (Gal 1:23; 1 Tim 2:7; 5:8; 6:10; 6:12; 2 Tim 3:8; Titus 1:13b).
- The act of believing, that is, acceptance of the gospel message, resulting in committing oneself to Jesus as Saviour. Whenever the New Testament talks of faith in Jesus or in Christ or in the Son of God, it is this personal response to the message of salvation and the accompanying promises of God that is in view (see Gal 1:16; 2:20).
- The ethical quality of faithfulness, that is, "the quality of being worthy of belief – faithfulness, trustworthiness, loyalty" (Bruce, 254).

[322] George, 404.

[323] Longenecker, 262; see also Burton, 317.

[324] Cited in Bruce, 254 and Longenecker, 262. The classical Greek spelling of this word is *praotēs*, rather than *prautēs*, which is used in the New Testament.

[325] In the New Testament, *enkrateia* occurs four times as a noun (Acts 24:25; Gal 5:22; and twice in 2 Pet 1:6), once as an adjective (Titus 1:8) and twice in verb form (1 Cor 7:9; 8:25).

[326] *The Daily Nation*, July 12, 2007, citing Dr. Enock Kibunguchy, Assistant Minister for Health in Kenya.

[327] The Greek in 5:17 includes a *hina* clause that can be interpreted in various ways. Some argue that it is final or telic, communicating the purpose of the two things pulling in opposite directions. Thus the TNIV translation reads, "so that you are not to do whatever you want". It seems better, however, to take this as a consecutive use of *hina*, communicating the result of the opposition. This interpretation is supported by its being positioned between 5:16 "walk by the Spirit and you will not fulfil the desire of the flesh" and 5:18 "But if you are led by the Spirit...". The focus in these two verses is on "you", and thus the focus in 5:17 seems to fall on why "you" fail to live by the Spirit all the time.

[328] Burton (302) puts it like this: "Does the man choose evil, the Spirit opposes him; does he choose good, the flesh hinders him."

[329] Paul uses a third class condition (*ean* and subjunctive mood for the verb translated "is caught") to allow for the idea that while it is not certain that this will happen, the odds are that it will.

[330] The Greek *prolēmphthē* is an aorist passive subjunctive from *prolambanō*, meaning "detect", "overtake", "surprise" (F. Wilbur Gingrich, *Shorter Lexicon of the Greek Testament*. Chicago: University of Chicago Press, 1957, 184). See also George, 409.

[331] The choice of the word *paraptōma* signifies "an isolated action which may make the person who does it feel guilty" (Bruce, 260).

[332] Some suggest that Paul uses the phrase *humeis hoi pneumatikoi* (you who are spiritual) as a designation for those who are libertine in their outlook as opposed to those who are legalistic, or see this phrase as a code term for those who are Gnostic as opposed to those who are not. However, these suggestions do not reflect a fair reading of Galatians. Paul assumes that all the Galatians are participants in things spiritual (see 3:2). See Longenecker, 273; George, 409–410.

[333] Hansen, 186.

[334] The Greek uses the word *baros* (burden) in 6:2 but *phortion* (load) in 6:5.

[335] There are two persons here: the one who is instructed (*katēchoumenos* – whence the term catechumen) and the one who instructs (*katēchon* – whence the term catechist).

[336] Guthrie, 145.

[337] Longenecker, 283.

[338] Ibid.

[339] Bruce, 266.

[340] There is considerable debate about who constitutes the "Israel of God" in the phrase, "Peace and mercy to all who follow this rule – to the Israel of God" (6:16). The following are some of the options:

- "Israel of God" refers to the same group as "all" at the start of the sentence. In other words, the phrase "Israel of God" is epexegetical or explicative and defines "all". The *kai* connecting the two is then equivalent to "namely" or "that is". If one takes this position, then "Israel of God" is all believers, from both Jews and Gentiles. This position is supported by Lightfoot (225), Guthrie (152), Dunn (345) and Hansen (201).
- "Israel of God" refers to a subset of "all". The "all" includes all believers, both Jews and Gentiles, but the "Israel of God" are the Jews. The *kai* is then copulative and can be translated as "and" (NASB, NRSV, NKJV), "even" (NIV) and "also". This interpretation raises the further question of whether "all Israel" refers to pious Jews in general or only to Jews who believe in Christ. Burton (358) and Bruce (275) see it as applying to the Jewish nation (see Rom 11:26). Eadie (471) relates it only to Jewish believers.
- In the context of Galatians, where Paul repeatedly stresses that being a Jew by birth (and thus circumcised) does not secure a right relationship with God without faith in Christ, it seems unlikely that he would suddenly suggest that there is a special place for those who are Jews by birth. Thus it is more likely that the "Israel of God" are Jews who have believed in Christ. Paul is probably intending to communicate something like this: "I have been hard on Jews, but you who are both Jews and believers in Christ are definitely included in this blessing."

[341] There is some debate about whether "peace" is Paul's blessing on "all", and "mercy" his blessing on "the Israel of God" (HCSB, Burton, 375). This interpretation is not supported by all Greek texts. The UBS *Greek New Testament* and the Nestle-Aland *Novum Testamentum Graece* have peace and mercy in one phrase, with no comma to show that peace is for one group and mercy for the other. The Textus Receptus, which has a comma, is not very clear regarding the position of two groups. It literally reads: "peace upon them, even mercy, and upon the Israel of God" (*eirēnē ep' autous, kai eleos, kai epi ton Israel tou theou*).

[342] For a more complete listing, see Lightfoot, 225; Bruce, 275–276; Dunn, 346–347; George, 441–442.

[343] Taking the genitive *tou kuriou* of 6:18, to which *Iēsou Christou* is in apposition, as agent. Jesus came to dispense God's grace, taking "God" here as representing the totality of the divine being in three Persons. He is also the sphere in which this grace is found.

BIBLIOGRAPHY

Arichea, Daniel C. Jr. and Eugene A. Nida. *A Translators Handbook on Paul's Letter to the Galatians*. New York: United Bible Societies, 1975.
Barnes, Albert. "Galatians", in *Barnes' Notes on the New Testament: Complete and Unabridged in One Volume*. 1860? Repr. Grand Rapids: Kregel, 1962.
Bauer, Walter, William F. Arndt, and F. Wilbur Gingrich. *Greek-English Lexicon of the New Testament and Other Early Christian Literature*. Chicago: University of Chicago Press, 1957.
Bruce, F. F. *Commentary on Galatians*. New International Greek Testament Commentary. Grand Rapids: Eerdmans, 1982.
Burton, Ernest De Witt. *The Epistle to the Galatians: A Critical and Exegetical Commentary*. Edinburgh: T & T Clark, 1980.
Cole, Alan. *The Epistle of Paul to the Galatians*. Grand Rapids: Eerdmans, 1965.
Dunn, James G. *The Epistle to the Galatians*. Black New Testament Commentaries. Peabody: Hendrickson, 1995.
Eadie, John. *Galatians*. John Eadie Greek Text Commentaries. Grand Rapids: Baker, 1979.
George, Timothy. *Galatians: An Exegetical and Theological Exposition of Holy Scripture – NIV Text*. The New American Commentary. Nashville: Broadman & Holman, 1994.
Gingrich, F. Wilbur. *Shorter Lexicon of the Greek Testament*. Chicago: University of Chicago Press, 1957.
Guthrie, Donald. *Galatians*. New Century Bible Commentary. London: Oliphants, 1969.
Hendriksen, William. *Galatians and Ephesians*. The New Testament Commentary. Grand Rapids: Baker, 1968.
Liddell, Henry George and Robert Scott. *A Greek-English Lexicon*. New edition. Oxford: Clarendon, 1940.
Lightfoot, J. B. *The Epistle of St. Paul to the Galatians*. Grand Rapids: Zondervan, 1957.
Longenecker, Richard N. *Galatians*. Word Biblical Commentary. Dallas: Word, 1990.
Reicke, Bo. *The New Testament Era: The World of the Bible from 500 B.C. to A.D.100*. Philadelphia: Fortress, 1964.
Schürer, Emil. *A History of the Jewish People in the Time of Jesus Christ*. First Division. Volume Two. Peabody: Hendrickson, 1994.
Sanders, J. N. "Galatians", in *Peake's Commentary on the Bible*. Edited by Matthew Black and H. H. Rowley. London: Thomas Nelson and Sons, 1962.
Stein, R. H. "Jerusalem", in *Dictionary of Paul and His Letters*. Edited by Gerald F. Hawthorne, Ralph P. Martin and Daniel G. Reid. Downers Grove: InterVarsity Press, 1993.
Stott, John R. W. *The Message of Galatians*. The Bible Speaks Today. London: Inter-Varsity Press, 1968.
Wenham, J. W. *The Elements of New Testament Greek*. Based on earlier work by H. P. V. Nunn. Cambridge: Cambridge University Press, 1965.
Witherington III, Ben. *Grace in Galatia: A Commentary on Paul's Letter to the Galatians*. Grand Rapids: Eerdmans, 1998.

www.ingramcontent.com/pod-product-compliance
Lightning Source LLC
Chambersburg PA
CBHW070535170426
43200CB00011B/2429